KW-221-817

CONTENTS

ISBN 0 85147 604 X

First Edition   1972
Reprinted   1972
Reprinted   1972
Second Edition, fully revised   1973
Third Edition, fully revised   1975
Fourth Edition, fully revised   1976

© Autobooks Ltd 1976

850

Printed and bound in Brighton England for Autobooks Ltd by G. Beard & Son Ltd

C

Morris Marina 1971-76 Autobook

By Kenneth Ball

and the Autobooks Team of Technical Writers

Morris Marina 1.3, Super, 1971-75
Morris Marina 1.8, Super, TC, 1971-75
Morris Marina 2 1.3, Super, 1975-76
Morris Marina 2 1.8 Super, Special, 1975-76
Morris Marina 2 1.8 GT, HL, 1975-76
Austin, Morris Marina 1.1, 1.3 Van, 1972-76
Austin Marina 1.8 1973-76

Autobooks Ltd. Golden Lane Brighton BN1 2QJ England

The AUTOBOOK series of Workshop Manuals is the largest in the world and covers the majority of British and Continental motor cars, as well as all major Japanese and Australian models. For a full list see the back of this manual.

ACKNOWLEDGEMENT

We wish to thank British Leyland Motor Corporation Limited for their co-operation and also for supplying data and illustrations. Considerable assistance has also been given by owners, who have discussed their cars in detail, and we would like to express our gratitude for this invaluable advice and help.

ACKNOWLEDGEMENT

We wish to thank British Leyland Motor Corporation Limited for their co-operation and also for supplying data and illustrations. Considerable assistance has also been given by owners, who have discussed their cars in detail, and we would like to express our gratitude for this invaluable advice and help.

INTRODUCTION

This do-it-yourself Workshop Manual has been specially written for the owner who wishes to maintain his vehicle in first class condition and to carry out his own servicing and repairs. Considerable savings on garage charges can be made, and one can drive in safety and confidence knowing the work has been done properly.

Comprehensive step-by-step instructions and illustrations are given on all dismantling, overhauling and assembling operations. Certain assemblies require the use of expensive special tools, the purchase of which would be unjustified. In these cases information is included but the reader is recommended to hand the unit to the agent for attention.

Throughout the Manual hints and tips are included which will be found invaluable, and there is an easy to follow fault diagnosis at the end of each chapter.

Whilst every care has been taken to ensure correctness of information it is obviously not possible to guarantee complete freedom from errors or to accept liability arising from such errors or omissions.

Instructions may refer to the righthand or lefthand sides of the vehicle or the components. These are the same as the righthand or lefthand of an observer standing behind the vehicle and looking forward.

CHAPTER 1

THE ENGINE

1:1 Description

The Marina follows the modern trend in that the same basic body shell is designed to accept engines of differing capacities, and therefore power, so that, combined with various extras, the owner can choose a car or van whose performance will suit both his pocket and his requirements as to performance.

Three alternative sizes of engine are fitted to these vehicles: 1.1, 1.3 or 1.8 litre. All the engines follow the same basic design of the well-tried Series A engine and have many parts in common, differing only in details of specification among the three types. In the main one set of instructions will cover the servicing of these engines, but type differences will be mentioned as necessary. Full details of dimensions, etc. will be found in the **Technical Data** at the end of this manual. The engines will be referred to by their capacity only, thus 1.3 will mean the 1.3 litre engine or vehicle fitted with this engine.

A sectioned view of the 1.8 engine is shown in **FIG 1:1**. Apart from the 1800 cast in the side of the crankcase, the manifolds and oil pump the figure could just as well represent the 1.3 engine, though there are other differences which do not appear in this figure. All types of engine are a water-cooled, four-cylinder with overhead valves mounted vertically in the cylinder head. The valves are operated by rockers, pushrods and cam followers from the camshaft, which is mounted in the crankcase and revolves in three renewable steel-backed whitemetal bearings. The camshaft is driven from the crankshaft, using a roller timing chain and sprockets mounted at the front end of the engine. The crankshaft rotates in renewable steel-backed bearing shells mounted between the crankcase and bearing caps. On the 1.1 and 1.3 three main bearings are used but on the 1.8 the bearings have been increased to five. On all types of engine the crankshaft end float and thrust is taken by thrust washers acting at the centre main bearing. The end float of the camshaft is set by the locating plate at the front of the engine. The connecting rods use steel-backed renewable bearing shells for the big-ends, the shells being clamped between the connecting rod and a bearing cap. On some models fully-floating gudgeon pins are used, secured in the piston by a circlip at either end, but the majority of models will have gudgeon pins that are a float fit in the piston but pressed into the connecting rod.

Aluminium solid-skirt pistons are used in each type of engine and each piston is fitted with four piston rings

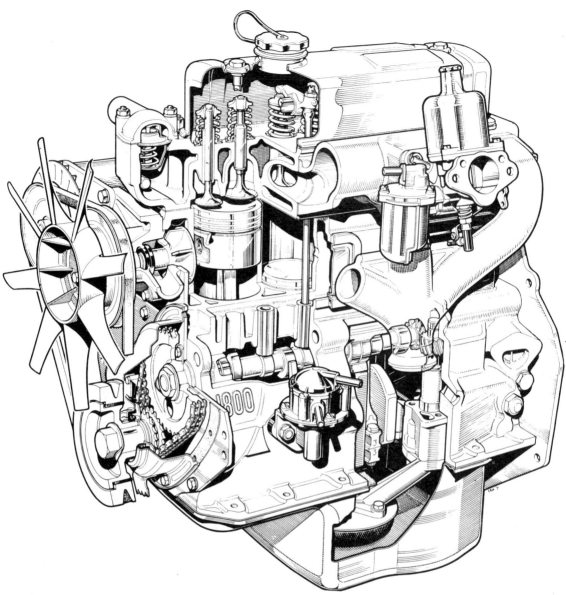

FIG 1:1   A sectioned view of the 1.8 engine

above the gudgeon pin. The design of the piston rings varies slightly but the upper three are compression rings and the bottom ring is an oil control ring.

Lubrication is by the oil pump drawing oil from the sump and then pumping it around the galleries under pressure. A relief valve is fitted to limit the maximum oil pressure when the engine is cold. The oil is drawn in from the sump through a gauze strainer in the pump inlet and it is passed through a renewable filter element before it passes into the engine oil gallery. The main bearings and camshaft bearings are fed directly from the oil gallery by internal passages. Drilled oilways in the crankshaft lead the oil from the main bearings to the big-end bearings. A

metered supply of oil is fed to the rocker assembly and this oil lubricates the valve operating gear as it passes down back to the sump.

The external components of the 1.8 engine are shown in **FIG 1 : 2** while the internal components are shown in **FIG 1 : 3**.

1 : 2 Removing the engine

The engine only can be removed, leaving the gearbox fitted to the car.

The sump and cylinder head can be removed with the engine still fitted to the car, as can the timing cover,

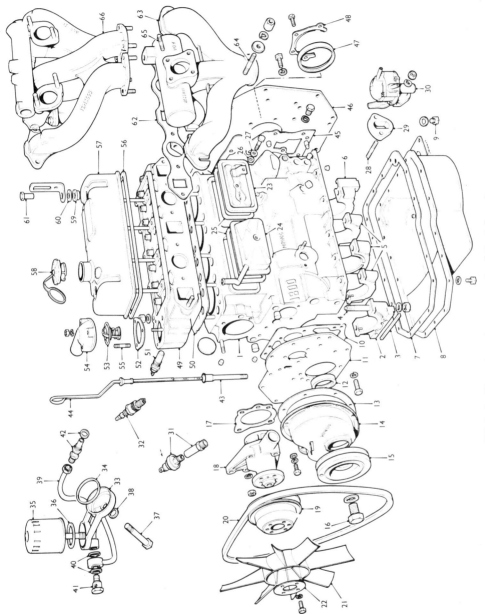

FIG 1:2 The external components of the 1.8 engine

Key to Fig 1:2 1 Cylinder block 2 Front mounting plate 3 Bearing capseal 4 Stud 5 Main bearing caps 6 Rear main bearing cap 7 Sump gasket 8 Sump
9 Sump drain plug 10 Gasket 11 Front mounting plate 12 Oil seal 13 Gasket 14 Timing cover 15 Crankshaft pulley 16 Bolt 17 Gasket 18 Water pump 19 Pulley
20 Fan belt 21 Fan 22 Lockwasher 23 Side cover 24 Oil separator 25 Gaskets 26 Rubber seal 27 Cup washer 28 Stud 29 Distance piece 30 Fuel pump
31 Oil pressure switch 32 Sparking plug 33 Oil filter support 34 Seal 35 Oil filter 36 Seal 37 Bolt 38 Sealing washer 39 Lubrication pipe 40 Sealing washers
41 Banjo bolt 42 Adaptor and seal 43 Dipstick tube 44 Dipstick 45 Gasket 46 Gearbox adaptor plate 47 Oil seal 48 Seal retainer 49 Cylinder head
50 Cylinder head gasket 51 Temperature transmitter 52 Gasket 53 Thermostat 54 Water outlet 55 Stud 56 Gasket 57 Rocker cover 58 Oil filler cap 59 Seal
60 Cup washer 61 Cap nut 62 Gasket 63 Single carburetter manifold 64 Stud 65 Stud 66 Twin carburetter manifold

MARINA

11

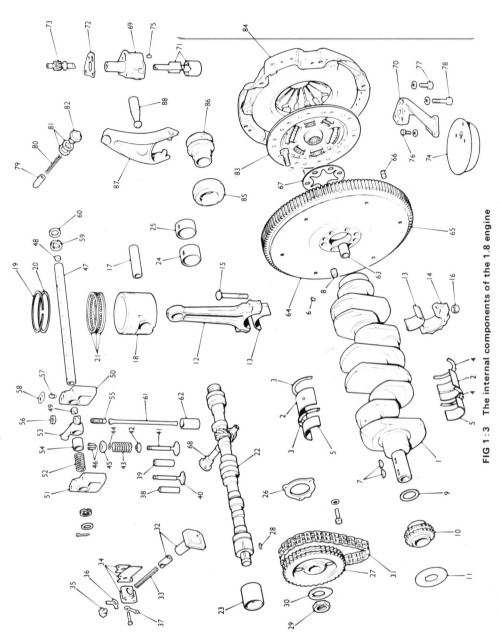

FIG 1:3   The internal components of the 1.8 engine

Key to Fig 1:3 1 Crankshaft 2 Main bearing 3 Thrust washer—upper 4 Thrust washer—lower 5 Main bearing 6 Oil restrictor 7 Key 8 Dowel 9 Shim 10 Timing gear 11 Oil thrower 12 Connecting rod 13 Big-end bearing 14 Big-end bearing cap 15 Bolt 16 Nuts 17 Gudgeon pin 18 Piston 19 Compression ring 20 Compression ring 21 Oil control ring 22 Camshaft 23 Camshaft bearing—centre 24 Camshaft bearing—front 25 Camshaft bearing—rear 26 Camshaft locking plate 27 Timing gear 28 Timing gear key 29 Camshaft nut 30 Lockwasher 31 Timing chain 32 Slipper head and cylinder 33 Spring 34 Tensioner body, plate and gasket 35 Plug for body 36 Lockwasher for plug 37 Lockwasher 38 Lockwasher 39 Inlet valve guide 40 Exhaust valve guide 41 Inlet valve 42 Valve spring collar 43 Valve spring 44 Packing ring 45 Valve cup 46 Valve cotter 47 Rocker shaft 48 Plain plug 49 Screwed plug 50 Pedestal with tapped hole 51 Pedestal 52 Spring 53 Valve rocker 54 Bush 55 Adjusting screw 56 Locknut 57 Locking screw 58 Locking plate 59 Spring washer 60 Washer 61 Pushrod 62 Cam follower 63 Crankshaft spigot bush 64 Flywheel 65 Starter ring 66 Dowel 67 Lockwasher 68 Distributor drive shaft 69 Oil pump body 70 Oil pump cover 71 Oil pump rotors 72 Gasket 73 Oil pump drive spindle 74 Oil pump strainer 75 Dowel 76 Bolt 77 Short bolt 78 Long bolt 79 Oil pressure relief valve 80 Spring for relief valve 81 Washer 82 Cap nut 83 Clutch plate 84 Clutch pressure plate 85 Clutch release bearing 86 Clutch throw-out sleeve 87 Operating lever 88 Fulcrum pin

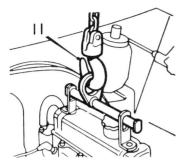

FIG 1:4 Lifting out the engine

valve timing gear and on the 1.1 and 1.8 even the camshaft. This means that the majority of operations on the engine can be carried out with it still fitted in the car. Practically the only exception is crankshaft removal for which it is essential to have the engine out of the car. If a major engine overhaul is being carried out it will be found easier if the engine is out of the car, as access to the parts will be so much better.

If the owner is not a skilled automobile mechanic it is suggested that he reads 'Hints on Maintenance and Overhaul' in the Appendix to this manual as it contains a great deal of useful information.

1 Drain the oil in the sump into a suitable container by removing the sump drain plug. Drain the cooling system and remove the radiator, and at the same time disconnect the heater pipes from their connections on the engine (see **Chapter 4**). Disconnect the battery. Remove the bonnet (hood) (see **Chapter 13**).

2 Remove the air cleaner. Disconnect the vacuum pipe, breather pipe and fuel pipe from the carburetter. Take off the nuts that secure the carburetter(s) to the inlet manifold and lay the carburetter(s) carefully to one side, still connected to the choke and throttle cables but taking care to collect the gaskets and insulators fitted. Disconnect the fuel line between the fuel tank and fuel pump at the fuel pump. If the tank is full and fuel syphons through, raise the pipe or plug it with a suitable bolt. Further instructions are given in **Chapter 2**. If the car is fitted with a brake servo, disconnect the vacuum hose from the inlet manifold. Remove the anti-roll bar if fitted.

3 Undo the two nuts and remove the clamp that secures the exhaust pipe to the exhaust manifold, carefully collecting the double-tapered ring between the two. Use penetrating oil on the nuts if they are stiff. The exhaust pipe is secured to the gearbox mounting plate by a bracket and clip. Free the clip, from underneath the car, and remove the bolt that secures the bracket. On all models, remove the two bolts that secure the sump connecting plate to the flywheel housing. Use a piece of string or wire to secure the exhaust pipe to the lefthand wing valance so that it is out of the way.

4 Disconnect all the electrical leads to the components and units on the engine. It is most advisable to label the leads so that there is no danger of reconnecting them to the wrong terminals when refitting the engine. The components which have electrical leads are the generator (or alternator), starter motor, distributor,

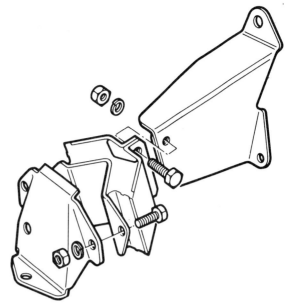

FIG 1:5 The front engine mounting for 1.3 engines

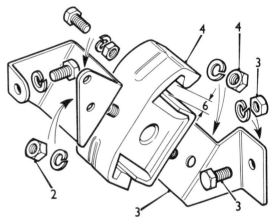

FIG 1:6 The engine mounting for 1.8 engines

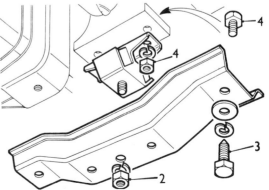

FIG 1:7 The rear engine mounting with 1.3 models, 1.8 models are very similar

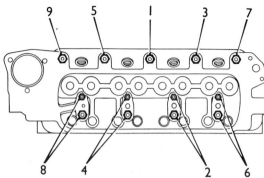

FIG 1:8 Sequence for tightening the cylinder head nuts on 1.3 models. 1.8 models have an additional nut at each end (see FIG 1:10)

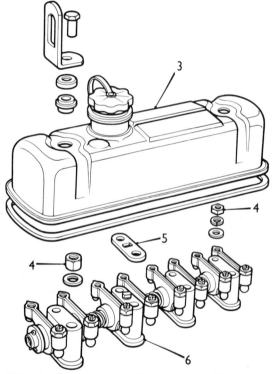

FIG 1:9 The rocker assembly on the 1.1 and 1.3 engine

ignition coil, temperature transmitter and oil pressure switch.

5 Use a hoist and sling on the engine lifting eyes, as shown in **FIG 1:4,** to take the weight of the engine. If the correct lifting tool is not available, a rope or wire sling may be used instead but **make absolutely sure that it can safely support the weight of the engine.** The sling should be positioned so that the lift is taken approximately at the centre of the engine, in line with the dipstick. Support the gearbox from underneath, using a small jack, and a pad of wood to stop the jack damaging the gearbox casing.

6 Remove the lower bolts that secure the flywheel housing, noting that on earlier models of the 1.3 only

the bolts that secure the sump connecting plate may be fitted. At the same time remove the remaining bolt that secures the starter motor so that the motor can be withdrawn and removed. Remove the upper bolts that secure the flywheel housing.

7 Remove the nuts from the bolts that secure the engine mountings to the brackets on the chassis. The engine mounting for a 1.3 engine is shown in **FIG 1:5** and that for a 1.8 engine is shown in **FIG 1:6. Check that there are no longer any attachments between the car and engine.** Slightly raise the engine to clear it from its mountings and, keeping it level, draw it forwards until the input shaft on the gearbox is well clear of the clutch, **taking great care to prevent the engine hanging on the input shaft.** Lift the engine out of the car, taking care that it does not swing or catch in the car.

The engine is refitted in the reverse order of removal, noting the following points:

1 Lightly lubricate the spigot bearing in the crankshaft end, into which the gearbox input shaft fits, with a little high-melting point grease.

2 Lower the engine back into place and make fine adjustments on the hoist and jack so that the gearbox input shaft is accurately aligned with the clutch. Slide the engine rearwards, without using force, so that the input shaft slides through the clutch. Turn the input shaft slightly if the splines do not line up. With the engine still on the hoist, align the engine mounting bolt holes and then fit and tighten the bolts. The upper flywheel housing bolts are fitted first, followed by the exhaust pipe clamp, starter motor and then lower bolts and sump connecting plate bolts. The bolts on the three types of engine are fitted as follows:

1.8 Longest flywheel housing bolt for upper starter motor flange. Bottom lefthand side bolt secures the exhaust pipe clamp. Engine earth strap is secured by the bolt immediately below the starter motor.

1.1 and 1.3 Longest flywheel housing bolt for lower starter motor flange. Earth strap secured by the long bolt through the lower starter motor flange. Second bolt from the bottom on the lefthand side secures the exhaust pipe clamp bracket.

3 Do not forget to refill the cooling system and engine sump. Check for leaks both before and after starting the engine.

Engine and gearbox removal:

If required, the complete power unit can be taken out of the car. There should not be many occasions when this is required as the gearbox can be taken out, leaving the engine in place. Note that this section does not cover removal of power units when automatic transmissions are fitted, and in such cases it is always best to remove the parts individually.

The connections of the manual gearbox are dealt with fully in **Chapter 6** while the propeller shaft attachments are dealt with in **Chapter 8.**

Start off as for removing the engine alone, carrying out operations 1 to 4 inclusive, without removing the sump connecting plate bolts.

Raise the car on jacks and place it onto axle stands so that the front wheels are clear of the ground by 15 inches

(381 mm). Support the engine with a sling and crane, as before, but this time the lifting point should be as near to the rear of the engine as possible.

Disconnect the engine earth cable from the chassis and disconnect the speedometer drive cable from the gearbox. Mark the flanges on the propeller shaft and disconnect it from the gearbox, tying the propeller shaft safely out of the way to a suspension torsion bar.

Remove the clip that secures the hydraulic clutch pipe to the bulkhead and then disconnect the pipe from the clutch master cylinder. The reservoir should be blocked or drained to prevent the hydraulic fluid from draining out.

The gearbox-to-chassis mounting is shown in **FIG 1 : 7**. The one shown is for the 1.3 engine but the 1.8 version is very similar except in the construction of the pad itself. The rubber is slightly different and instead of being secured to the gearbox by nuts and bolts, studs are embodied in the mounting and nuts secure the mounting to the gearbox. Remove the bolts 3 that secure the cross-member to the body. Lower the engine by approximately 3 inches (80 mm) and release the gearlever, by freeing the bayonet-type fitting, from the gearbox. Free the front engine mountings as described in operation 7.

Check that there are no longer any connections between the power unit and car. Slide a trolley into place under the car and lower the power unit onto it. Disconnect the hoist and sling and draw the power unit out from under the car.

The unit is refitted in the reverse order of removal. In addition to filling the cooling system and engine sump it will also be necessary to fill and bleed the clutch hydraulic system.

Engine mountings:

The different mountings are shown in **FIGS 1 : 5, 1 : 6** and **1 : 7**. If the rubber has perished or assumed a permanent set then the mounting should be renewed.

On the 1.8 model, the mounting shown in **FIG 1 : 6**, the lefthand mounting is fitted with a torque bump stop. When the engine is in place and not running, the clearance 6 should be a minimum of .312 inch (7.94 mm). If the clearance is less than the minimum then a new mounting should be fitted.

1 : 3 Removing the cylinder head

Whenever the cylinder head is refitted or its nuts torque-loaded then they must be turned in the order shown in **FIG 1 : 8**. If this precaution is not taken the cylinder head may easily become distorted. A distorted cylinder head will allow the cylinder head gasket to blow, and it can only be cured by specialist grinding or milling.

  1 Drain the cooling system as instructed in **Chapter 4**. The rocker cover and rocker assembly parts for the smaller engines shown in **FIG 1 : 9**. The parts for the 1.8 are very similar except that the locking washer 5 is fitted to the rear pedestal and the washer is of slightly different shape. Remove the two cap nuts that secure the lifting eyes and rocker cover, carefully collecting the sealing washers fitted under them. Lift off the rocker cover, noting that the vacuum pipe between distributor and carburetter will have to be disconnected. Take care not to damage the rocker

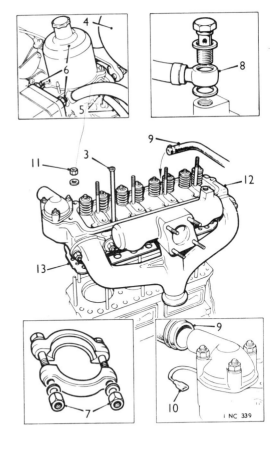

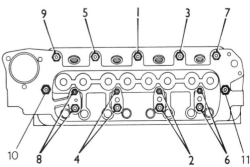

FIG 1 : 10   The attachment of the 1.8 cylinder head

cover gasket, but if it is broken or compressed flat it should be removed and a new gasket fitted in its place. Stick the new gasket to the cover, using a little jointing compound, and lay the cover onto a flat clean surface with a weight on top of it so that the new gasket is held in place until the jointing compound has a chance to set. Evenly and progressively slacken the eight bolts that secure the rocker assembly, marked 2, 4, 6 and 8 in **FIG 1 : 8,** and lift off the rocker assembly, noting the shims under the two centre brackets on 1.8 engines.

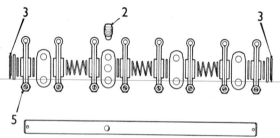

FIG 1:11 The components of the 1.3 engine rocker assembly

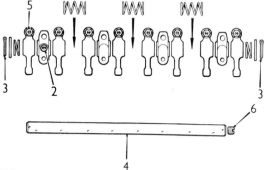

FIG 1:12 The components of the 1.8 engine rocker assembly

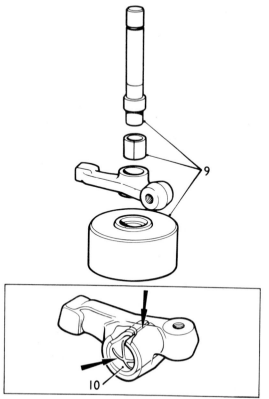

FIG 1:13 Fitting a new bush to a forged rocker arm

2 The attachments on the 1.8 engine are shown in **FIG 1:10**, and those on the 1.1 and 1.3 engine are similar except that there is a bypass hose between the head and water pump. Remove the air cleaner 4 and disconnect the breather and fuel hoses 5 from the carburetter. Take off the flange nuts 6 so that the carburetter can be freed from the inlet manifold. Collect the gaskets and insulators. Lay the carburetter safely out of the way, still attached to its throttle and choke cables. Remove the clamp 7 that secures the exhaust pipe to the exhaust manifold and disconnect the banjo union 8 from the inlet manifold. The union 8 is for the brake servo and will therefore not be fitted on 1.3 models. Disconnect the heater and radiator top hoses 9 as well as the bypass hose on the 1.3 engine. On the 1.3 engine a metal pipe runs along above the manifolds for taking the heater water from the pump to the hose. Remove the manifold nut and washer that also secure the support for this pipe. Disconnect the lead 10 to the temperature transmitter.

3 Lift out the eight pushrods 3 and store them in their correct order, as they must not be interchanged. Disconnect the four HT leads from the sparking plugs. Remove the remaining cylinder head nuts 11 and their washers (nuts 1, 3, 5, 7 and 9 in **FIG 1:8**). Free the cylinder head 12 and lift it squarely up and off its studs. If the cylinder head sticks try tapping upwards gently with a hide-faced or rubber mallet. As a last resort flick the engine over on the starter motor so that the compression breaks the seal. Make sure that the cylinder head is lifted squarely otherwise it will jam on its studs. Remove the old cylinder head gasket 13.

Reassembly:

The cylinder head is refitted in the reverse order of removal. Service the cylinder head as described in the next section. **Make sure that the mating faces of the cylinder head and block are scrupulously clean and free from any small particles or dirt.** Wash all the cylinder head nuts in clean fuel or suitable solvent to make sure that their threads are clean. Similarly make sure that the threads on the studs are clean and check that the nuts run up and down them freely.

Carefully slide a new cylinder head gasket into place down the studs. If need be the gasket can be lightly smeared with grease on both sides to act as an additional seal, but if jointing compound is required then suspect distortion of the head or cylinder block faces. All the gaskets are labelled 'TOP', and this marking should be upwards, and some gaskets are also marked 'FRONT'. Using the old cylinder head gasket is likely to lead to leaks.

Lower the cylinder head back into position. Refit the eight pushrods into their original positions, making sure that their bottom ends seat into the cam followers (tappets). Refit the rocker assembly onto its four studs and carefully fit all the ball-end adjusters on the rockers into the cups in the tops of the pushrods. Evenly and progressively tighten the cylinder head and rocker assembly nuts in the order shown in **FIGS 1:8** or **1:10**. Set all the nuts fingertight and then partially tighten them further in order, carrying on in sequence until they are all at the correct torque load. On all models the correct torque load for the four nuts on the rocker assembly studs is 25 lb ft (3.4 kg m). The cylinder head nuts on 1.1 engines must be tightened to a torque of 40 lb ft (5.5 kg m), on 1.3 engines to 50 lb ft (6.9 kg m) and on 1.8 engines to 45 to 50 lb ft (6.2 to 6.9 kg m).

When the cylinder head nuts are correctly tightened set the valve clearances, as described in **Section 1 : 5**. Refit the remainder of the parts and connect all hoses and leads. Fill the cooling system.

1 : 4 Servicing the cylinder head

Removal of the cylinder head is dealt with in the previous section.

Rocker assembly:

Renewal of the rocker cover gasket has been dealt with in the previous section. Wipe out the sludge in the cover using newspaper or rags and then wash it out with fuel or paraffin. The oil filler cap in the cover should be renewed at the same time as the oil filter and it is advisable to renew it at major engine overhauls as well.

The rocker assembly parts for the 1.1 and 1.3 engine are shown in **FIG 1 : 11** and those for the 1.8 in **FIG 1 : 12**. To dismantle the parts, take out the shaft locking screw 2 and extract the splitpins 3 from the ends of the shaft. The components can then be slid off the shaft, but store them in the correct order for reassembly.

Wash the parts in clean fuel and make sure that all the oilways are clean. Renew the adjusters if their ball ends show signs of wear. If the tips of the rockers show signs of wear, try gently smoothing them down with an oil stone (while keeping the original contour) but if the damage is too deep then the rocker arm must be renewed. Bushes are fitted into the rocker arms. If the pressed rocker arms are fitted and the bushes found to be worn then new rocker arms must be fitted. The bushes can be renewed in the forged rocker arms. The method is shown in **FIG 1 : 13** using the tools 18G.226 and 18G.226A, making sure that the oil grooves are at the bottom and the butt joint at the top as shown. Once new bushes have been fitted into the forged rocker arms the bushes must be burnish reamed. The final diameter for 1.1 and 1.3 engines is .5630 to .5635 inch (14.30 to 14.31 mm) while that for 1.8 engines is .6255 to .626 inch (15.8 to 15.9 mm).

On 1100 cc engines a small plug will be found in the end of the rocker arm, this is a guide for an oil way between the adjuster screw and the rocker bush.

Remove the adjuster screw, drill out the plug with a No. 43 drill (2.26 mm) and continue the oilway through to the bush. Reseal the end hole with a rivet welded in position.

Continue the hole, which will be found in the top of the rocker barrel, with a No. 47 drill (1.98 mm).

The parts are reassembled in the reverse order of dismantling, making sure that the shims and parts are refitted into their original positions and using new splitpins to secure the end washers. Do not forget to refit the lockwasher for the screw 2 before refitting the nut that secures the pedestal to the engine.

Note that on 1100 cc engines the following shims, present on 1.3 engines, are omitted:

1 Shims on either side of Nos. 1 and 8 rockers.

2 Shim behind No. 2 rocker shaft bracket.

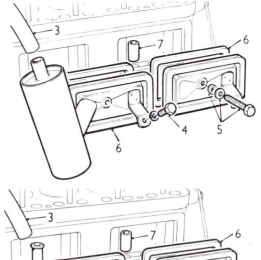

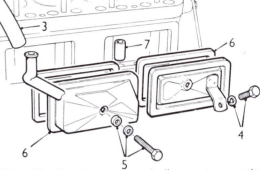

FIG 1 : 14   The side covers and oil separators on the 1.8 engine

3 Shim in front of No. 3 rocker shaft bracket, but double coil spring washers are fitted at either end of the rocker shaft.

Cam followers (Tappets):

On the 1.3 engine these are extracted downwards and can therefore only be removed after the camshaft has been taken out (see **Section 1 : 11**) with the cylinder head, pushrods and sump removed.

On the 1.1 and 1.8 engines the cam followers can be removed after the pushrods have been removed and the side covers taken off. The attachments of the side covers on the 1.8 engine are shown in **FIG 1 : 14**, the difference being the oil separator canister. Disconnect the breather hose 3 and free the heater pipe by taking out the bolts 4. Take out the bolts 5, collecting the washers and seals, and then remove the covers and their gaskets 6. The cam followers 7 can then be lifted out. Keep the cam followers in order as they should not be interchanged.

Check that each cam follower is a free fit in its bore, without excessive play. Renew any cam followers that show wear, scoring or chipped faces.

Decarbonizing:

The parts of the 1.3 cylinder head are shown in **FIG 1 : 15** and those of the 1.8 in **FIG 1 : 16**. Remove the sparking plugs 2, thermostat cover 3 and thermostat valve 4, temperature transmitter 5, heater pipe 6. Take off the nuts and washers that secure the manifold assembly 7 and remove the manifolds with the gasket. Leave the valves fitted at this stage as they will protect the valve seats.

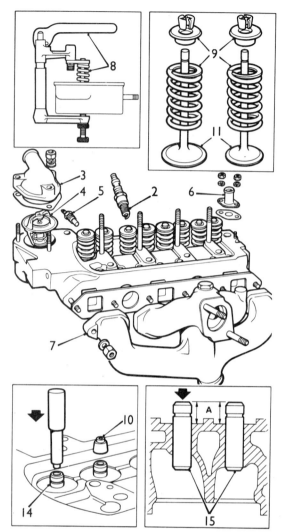

FIG 1:15   The cylinder head details on the 1.3 engine. The 1.1 is very similar

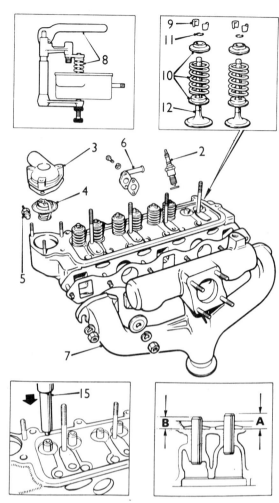

FIG 1:16   The cylinder head details on the 1.8 engine

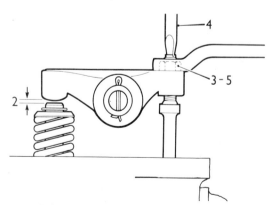

FIG 1:17   Adjusting the valve clearances

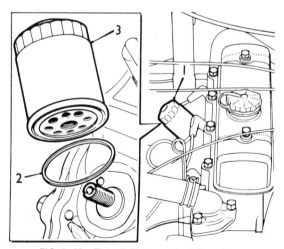

FIG 1:18   The oil filter on the 1.3 engine

Remove the carbon from the combustion chambers and ports. Aluminium alloy must be treated with great care and carbon should only be removed using a sharpened stick of solder or hardwood and provided that all abrasive particles can be washed away it may be lightly polished using worn emerycloth dipped in paraffin. On cast iron head more drastic methods can be used. Scrape off the worst of the deposits. The best method of removing the remainder is to use a rotary wire brush in an electric drill. Remove the valves and clean the ports by similar method, **but take great care not to damage the valve seats in the head or the valve guides.**

Scrape the carbon away from around the valves, **taking great care not to damage the seats or the ground portion of the valve stems.** The valves can be lightly polished using emerycloth, but not on the seats or stems.

Clean the bores of the valve guides. Special wire brushes are made for the purpose, where both ends of the wires are trapped, but if these are not available soak a long thin piece of rag in fuel and pull this through the valve guide several times, following up with a clean strip of rag.

Blank off the oilways and water passages in the block with pieces of rag. Turn the engine until two pistons are nearly at TDC. The ring of carbon around the periphery of the piston acts as an additional oil seal and heat shield for the top compression ring, so this carbon should be left in place. The best method of protecting this carbon is to spring an old piston ring into the bore above the piston. Before removing carbon from the piston crowns, smear a little grease around the top of each bore to trap loose dust and carbon. Use a sharpened stick of solder or hardwood to scrape away the carbon. **No other tools may be used and no form of abrasive should be used.** Repeat the procedure with the other pair of pistons nearly at TDC. Blow away loose dust and dirt and wipe out the grease and dirt from the tops of the bores. Remove all the pieces of rag from the water passages and oilways, making absolutely sure that none have fallen into the block.

Mating faces:

Make sure that these are scrupulously clean before reassembling the parts. Slight deposits of carbon will build up on the face for the manifold and these should be carefully removed with a scraper or steel rule. Check the faces using a long steel straightedge. A better method is to use engineer's blue spread onto a surface table or plate glass as this will show high spots. High spots can be carefully removed using a scraper or smooth file but if the surface is badly distorted, specialist regrinding is the only cure. When checking the face of the cylinder block it may be necessary to remove the cylinder head studs. Special stud extractors are made but, if these are not available studs can often be removed by locking two nuts together on the threads and unscrewing the stud using a spanner on the lower nut.

Valve removal:

A valve spring compressor will be required. Use the tool as shown in the insert 8 to compress the valve spring. Lift out the split collets and carefully release the compressor. Note the differences between the valves on the 1.3 and 1.8 engines. On the 1.3 engine the valve seals 10 are fitted directly onto the inlet valve guides and no lower spring collars are fitted. On the 1.8 engine, packing rings 11 are fitted under the split collets 9. In both cases the seals should be discarded and new ones fitted on re-assembly.

Once the collets have been removed, lift off the spring cup, valve spring (and collar if fitted) so that the valve can be slid out from the combustion chamber side.

Store the valves in their correct order as they must be refitted into their original positions.

Refit the valves in the reverse order of removal, after they have been examined and serviced.

Valve examination:

Check the seat width on the valve and if it is so wide that it is making a sharp edge with the end of the valve then the valve should be discarded and a new one fitted in its place. Examine the ends of the valve stems and use an oil stone to smooth them down if they are rough or slightly worn.

Renew any valves that have scored or bent valve stems. Use a steel rule for checking the valve stems for bend.

Grinding-in valves:

The best method is to use garage equipment to break the glaze and then cut the seats in the head. The valves are ground on a special grinder to remove pits and a final finish is given by lapping the seats together using grinding paste.

Grinding paste alone will usually be sufficient for the owner, but check the seats both in the head and on the valves for deep pitting and have them cut on garage equipment to remove these pits. The use of grinding paste will remove excess metal from the mating seat.

Fit the valve back into its guide, with a light spring between the valve head and cylinder head. Smear a little medium-grade grinding paste evenly around the seat and then use a suction tool to press the valve down against the spring. Grind with a semi-rotary motion, frequently allowing the valve to rise up and turning it through a quarter turn before pressing it down again and continuing grinding. When the pits have been removed, take out the valve and clean away all traces of grinding paste. Repeat the procedure using fine-grade paste until both seats are even and matt-grey with no pits or scores. Remove the valve, clean away grinding paste and repeat the procedure on the remaining valves.

When all the valves have been ground-in, wash the parts thoroughly to remove all traces of abrasive from the valves, ports and cylinder head.

Valve seats:

The seats in the head should not be allowed to become too wide. For inlet valves the best width is approximately $\frac{1}{16}$ inch and for exhaust valves $\frac{3}{32}$ inch. Wide seats can be reduced by using different angle cutters. A large angled cutter will remove material from the outside of the seat and a narrow cutter will remove material from inside the port. Both angles of cutter should be used to bring the seat width to the correct limit while still allowing the seat to meet the valve sealing face centrally. If the cylinder head seats cannot be restored by the use of cutters or the valve sinks into the seat so that its face is flush or below

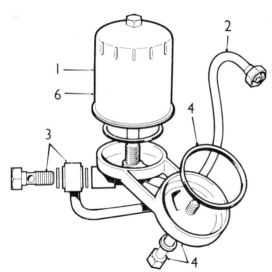

FIG 1:19   The oil filter assembly for the 1.8 engine

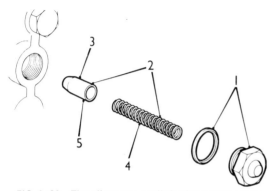

FIG 1:20   The oil pressure relief valve components

the combustion chamber, then the head should be taken to an agent for seat inserts to be fitted and cut to size.

Valve springs:

Rigs are available for testing valve springs, and the spring data is given in Technical Data at the end of this manual. A check can be made by using a modified spring balance and steel ruler to measure the compression under load. As a rough test, mount the old spring end-to-end onto a new spring and compress the pair between the jaws of a vice. If the old spring has weakened it will be appreciably shorter than the new one, while both are under equal pressure.

If any of the valve springs are weak, the complete set should be renewed.

Valve guides:

The valve guides must be renewed if they are worn (check using a new valve) as they will allow oil to leak past them into the combustion chamber. The method of renewing valve guides is shown in FIGS 1:15 and 1:16. Press the old guides out, in the direction of the arrow, so that they come out through the combustion chamber.

Press the new guides back into place, again in the direction of the arrow, until the projection A or B of the guide above the spot face in the cylinder head is correct. On the 1.1 and 1.3 engines both guides are pressed in until the dimension A is .54 inch (13.72 mm). On the 1.8 engines the inlet guides are pressed in until the dimension A is correct at .75 inch (19.05 mm) and the exhaust guides until the dimension B is correct at .625 inch (15.87 mm).

When new valve guides have been fitted, the valve seats in the head must be recut to ensure concentricity.

Reassembly:

The parts are all reassembled in the reverse order of dismantling. Lubricate all bearing surfaces liberally with clean engine oil. Discard old seals and gaskets, using new ones (available in 'decoke' kits). Soak the oil seals in oil before refitting them.

Check the pushrods and renew any that are bent (use a steel straightedge or roll them along a flat surface) as well as any that have damaged or worn cups or ball ends. Slacken off the adjusters on all the rocker arms to ensure that there is plenty of clearance when the cylinder head is refitted, otherwise there may be no clearance and the pushrod will bend as the cylinder head nuts are tightened. Adjust the valve clearances, as described in the next section, after the cylinder head has been refitted but before the rocker cover is fitted.

1:5   Adjusting valve clearance

The method of adjusting the valve clearance is shown in FIG 1:17. On the 1.1 and 1.3 engine the gap 2 on all valves, with the valve fully open, should be .012 inch (.3 mm) while on the 1.8 engine the gap should be .013 inch (.33 mm). The setting is done with the engine cold.

Remove the valve rocker cover to expose the rocker assembly. The engine must be turned over while setting the valves. Try turning it using a spanner on the crankshaft pulley bolt or by pulling it around with the pulley and fan belt. Another method is to jack up one rear wheel, engage a high gear, and turn the engine by turning the jacked-up wheel. In all cases the engine will be easier to turn if the sparking plugs have been removed.

Turn the engine until number 8 (rearmost) valve is fully open with the rocker down and valve spring compressed. No. 1 (front) valve can now be adjusted.

Hold the adjuster with a screwdriver 4 while the locknut 3 is slackened with a spanner 5. Insert a feeler gauge of the correct thickness into the gap 2 and turn the screwdriver 4 until the feeler gauge is just lightly nipped between the rocker tip and top of the valve stem. Slacken back the adjuster very slightly until the feeler gauge is a sliding fit but light drag is felt as it is moved. While checking the gap, apply downwards pressure on the screwdriver to take up any backlash in the system and break any oil film. When the gap is correct, hold the screwdriver to prevent the adjuster from turning and tighten the locknut 3. Check that the gap has not altered while tightening the locknut, as small movements of the adjuster make quite a difference.

The valves are best checked in the following sequence:
Check No. 1 valve with No. 8 valve fully open
Check No. 3 valve with No. 6 valve fully open
Check No. 5 valve with No. 4 valve fully open
Check No. 2 valve with No. 7 valve fully open

Check No. 8 valve with No. 1 valve fully open
Check No. 6 valve with No. 3 valve fully open
Check No. 4 valve with No. 5 valve fully open
Check No. 7 valve with No. 2 valve fully open

The valves are counted as No. 1 at the front and No. 8 at the rear. Note that the numbers in each line add up to 9 so that, though the sequence given will require minimum turning of the engine, the sequence can be started at any point and constant reference to the table will not be necessary.

Refit the valve rocker cover, using a new gasket if required. Check for oil leaks after the engine has been running for some time.

1 : 6 The oil filter and relief valve

The oil filter element, engine oil and oil filler cap should all be changed at intervals of 6000 miles (10,000 kilometres) or 6 months, whichever occurs the sooner.

Take the car for a short run to warm the oil and bring all dirt into suspension. Remove the drain plug from the sump and allow the oil to drain into a suitable container. The drain plug is fitted with a copper washer so renew the washer at every other oil change or if it appears damaged.

The filter assembly on the 1.3 engine is shown in **FIG 1 : 18** (the 1.1 type is similar but mounted vertically) and that on the 1.8 engine in **FIG 1 : 19**. Unscrew the old canister and discard it, together with its seal. Check the seal on the new canister, smear it lightly with engine oil and screw the complete canister back into place handtight.

Refit the sump drain plug and fill the engine to the upper mark on the dipstick, through the oil filler on the rocker cover, using fresh oil. Start the engine and leave it to run while checking for oil leaks around the oil filter. Stop the engine and leave it for at least five minutes before checking the level and topping up as required.

If the seal around the filter support on the 1.8 models leaks then the complete unit must be removed and a new seal 4 fitted.

Relief valve:

The parts of the relief valve are shown in **FIG 1 : 20**. Dirt under the seat 3, a pitted or scored valve 5, or weak spring 4, will cause a drop in oil pressure.

Unscrew and remove the cap nut with its seal 1 so that the spring and plunger assembly 2 can be drawn out. Check the spring against the dimensions given in Technical Data and renew it if worn or broken. Renew the plunger 5 if it is scored or damaged. A stick of hardwood can be used to clean out the seat in the cylinder block but a special tool 18G.69 is made for lapping the seats.

Refit the parts in the reverse order of removal.

1 : 7 The sump and oil pump

Both the sump and oil pump differ between the two types of engine. The sump and oil strainer for the 1.1 and 1.3 engine are shown in **FIG 1 : 21** while the sump and oil pump for the 1.8 engine are shown in **FIG 1 : 22**.

Sump removal:

Drain the oil from the sump into a suitable container, leaving it to drain for as long as possible as this will reduce oil drips when the sump is removed. Remove the

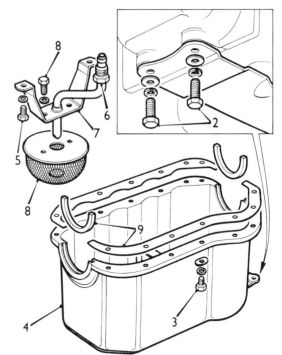

FIG 1 : 21   The sump and oil strainer on the 1.1 and 1.3 engine

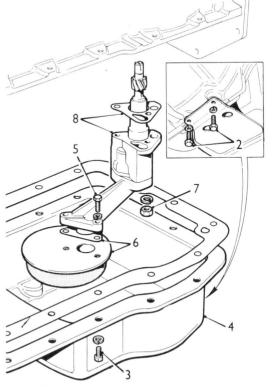

FIG 1 : 22   The sump and oil pump on the 1.8 engine

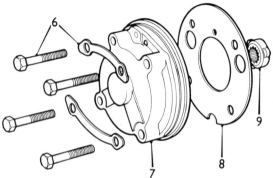

FIG 1:23 The oil pump and its attachments on the 1.3 engine

bolts 2 that secure the sump connecting plate to the fly-wheel housing. Remove the bolts 3 that secure the sump to the crankcase, carefully collecting all the lockwashers and load spreader washers (if fitted). Leave four bolts loosely in place, one in each corner, until the sump 4 is ready for removal and then take out these bolts and lower the sump from the car.

Whenever the sump is removed, check and clean the strainer for the inlet to the oil pump. Wash the strainer in clean fuel to remove any sludge and renew it if the gauze has broken.

Refit the sump in the reverse order of removal. It is most advisable to renew the gaskets 9. Wash and wipe out the sump so that it is clean both on the inside and outside. Secure the gaskets in place with a little grease and then carefully lift the sump up so that the gaskets are not displaced. Hold the sump in place with a bolt at each corner, only just tightened, and then fit the remainder of the bolts loosely before tightening them all progressively to the correct torque of 6 lb ft (.8 kg m). Refill the sump to the correct level with fresh engine oil and check for leaks after the engine has been run for a short while.

Engine oil pump, 1.1 and 1.3 litre:

In both engines this is mounted at the rear of the engine and driven from the camshaft. The 1.3 is shown in **FIG 1:23**, that on the 1.1 engine is very similar. In order to gain access to the pump the clutch and flywheel must be removed (see next Section). Remove the gearbox adaptor plate. Unlock and remove the bolts 6 and withdraw the oil pump 7. Remove the gasket 8 and extract the oil pump drive coupling 9 from the end of the camshaft.

Refit the pump in the reverse order of removal. Use a new gasket 8 and tighten the bolts 6 to a torque of 9 lb ft (1.2 kg m).

The components of the oil pump and the dimensions to be checked are shown in **FIG 1:24**. Dismantle the pump by taking out the screws 2 but note that the parts of the body are aligned by dowels. Clean all the parts and then use feeler gauges to measure the clearances shown. If the clearances are greater than given then the complete pump must be renewed.

Lubricate the parts liberally with engine oil before reassembling the pump, and check that the pump rotates freely when assembled.

Engine oil pump, 1.8 litre:

The attachments of the pump are shown in **FIG 1:22**. With the sump removed, take out the bolts 5 and remove the strainer with its gasket 6. Take off the attachment nuts 7 and withdraw the oil pump with its gasket 8.

The pump is refitted in the reverse order of removal. Tighten the nuts 7 and bolts 5 to a torque load of 14 lb ft (1.9 kg m).

The components of the oil pump and the dimensions to be checked are shown in **FIG 1:25** and the servicing is carried out in a similar manner to that on the 1.3 pump. The cover attachment bolts are tightened to a torque of 10 lb ft (1.38 kg m).

1:8 The clutch and flywheel

This section only deals with the removal and refitting of the clutch and all other matters relating to the clutch will be found in **Chapter 5**.

The parts are only accessible after the engine has been separated from the gearbox. Depending on what further work is to be carried out remove the engine from the car (see **Section 1:2**) or remove the gearbox from the car (see **Chapter 6**).

The attachments of the clutch are shown in **FIG 1:26**. Make alignment marks 2 and 8 on the clutch cover and flywheel so that the parts will be reassembled in their original alignment. Progressively and diagonally slacken the attachment bolts 3. **The bolts must be progressively slackened otherwise the pressure of the spring will distort the clutch cover.** When all the bolts are free lift off the clutch assembly and remove the driven plate 6.

The attachments of the flywheel on 1.8 engines are shown in **FIG 1:27**. On the 1.1 and 1.3 engine there is no rear oil seal retainer 7 or oil seal, so references to these parts can be ignored, but the oil pump is fitted behind the gearbox adaptor plate. Note that on the 1.3 engine the oil pump is fitted with its flange between the gasket and adaptor plate. Turn the engine until the 1-4 TDC mark is uppermost and make light marks 4 on the flywheel 6 and end of the crankshaft. Unlock and remove the flywheel attachment bolts and lockplate 5. Carefully pull the fly-wheel 6 back off the dowels and remove it.

Take out the bolts and remove the oil seal retainer 7. Take out the adaptor plate securing bolts 12 and remove the adaptor plate and gasket 8 as well as the rear crank-shaft oil seal.

Reassembly:

The parts are refitted in the reverse order of removal. Renew any parts, gaskets or seals that are damaged.

When refitting the gearbox adaptor plate on the 1.8 engine, use the tool 18G.1108 (see item 11 in the inset) to protect the oil seal as the plate is fitted back into position. Tighten the adaptor plate bolts 12 to a torque of 30 lb ft (4.15 kg m) on 1.8 models and 25 lb ft (3.4 kg m) on 1.1 and 1.3 models. The oil seal retainer on the 1.8 has its bolts tightened to 25 lb ft (3.4 kg m).

Refit the flywheel, making sure that the contact faces are perfectly clean and aligning any previously made marks. Use a new lockplate if the old one is damaged and tighten the bolts 5 to a torque of 40 lb ft (5.5 kg m) before locking them.

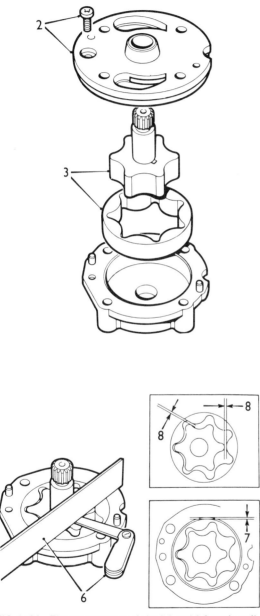

FIG 1:24 The components of the 1.1 and 1.3 engine oil pump, showing the dimensions to be checked

Key to Fig 1:24   2 Pump cover and screws   3 Rotors
6 Rotor end float .005 inch (.127 mm)   7 Outer rotor to body
clearance .010 inch (.254 mm)   8 Lobe clearances .006 inch
(.152 mm)

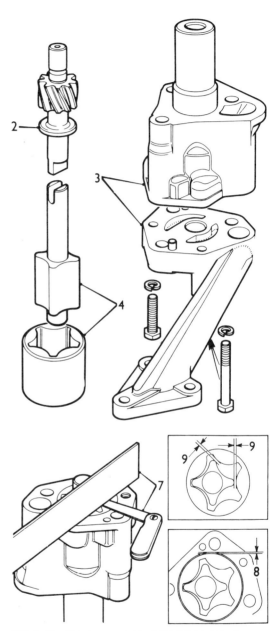

FIG 1:25 The components of the 1.8 engine oil pump, showing the dimensions to be checked

Key to Fig 1:25   2 Drive spindle   3 Cover and body
4 Rotors   7 Rotor end float .005 inch (.127 mm)   8 Outer
rotor to body clearance .010 inch (.254 mm)   9 Lobe clearances
.006 inch (.152 mm)

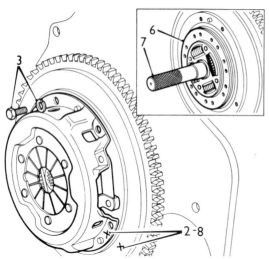

FIG 1:26 The clutch attachments. Inset shows centralizing mandrel fitted

Fit the driven plate to the flywheel with the spring housing facing outwards and hold it in place with the centralizing mandrel as shown. On the 1.8 engines use mandrel No. 18G.1195 and on the 1.3 engines No. 18G.1196. **The mandrel is essential as it centralizes the driven plate so that the gearbox input shaft can be passed through it into the spigot bearing, when refitting the gearbox.** Refit the clutch cover assembly, aligning the marks, and secure it in place by evenly and progressively tightening the attachment bolts. Tighten the bolts to a torque of 25 to 30 lb ft (3.4 to 4.1 kg m).

Starter ring gear:

If the teeth on the ring are badly worn or damaged a new ring can be fitted to the flywheel. Remove the flywheel. Carefully drill through partially at the root of a tooth and use a cold chisel to split the ring at this weak point. **Take great care not to damage or mark the flywheel itself.**

Thoroughly clean the periphery of the flywheel by scrubbing it with a wire brush and removing high spots with emerycloth.

Heat the new starter ring gear to a temperature of 300° to 400°C (572° to 752°F)—indicated by a light blue surface colour of the paint indicator. The best method is to use a stove to heat the ring but it can be heated using two or more blow lamps while laid on a sheet of asbestos. If blow lamps are used keep the flames moving so that local overheated spots do not develop. **Overheating will ruin the temper of the metal.** When the ring is hot, lay it into place on the flywheel and tap it fully into place with soft-metal drifts. The lead-in on the teeth should face towards the clutch side of the flywheel. Leave the ring to cool fully before moving the flywheel.

Spigot bush:

Whenever the clutch is removed, the spigot bush in the end of the crankshaft should be checked for wear or chatter marks. Renew the bush if it is damaged.

The bush can possibly be removed by tapping a thread in it and using a bolt screwed in to pull it out. If this does not succeed find a suitable tube as a spacer and in combination with a flat washer make an extractor so that the bush is pulled out as the bolt is tightened. If a tap is not available, or a suitable internal extractor, find or turn a piece of rod that is a snug fit in the bush. Fill the bush and recess in the crankshaft with grease, avoiding air pockets. Press the rod into the bush and with light hammer blows on the end of the rod the hydraulic pressure of the grease will force the bush out.

Press a new bush into place and lubricate it lightly with high melting-point grease.

1:9 The distributor drive gear

The parts of the drive are shown in **FIG 1:28** and they are similar in appearance on all models.

Removal:

Remove the distributor, by taking off the cap and disconnecting the low-tension lead and vacuum pipe, followed by removal of the two bolts that secure the clamp and withdrawing the distributor.

Take out the special bolt 2 that secures the housing 4 to the crankcase. Screw a $\frac{5}{16}$ UNF bolt 3, approximately $3\frac{1}{2}$ inch (90 mm) long into the threaded portion of the drive shaft 5. Turn the engine until No. 1 piston is 90 deg. before or after TDC so that all four pistons are halfway up the bores. Withdraw the distributor housing 4 and drive shaft 5.

Reassembly:

If the engine has been turned after the drive shaft has been removed turn it back to the position where No. 1 piston is 90 deg. before or after TDC and insert the drive shaft 5 back into position. Turn the engine until No. 1 piston is at TDC on the compression stroke. This can be found by removing the rocker cover and turning the engine until the valves of No. 4 (rear) cylinder are at the point of balance, with the inlet valve just opening and the exhaust valve just closing. Another method is to remove the sparking plug from No. 1 (front) cylinder and turn the engine until a rise in pressure is felt in the cylinder when the plug hole is blocked with a thumb, indicating the compression stroke. With the second method, accurately find TDC using the timing marks on the timing cover and crankshaft pulley (or on the flywheel). The 1.1 and 1.3 engines should be set to 5 deg. BTDC while the 1.8 is set at TDC.

Partially withdraw the drive shaft 5 so that it is no longer in mesh and on 1.8 engines turn it to the position shown in the inset 8. On 1.1 and 1.3 engines the larger offset must still be uppermost, but the slot should be in the 'ten to four' position. Lower the drive shaft down, allowing it to rotate as it meshes with the camshaft. When the drive shaft is fully in place, the offset will have turned in an anticlockwise direction to the two o'clock position.

Refit the housing 4 and secure it with the special bolt 2, making sure that the head of the bolt does not protrude above the face of the housing. On the 1.8 engine a countersunk screw is used in place of the bolt shown.

Take out the bolt 3 that was used to hold the drive shaft. Refit the rocker cover if it has been removed and refit the distributor.

If marks are made on the clamp and crankcase before the distributor is removed and the clamp is not slackened on the distributor, the ignition timing need not be lost when refitting the distributor if the marks are again set in alignment. Slide the distributor into place and rotate its shaft until the drive dog aligns with the offset in the drive and press the distributor fully home. If there is any doubt check with the instructions in **Chapter 3** and reset the ignition timing.

1:10 The valve timing gear

The details of the timing cover on the 1.3 engine are shown in **FIG 1:29**. The 1.8 engine is exactly similar with the exception of the oil separator, which is mounted on a side cover instead of the timing cover, so that the hose 7 can be ignored.

Removing timing cover:

1 Drain the cooling system and remove the radiator. Slacken the three generator attachment bolts 3 and push the generator down in the opposite direction to the arrow 5 so that the fan belt tension is released and the fan belt 4 can be removed. Pull the generator up in the direction of the arrow 5 to keep it out of the way. Take out the bolts and remove the cooling fan and water pump pulley 6. Full and further instructions on the work in this operation will be found in **Chapter 4**. As a safety precaution, disconnect the battery before starting work.

2 Disconnect the breather hose 7 (if fitted). Unlock and remove the crankshaft pulley bolt 8, preferably using the special spanner 18G.98A as this has an end made for hammering on if the nut is tight. Remove the pulley 9 from the crankshaft. A two-legged extractor should be used but if care is taken the pulley can be levered off using two screwdrivers.

3 Take out the bolts and remove the timing cover 10 with its gasket 14.

4 If there have been oil leaks check the condition of the gasket 14 and the oil seal 11, renewing them if necessary. At the same time check the hub of the crankshaft pulley and renew the unit if the hub is scored or worn.

Refitting the timing cover:

Wash the cover in fuel to remove sludge from the inside and dirt from the outside. If the oil seal 11 has been removed, fit a new one in its place using the tools 18G.134 and 18G.134BD, making sure that the lips of the seal face into the engine.

Refit the timing cover and use the tool 18G.1046 to centralize the oil seal about the crankshaft before tightening the attachment bolts.

The remainder of the parts are refitted in the reverse order of removal. Note that the hub of the crankshaft pulley should be oiled before pushing the pulley back into place.

Adjust the fan belt tension and refill the cooling system.

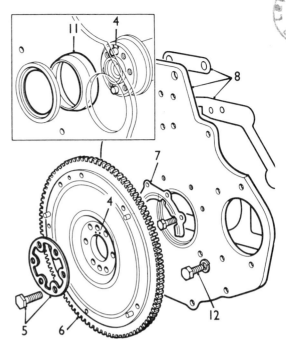

FIG 1:27 The attachments of the flywheel and adaptor plate on the 1.8 engine

Timing chain and sprockets:

Remove the timing cover as just described. The tensioner and parts on the 1.3 engine are shown in **FIG 1:30**; note that some earlier models are not fitted with a tensioner. The parts on the 1.8 engine are shown in **FIG 1:31**. Note that a hydraulic chain tensioner is fitted.

1 Remove the oil thrower 2. On the 1.3 models, remove the pivot bolt and withdraw the tensioner 3. On the 1.8 models, free the tab and unscrew the bolt 3 from the body of the tensioner. Insert a $\frac{1}{8}$ inch (3.2 mm) Allen key through the hole where the bolt 3 fitted and turn the key in a clockwise direction until the pressure

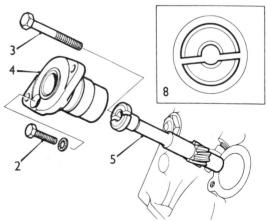

FIG 1:28 The distributor drive shaft assembly. Inset shows the correct position of the offset before the shaft is lowered back into full mesh, with No. 1 cylinder at TDC (1.8 engines)

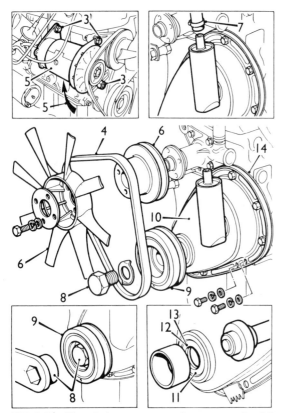

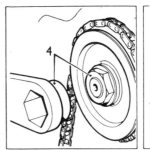

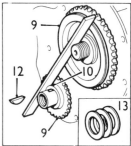

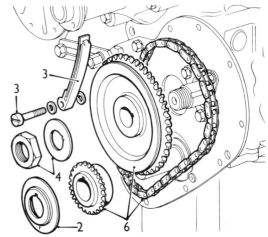

FIG 1 : 29 The timing cover attachments on the 1.3 engine. The 1.8 engine is similar apart from the oil separator canister shown in inset 7

FIG 1 : 30 The timing chain, sprockets and tensioner on the 1.3 engine. Not all models are fitted with the tensioner. Later 1.3 engines have a duplex chain, the single chain being retained on 1.1 engines

of the tensioner on the chain is reduced. **Note that on the hydraulic tensioner the Allen key must always be turned clockwise, whether tightening or slackening the tensioner, and the slipper must never be forced back into the body. Turning the Allen key anticlockwise will damage the tensioner.** Once the tension is reduced, take out the bolts and remove the tensioner assembly 5.

2 Use the special spanner 18G.98A to undo and remove the nut and washer 4 that secure the camshaft sprocket to the camshaft. Withdraw both sprockets evenly from their shafts and remove them complete with the timing chain. Suitable two-legged extractors should be used but if care is taken it should be possible to draw them off by levering each one with two screwdrivers.

3 Check the timing chain and sprockets for wear. Excessive sideways movement of the chain is one indication of wear and noise when it is operating is another. Renew the chain if it is worn and usually it is advisable to renew the sprockets at the same time, as worn sprockets will quickly wear a new chain. Examine the sprocket teeth for wear and if the teeth are worn to a hook shape then the sprockets must be renewed.

The parts are refitted in the reverse order of removal, setting the valve timing and making sure that the sprockets align.

Shims 13 are fitted behind the crankshaft sprocket to bring the two sprockets into alignment. Refit the sprockets without the timing chain, and omitting the keys if they have been taken out. Press the sprockets fully and tightly against the engine and lay a straightedge across them as shown in the inset. Measure, with feeler gauges, the gap between the straightedge and crankshaft sprocket and select shims 13 to reduce this gap to zero. Once the correct shims have been selected, and tried, remove the sprockets and leave the shims on the crankshaft. Refit the key 12 into the crankshaft, as well as the key in the camshaft if this too has been removed.

Turn the crankshaft until the pistons are all approximately halfway down their bores. This ensures that there is no danger of the valves hitting the piston crowns when the camshaft is turned. Turn the camshaft until its key is approximately at two o'clock, as shown in **FIG 1 : 32**. Turn the crankshaft until its keyway is vertical. Encircle the sprockets with the timing chain so that their dimples are in line and then press them both back onto the crankshaft and camshaft, with the chain fitted. When the sprockets are in place, make sure that their dimples are still in line. Secure the camshaft sprocket in place with the nut and washer 4.

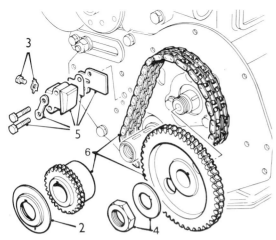

FIG 1:31 The timing chain, sprockets and hydraulic tensioner on the 1.8 engine

Refit the chain tensioner. On the 1.3 engine, make sure that the washers are fitted on either side of the tensioner. On the 1.8 engine, slacken off the tensioner by turning the Allen key clockwise, refit the tensioner and adjust it by turning the Allen key clockwise until the slipper pad is in contact with the timing chain. Fit the bolt 3 with a new lockwasher back to the tensioner body.

Refit the oil thrower 2 with the face marked F facing forwards. Refit the timing cover in the reverse order of removal.

1:11 The camshaft

On the 1.1 and 1.8 engine the camshaft can be removed with the engine still fitted to the car. On the 1.3 engine, the engine must be removed from the car and laid on its side (or inverted) when removing the camshaft otherwise the cam followers will fall and jam the camshaft as it is withdrawn.

1.8 and 1.1 litre engines:

The instructions given cover the removal of the camshaft with the engine still fitted in the car. If the engine has been removed the instructions relevant to the engine mountings, cooling system and air intake grille can be ignored.

1 Drain the cooling system and remove the radiator. Disconnect the battery. Remove the rocker cover, rocker shaft assembly and pushrods but leaving the cylinder head fitted, and take out the cam followers (see **Sections 1:3** and **1:4**). Remove the distributor and its drive shaft (see **Section 1:9**). Remove the timing cover, timing chain and sprockets as described in the previous section. Remove the fuel pump (see **Chapter 2**).

2 The manufacturers instructions do not require removal of the sump and oil pump but if the owner is not skilled he may have trouble unmeshing and meshing the oil pump drive gears. If difficulty is found then be prepared to have to remove the sump and oil pump as well (see **Section 1:7**).

3 Remove the camshaft locating plate 8, shown in **FIG 1:33**. Support the engine from underneath with a

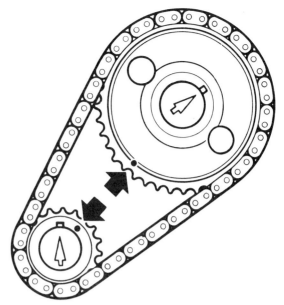

FIG 1:32 The correct positions of the keys and the valve timing marks on the sprockets correctly aligned

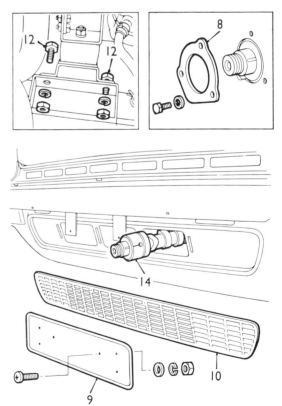

FIG 1:33 Removing the camshaft, with the engine fitted, on 1.8 models

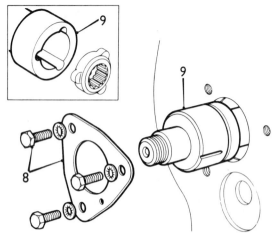

FIG 1:34 The camshaft locating plate on 1.3 engines. Note the oil pump drive coupling shown in the inset

jack and pad of wood and free the front engine mounting bolts 12. Remove the number plate 9 and carefully drill out the pop rivets that secure the air intake grille 10. Lower the jack under the engine until the camshaft can be drawn out through the aperture as shown in the figure. These latter operations are not necessary on 1.1 litre engines.

The camshaft is refitted in the reverse order of removal. Before refitting the camshaft, check the end float. Refit the locating plate and sprocket to the camshaft and use feeler gauges to measure the gap between locating plate and sprocket. If the gap is not within the correct limits of .003 to .007 inch (.076 to .178 mm) a new locating plate must be fitted to correct the end float.

Use .125 inch (3.17 mm) diameter pop rivets to secure the air intake grille back in place.

1.3 litre engine:

1 Remove the engine from the car (see **Section 1:2**). Remove the rocker cover, rocker assembly and pushrods but leaving the cylinder head fitted (see **Sections 1:3** and **1:4**). Remove the distributor drive shaft (see **Section 1:9**). Remove the fuel pump (see **Chapter 2**). Remove the timing cover and valve timing gear as instructed in the previous section.

2 Lay the engine on its side, or invert it. Take out the bolts and remove the camshaft locating plate 8, shown in **FIG 1:34**, and then withdraw the camshaft 9. The oil pump drive coupling is fitted to the rear of the camshaft as shown in the inset and great care must be taken to avoid it being drawn out with the camshaft and falling into the sump.

3 If the cam followers require removal, take off the sump and draw them out of their bores, storing them in the correct order for reassembly. Obviously the sump must be removed if the oil pump coupling or cam followers accidentally fall out of position.

Check the end float between the locating plate and sprocket, with the parts fitted to the camshaft, and renew the locating plate of the end float is outside the limits of .003 to .007 inch (.076 to .178 mm).

Refit the camshaft in the reverse order of removal.

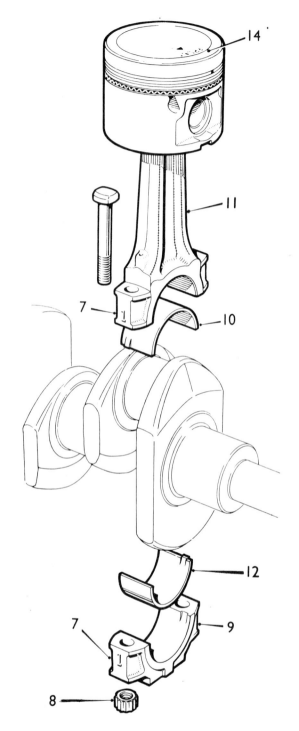

FIG 1:35 Typical piston and connecting rod assembly

Key to Fig 1:35   7 Identification number   8 Nut
9 Bearing cap   10 Bearing shell for connecting rod
11 Connecting rod   12 Bearing shell for cap   14 Front identification mark on piston

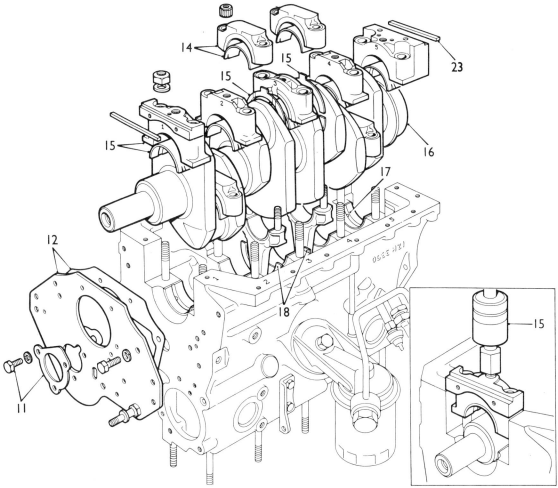

FIG 1:36 The 1.8 engine crankshaft and bearings

Camshaft bearings:

The camshaft rotates in three renewable steel-backed whitemetal bearings. If there is excessive sideways play of the camshaft, remove the camshaft and measure the journals with a micrometer. Undersize bearings are not available so if the journals are worn a new camshaft must be fitted.

With the camshaft removed, check the bearings. The diametrical clearance on each bearing should be .001 to .002 inch (.0254 to .0508 mm) but if this is only slightly exceeded or the bearings are slightly scored it is worth leaving them because of the work involved in changing the bearings.

Before the camshaft bearings can be renewed the engine must be fully stripped down to the crankcase. This includes removing cylinder head, pistons and connecting rods, crankshaft as well as all the valve timing gear and camshaft.

A whole series of special tools is used to extract the old bearings and draw the new bearings back into place. Once the new bearings have been fitted they must be accurately line-reamed. Because of the complexity, the work should be left to an agent. However, a great deal of money can be saved if the crankcase alone is taken to the agent, provided that this has been arranged beforehand. Since the engine must be dismantled so fully, the opportunity should be taken to carry out a major engine overhaul.

1:12 The pistons and connecting rods

A typical assembly is shown in **FIG 1:35**. On some earlier models and all 1.1 engines fully-floating gudgeon pins are used (secured in the piston by circlips) but generally it will be found that the gudgeon pins are an interference fit in the connecting rod small-end. On the models fitted with interference-fit gudgeon pins the pistons should not be separated from the connecting rods unnecessarily.

To change the big-end bearings, only the sump needs to be removed (see **Section 1:7**) but if the connecting rods and pistons are to be removed the cylinder head must be removed as well (see **Section 1:3**), leaving the engine fitted in the car.

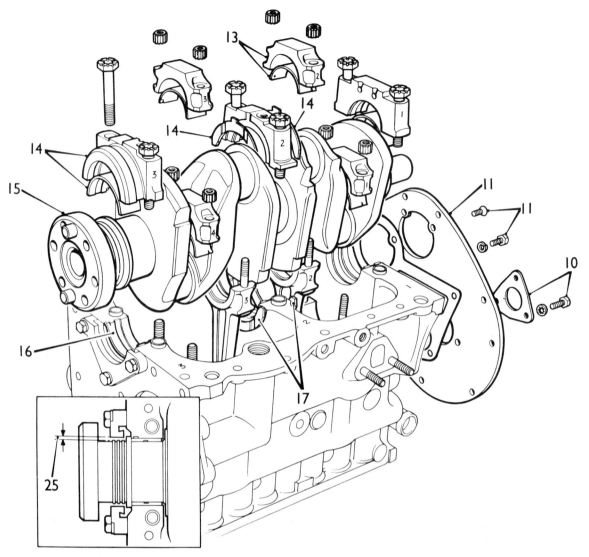

FIG 1:37   The 1.3 engine crankshaft and bearings

Big-end bearings:

The crankshaft main bearings and big-end bearings for the 1.8 engine are shown in **FIG 1:36** while those for the 1.3 engine are shown in **FIG 1:37.**

1 Refer to **FIG 1:35,** though noting that details are also shown in **FIGS 1:3, 1:36** and **1:37.** Check that the connecting rods and bearing caps are numerically marked, as shown at 7, and that the numbers face towards the camshaft side of the engine. If new parts have been fitted they should be lightly marked with a code of punch dots.

2 Turn the engine to a position where access to the big-ends is easiest (usually with all the pistons half-way up their bores). Remove the two nuts 8 that secure the bearing cap 9 and pull off the cap together with its bearing shell 12. Remove the remaining three bearing caps in a similar manner.

3 Push the pistons and connecting rods 11 up the bores of the cylinders so that the connecting rods clear from the crankshaft crankpins. Slide the bearing shells 10 and 12 out of the caps and connecting rods and lay the caps and shells out in the correct order, as the bearing shells must be refitted into their original positions if they are used again.

4 Examine the bearing shells and renew the complete set if any show signs of wear, scoring or pitting. New shells are fitted exactly as received, apart from cleaning off any protective, and do not require scraping or boring.

5 Clean the crankpins and measure each one at several points, using a micrometer gauge. If the crankpins

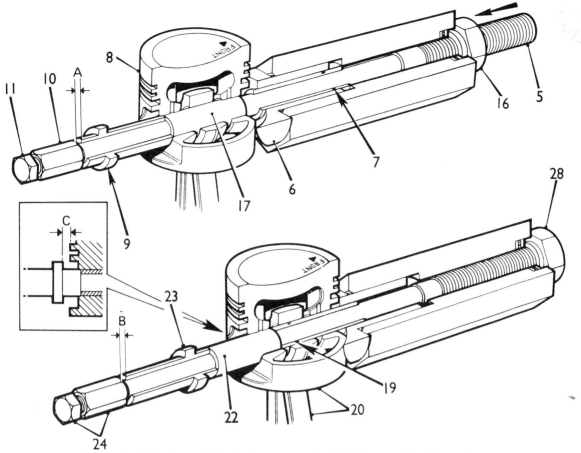

FIG 1:38 Using the special tools to remove and refit interference fit gudgeon pins

are excessively worn, scored, tapered or oval the crankshaft must be removed and sent away for specialist regrinding. **Under no circumstances file the connecting rods or caps in an attempt to take up wear in a bearing.**

6 Clean the crankpins and shell seats very thoroughly and wipe the shells clean with a piece of leather or lint-free cloth. Refit the bearing shells into their correct positions, making sure that the tags are fully and correctly located.

7 Lubricate the crankpins and bearings liberally with clean engine oil and pull the connecting rods down into position on the crankpins. **Take care not to trap the connecting rods between crankshaft throws and crankcase if the engine has to be turned.** Refit the bearing caps, making sure that the number on each one corresponds to the number on the connecting rod and that all numbers face the camshaft side of the engine.

8 Tighten the cap nuts 8 to the correct torque load and check that the engine rotates freely. The correct torque for the 1.3 engine is 35 lb ft (4.8 kg m) while that for the 1.8 engine is 33 lb ft (4.6 kg m).

9 Refit the sump and fill the engine correctly with fresh oil.

Removing the parts:

Remove the sump and cylinder head. Disconnect the big-ends as just described and push the connecting rods right up the bores so that the pistons pass out of the bores and the assemblies can be removed from the engine.

Do not separate the pistons from the connecting rods unnecessarily, noting that special tools must be used on the interference fit gudgeon pins. The majority of servicing can be carried out without separating the pistons.

Gudgeon pins:

On some earlier models, fully floating gudgeon pins are used. Remove the circlips that hold the gudgeon pins in place and press the gudgeon pin out to separate the piston from the connecting rod. The task will be easier if the piston is heated in boiling water and thumb pressure should be sufficient. Renewable bushes are fitted into the small-end of the connecting rod and if they are worn they can be removed with a press and mandrel, and new bushes fitted. Once new bushes have been fitted they must be accurately jig-reamed so renewal of bushes is best left to an agent. Refitting the piston to the connecting rod is the reversal of the dismantling procedure, heating the piston if necessary, but making sure that the

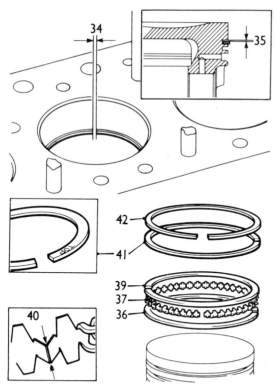

FIG 1 : 39   The piston rings for the later 1.8 engines

1 : 39. Note that this model has only three piston rings whereas earlier versions and all 1.1 and 1.3 engines are fitted with four rings. The actual types of rings have also varied slightly.

Before fitting a new ring, check that the gaps between the ends, when fitted, are correct. Spring the ring into the cylinder bore and use an inverted piston to press it squarely down the bore until it is approximately 1 inch from the top. Measure the gap 34 with feeler gauges and adjust to the correct limit by carefully filing the ends of the ring. Use feeler gauges to check the gap 35 between the ring and piston groove. If the gap 35 is excessive with a new ring fitted the piston itself must be renewed otherwise oil consumption will be high.

The piston rings are refitted in the reverse order of removal. On some earlier models a single-part oil control ring is fitted and this can be treated as an ordinary compression ring.

Fit the bottom rail 36 of the oil control ring into the bottom piston groove, followed by the expander 37 and finally the top rail 39. Make sure that the ends of the expander 37 are abutting but not overlapping, as shown in the inset 40. Turn the parts of the oil control ring so that their gaps are at 90 deg. to each other but no gap is on the thrust side of the piston. Refit the compression rings 41 and 42, making sure that the markings 'TOP' on the lower compression rings face upwards to the crown of the piston. When all the rings are in place, stagger their gaps at 90 deg. to each other without having any gaps on the thrust side of the piston.

The details of the rings and their dimensions are given in Technical Data.

Pistons:

Once the piston rings have been removed clean the ring grooves in the piston, using an old broken piston ring to scrape out the carbon. **Take great care not to remove metal from the piston grooves otherwise the oil consumption will be increased.** Clean the oil return holes behind the oil control ring with a blunt-ended piece of wire.

The piston crowns can be lightly polished using worn emerycloth dipped in paraffin, as all traces of abrasive can be washed away before reassembly. Do not use abrasive on the sides of the pistons and any lacquering indicative of gas blown-by past the rings should only be removed with a solvent such as methylated spirits or trichlorethylene.

If the pistons are scored or the ring grooves excessively worn then new pistons should be fitted.

Cylinder bores:

These can best be inspected and measured after the pistons have been removed. They can be checked without removing the pistons, once the cylinder head has been removed, and the depth of the unworn ridge around the top of the bore will give a good guide to the overall wear. The accurate method is to use a special form of Dial Test Indicator to measure the bore at several points. If the bores are excessively worn, tapered, out of round or scored then they should be rebored by a specialist firm and new oversize pistons and rings fitted.

If wear is such that reboring will make the bore larger than oversize pistons available then the cylinders can be bored out oversize and liners pressed into them. The

'Front' marking on the piston crown will be forwards when the number on the connecting rod is facing the camshaft side of the engine. **Make sure that the circlips rest fully in their grooves.**

On the models with the interference fit gudgeon pins special tools 18G.537 and 18G.1150 must be used for removing or refitting the gudgeon pins. In addition to these special tools, 18G.1150A must be used for 1.3 engines and 18G.1150B for 1.8 engines as well as a torque wrench. The tools are shown fitted in **FIG 1 : 38** but the work is best left to an agent as damage can be caused by incorrect fitting.

Piston rings:

The best method of removing and refitting piston rings is to use a ring spreader which grips the ring by the ends and then gently parts the ends so that the ring expands and can be lifted out of its groove and up off the piston. If the correct spreader is not available, three shims, such as discarded feeler gauges, can be used instead. Remove the top ring first and refit it last. Lift out one end of the ring and slide a shim under it. Work the shim around under the ring while gently pressing the ring as it comes free onto the piston land above it, taking great care not to force the ring as it is brittle and will snap easily. When all the ring is on the piston land, slide the other two shims under the ring and use them as guides to slip the ring up and off the piston. Gently parting the ends of the ring with the thumb nails will help, but take great care that the back of the ring does not scrape the piston.

The ring details on the 1.8 engine are shown in **FIG**

liners are then honed out to standard size so that standard pistons can be used, allowing for further rebores if necessary. The fitting of liners is again a specialist task and should not be carried out by the owner.

If wear is not sufficient to warrant reboring but it is still sufficient to give a high oil consumption consideration should be given to fitting new piston rings. If new rings are fitted without reboring the unworn ridge around the top of the bore must be removed using garage equipment. The new top ring will not be worn and therefore it will hit the ridge on every stroke and rapidly break up.

Connecting rods:

The small-ends and big-ends have been dealt with earlier in this section.

If the pistons have to be separated from the connecting rods it is worthwhile having the connecting rods checked for bend and twist by the agent. This can be done by the owner but V-blocks, suitable mandrels and a DTI (Dial Test Indicator) are required as well as a hydraulic press to straighten the connecting rod if it is found to be bent.

Reassembly:

The refitting of the individual parts have been dealt with throughout this section so it is a matter of refitting the assembly into the bore. First check that when the triangle or 'FRONT' mark on the piston crown is facing forwards the number on the connecting rod will face the camshaft side of the engine. On the 1.1 and 1.3 engine, the connecting rods are offset and they must be fitted as shown in **FIG 1:40**. If the rings have moved, rotate them in their grooves until their gaps are staggered at 90 deg. with no gaps on the thrust side of the piston.

Lightly oil the piston rings and compress them into their grooves with a suitable ring clamp. If a suitable ring clamp is not available a large worm-driven hose clip can be used but more care will be required. Lower the connecting rod down the bore, making sure that the mark on the piston is facing forwards, and enter the skirt of the piston into the cylinder. Lower the piston down and gently press it in, allowing the clamp to slide off the rings as they enter the bore. **Do not force the rings or allow them to escape from the tool before they are in the bore, otherwise they may well snap.**

Reconnect the big-ends and reassemble the engine in the reverse order of dismantling.

1:13 The crankshaft and main bearings

It is essential that the engine is removed from the car before the crankshaft is taken out or the main bearing shells renewed.

The parts of the 1.8 engine crankshaft are shown in **FIGS 1:3** and **1:36** while those for the 1.3 engine are shown in **FIG 1:37**.

Removal:

1 Remove the engine from the car as described in **Section 1:2**. Remove the sump and on 1.1 and 1.3 models remove the oil strainer, but on 1.8 models remove the oil pump complete (see **Section 1:7**). Remove the clutch, flywheel and gearbox adaptor plate

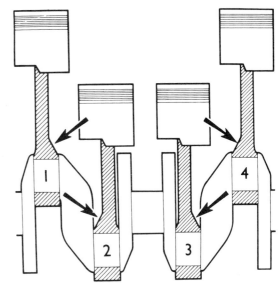

FIG 1:40 The connecting rod offsets correctly positioned on the 1.1 and 1.3 engine

(see **Section 1:8**) leaving the oil pump fitted on the 1.3 models. Remove the timing cover, sprockets and timing chain (see **Section 1:10**) and also remove the camshaft locating plate but leave the camshaft fitted. Remove the cylinder block front plate and its gasket. Disconnect the big-ends and push the connecting rods into the bores so that they are clear of the crankshaft. Take great care when turning the crankshaft not to trap the big-ends of the connecting rods between the throws and crankcase.

2 Check that the main bearing caps are marked with numbers in the correct numerical order, counting the front bearing as No. 1. On the 1.1 and 1.3 engine the numbers should be facing the corresponding numbers on the crankcase and towards the camshaft side of the engine while on the 1.8 engine the marks should face forwards. If the caps are not numbered then identify them with a code of light punch dots.

3 Evenly and progressively slacken and remove all the nuts that secure the main bearing caps, noting that bolts are fitted on the 1.1 and 1.3 engine. Remove the bearing caps and store them in order. On the 1.8 engine the safety method of removing the caps is to use the impact extractor 18G.284 with adaptors 18G.284A and AC as shown in inset 15. If the tools are not available use a plastic hammer to tap them very carefully and squarely up the studs.

4 Lift out the crankshaft. Remove the main bearing shells from the caps and recesses in the crankcase and store them in order and position. Note that thrust washers are fitted on either side of the centre main bearing and that the lower pair of thrust washers will come free when the cap is removed.

Examination:

Check the bearing shells and renew the complete set if any show signs of wear, scoring, pitting or cracking. If the crankshaft has to be reground new undersize bearings must be fitted. New bearing shells are fitted exactly as received and do not require scraping or boring.

Measure each journal at several points with a micrometer gauge. The crankshaft must be sent away for specialist regrinding of the journals.

Cleaning:

All the parts must be scrupulously clean. Pay particular attention to the joint faces of the bearing caps. Wipe the shells clean with a piece of leather or lint-free cloth.

Clean the oilways in the crankshaft. This is particularly important if a bearing has run or the crankshaft has been reground. Blow through them with paraffin under pressure, from a syringe if the proper equipment is not available, and then dry them with compressed air, preferably from an air-line but using a tyre pump as an alternative.

Reassembly:

1 Refit the bearing shells into their locations, making sure that the tags on the shells are fully seated in their recesses. Fit the semi-circular thrust washers with tags on either side of the centre main bearing cap, so that the oilways face away from the cap. The other two thrust washers are similarly fitted on either side of the centre main bearing in the crankcase.

2 Liberally lubricate the journals with clean engine oil and lower the crankshaft back into place. Refit the bearing caps, complete with shells, and progressively tighten the nuts (or bolts) to the correct torque load. The nuts for the 1.8 engine should be torque-loaded to 70 lb ft (9.7 kg m) and the bolts for the 1.1 and 1.3 engine to 60 lb ft (8.3 kg m). Check that the crankshaft rotates freely. If the crankshaft is stiff, loosen each bearing in turn and then tighten it until the tight bearing is found. A tight bearing can be aligned by giving it gentle taps with a hide-faced hammer at the base.

3 Check the end float of the crankshaft. Mount a DTI on the crankcase so that its stylus rests vertically on the end of the crankshaft, or as an alternative use feeler gauges between a main bearing and the crankshaft. Lever the crankshaft firmly backwards and forwards so that the end float can be measured. The correct end float should be .002 to .003 inch (.051 to .076 mm) on all models. If the end float is incorrect selectively fit thrust washers on either side of the centre main bearing to bring it within limits. If the end float is just too small, lightly lap down the face of the thrust washer that is against the bearing cap and crankcase using fine-grade emerycloth spread on plate glass or a surface table. Do not lap down the sides in contact with the crankshaft.

4 Reassemble and refit the engine in the reverse order of dismantling and removal. On the 1.8 engine, lightly coat the horizontal face of the rearmost cap with jointing compound. Soak new cork seals in oil and fit them to the front and rear bearings.

Crankshaft oil seals:

The front oil seal on all models is fitted in the timing cover and is dealt with in **Section 1:10**. Note that this seal can be renewed with the engine still fitted in the car.

1.8 litre engine:

A conventional oil seal is fitted into the gearbox adaptor plate. If the seal is defective, press it out and press a new one back into position so that its lip faces towards the engine and is flush with the front face of the plate. Mandrels 18G.134 and 18G.134CQ are made for pressing the seal back into place. Lubricate the seal with oil before refitting the adaptor plate. Note that if the area on which the seal acts on the crankshaft is scored or burred oil leaks will be unavoidable.

1.1 and 1.3 litre engine:

A labyrinth type seal is used and it is shown in the inset in **FIG 1:37**. There should be no metal-to-metal contact and check that there is a clearance of .004 inch (.010 mm) between the oil return thread and the oil thrower, as shown at 25. If the engine is run with excessively worn main bearings then metal-to-metal contact can take place and the ensuing wear will allow oil to leak into the clutch.

1:14 Reassembling a stripped engine

All the operations have been dealt with in the relevant sections so it is only a question of tackling the work in the best order.

Make sure that all parts are scrupulously clean before reassembling them. It is advisable to wash the parts in fuel as they are dismantled and then wipe over bright metal parts with an oily rag to prevent them from rusting. Wash the parts again in fuel or suitable solvent to remove the protective film and any dirt picked up in storage.

Swill small parts and all nuts and bolts in a tin of fuel to clean threads and use a wire brush to clean threads on studs. Cleanliness will not only ensure longer engine life but also make the assembly work easier.

Discard all old gaskets and seals and fit new ones on reassembly. Kits of seals for the different parts are available so that there should be no excuse for having to use old gaskets. Make sure that jointing faces are free from old bits of gaskets and jointing compound. They can usually be scraped clean but brushing with trichlorethylene will soften old jointing compound and make it easier to remove.

Start by fitting the crankshaft followed by the front engine plate. Refit the pistons and connecting rods followed by the valve timing gear and camshaft. On the 1.3 engine do not forget to refit the cam followers before sliding the camshaft back into place. Refit the gearbox adaptor plate, not forgetting to refit the oil pump first on the 1.3 engine. The flywheel and clutch can then be fitted. Refit the cylinder head and rocker assembly. Do not forget to refit the cam followers on the 1.8 engine before refitting the cylinder head. Set the valve clearances as this is the easiest time to do them. Refit the oil pump (oil strainer on the 1.3) followed by the sump. Refit the distributor drive shaft. Leave external accessories and covers until last. Items like the distributor, generator and manifolds can even be left off until the engine has been refitted in the car.

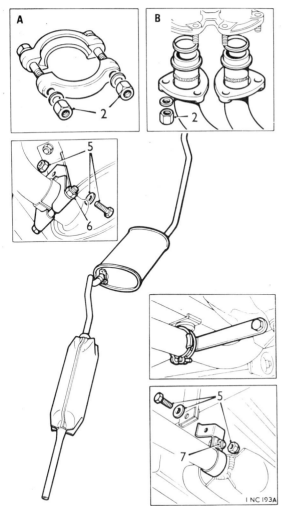

FIG 1:41 Removing and refitting the exhaust system, showing single pipe manifold joint **A** and twin joint **B**

1:15 The exhaust system

There are two silencers or expansion chambers with a single connecting pipe connecting them but there may be either one or two downpipes from the exhaust manifold. A single downpipe is attached by means of a split clamp, while twin pipes use a flange fitting as shown in **FIG 1:41**. Instructions for removing and refitting both types are given, the relevant items being as follows:

Front pipe SC 1 to 6
Rear pipe SC 1 to 7
Front pipe TC 1, 2, 4 and 6
Rear pipe TC 1, 2 and 4 to 7

Removing:

1 Support the front pipe on a temporary sling.
2 Release the front pipe(s) from the manifold.
3 Single pipe: Release the clip from the stay (1.8).
4 Jack up the lefthand side of the car, release the damper from its mounting plate and swing it inwards.

5 Detach both clamps from their supporting straps, raise the exhaust pipe assembly clear of the rear axle and remove it from the car.
6 Slacken the front clamp and separate the front and rear pipes.
7 Slacken and remove the rear clamp.

Refitting:

Reverse the above procedure, noting:
On single pipes, apply manganese paste to the exhaust manifold flange.
On twin pipes use two new joint gaskets.
Do not tighten any of the clamps until after the complete exhaust system has been fitted.

1:16 Fault diagnosis

(a) Engine will not start

1 Defective ignition coil
2 Faulty distributor capacitor
3 Dirty, pitted or incorrectly set ignition contact points
4 Ignition wires loose or insulation faulty
5 Water on sparking plug leads
6 Battery discharged, terminals corroded
7 Faulty or jammed starter motor
8 Sparking plug leads incorrectly connected
9 Vapour locks in fuel line (hot weather only)
10 Defective fuel pump
11 Over or underchoking
12 Blocked fuel filter, jammed float chamber needle valves or blocked carburetter jet(s)
13 Leaking valves
14 Sticking valves
15 Valve timing incorrect
16 Ignition timing incorrect

(b) Engine stalls

1 Check 1, 2, 3, 4, 5, 10, 11, 12, 13 and 14 in (a)
2 Sparking plugs defective or gaps incorrect
3 Retarded ignition
4 Mixture too weak
5 Water in fuel system
6 Petrol tank vent blocked
7 Incorrect valve clearances
8 Sticking air valve in carburetter

(c) Engine idles badly

1 Check 2, 7 and 8 in (b)
2 Air leaks at manifold joints
3 Worn piston rings
4 Worn valve stems or valve guides
5 Weak exhaust valve springs

(d) Engine misfires

1 Check 1, 2, 3, 4, 5, 10, 12, 13, 14, 15 and 16 in (a) and 2, 3, 4 and 7 in (b)
2 Weak or broken valve springs
3 Defective HT lead

(e) Engine overheats (see **Chapter 4**)

(f) Compression low

1 Check 14 and 15 in (a); 3 and 4 in (c) and 2 in (d)
2 Worn piston ring grooves
3 Scored or worn cylinder bores

(g) Engine lacks power

1 Check 3, 10, 11, 13, 14, 15, 16 and 17 in (a); 1, 2, 3 and 6 in (b); 3 and 4 in (c) and 2 in (d). Also check (e) and (f)
2 Leaking cylinder head gasket
3 Fouled or worn out sparking plugs
4 Automatic advance not operating

(h) Burnt valves or seats

1 Check 14 and 15 in (a); 6 in (b) and 2 in (d). Also check (e)
2 Excessive carbon in combustion chamber and on valve

(j) Sticking valves

1 Check 2 in (d)
2 Bent valve stem
3 Scored valve stem or guide
4 Incorrect valve clearance
5 Gummy deposits on valve stem

(k) Excessive cylinder wear

1 Check 11 in (q) and also check (e)
2 Lack of oil
3 Dirty oil

4 Piston rings gummed up or broken
5 Connecting rod bent
6 Gudgeon pin loose or incorrectly fitted

(l) Excessive oil consumption

1 Check 4 in (k) and also check (f)
2 Oil return holes in piston choked with carbon
3 Oil level too high
4 External oil leaks

(m) Crankshaft or connecting rod bearing failure

1 Check 2, 3 and 5 in (k)
2 Restricted oilways
3 Worn journals or crankpins
4 Loose bearing caps
5 Extremely low oil pressure

(n) Low oil pressure

1 Check 2 and 3 in (k) and 2, 3 and 4 in (m)
2 Choked oil filter
3 Weak relief valve spring or dirt under seat
4 Faulty gauge, switch or connections

(o) Internal coolant leakage (see Chapter 4)

(p) Poor coolant circulation (see Chapter 4)

(q) Corrosion (see Chapter 4)

(r) High fuel consumption (see Chapter 2)

CHAPTER 2

THE FUEL SYSTEM

2:1 Description

The fuel system is basically similar on all the variants of the Marina. Fuel is stored in a tank under the rear of the car and is drawn through a system of two flexible hoses and a metal pipe which runs along under the car and across the front. A mechanically operated fuel pump draws the fuel from the tank and supplies it under slight pressure to the float chamber(s) of the carburetter(s). One of the flexible hoses connects the metal pipe to the tank and the other hose connects the fuel pump to the pipe.

SU carburetters are used as standard on all versions. A single carburetter is used on all models, except the 1.8TC which is fitted with twin carburetters.

The 1.3 engine is fitted with an SU HS4 carburetter and the 1.8 with an HS6, while the 1.8TC uses twin HS4 carburetters and the 1100 Van has an HS2. The general construction details of all the carburetters are similar. An SU mechanical fuel pump is fitted to all versions.

The fuel pump contains a gauze filter and sediment chamber to ensure that only clean fuel reaches the carburetter. On some models the filter is not fitted to the pump but a filter is fitted on the inlet in the tank unit. An air cleaner is fitted to the intake of the carburetter to filter the air entering the engine and also to silence the roar in the carburetter intake.

2:2 Routine maintenance

1 At intervals of 6000 miles (10,000 kilometres) or 6 months, whichever occurs the sooner, unscrew and remove the plug and damper 7 from the top of the carburetter 8, shown in **FIG 2:1.** Add a little engine oil, if necessary, to bring the level approximately $\frac{1}{2}$ inch (13 mm) above the top of the hollow piston rod, as shown by the arrows. Push the damper back into position and tighten the plug firmly.

2 At the same time as topping up the carburetter damper, check the carburetter linkages for full and free move-ment, cleaning and lightly lubricating the pivot points. Adjust the carburetters and their linkage if performance or economy have dropped or the opera-tion seems poor.

Single carburetter air cleaner:

The element should normally be renewed at intervals of 12,000 miles but if the car is used in very dusty conditions the period between servicing should be reduced. The air cleaner parts are shown in **FIG 2:2.** It is best to

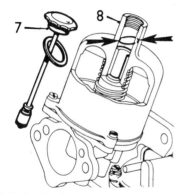

FIG 2:1 Topping up the carburetter damper

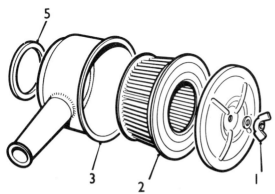

FIG 2:2 The air cleaner fitted with single carburetters

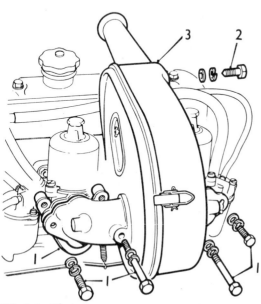

FIG 2:3 The attachments of the air cleaner fitted with twin carburetters

remove the air cleaner complete as this ensures that no dirt will fall into the carburetter intake.

Unscrew the thumb nut 1 and collect the fibre washer under it. Gently pull the complete assembly off the intake and check that the seal 5 is undamaged and in position. Remove the cover from the body 3 and discard the old element 2. The element can be partially cleaned by tapping it onto a firm flat surface and using a soft brush to remove loose dirt from the folds. This should only be done if the air cleaner is removed for reasons other than element renewal and must not be done at the servicing interval. **Do not wash the element in any form of solvent.**

Wipe out the inside of the cover and body, fit the new element and refit the air cleaner in the reverse order of removal, making sure that the seal 5 and fibre washer are in place.

Twin carburetter air cleaner:

The servicing interval and instructions for the element itself are exactly the same as for the single carburetter air cleaner.

The attachments of the unit are shown in **FIG 2:3**. To remove the air cleaner, take out the four flange attachment bolts 1 and remove the bolt 2 from the steady bracket. The assembly 3 can then be lifted out of the car, carefully collecting the flange gaskets.

The components of the air cleaner are shown in **FIG 2:4**. Unscrew the wing nut 4 and remove the intake elbows 5 with their gaskets. Remove the wing bolt 6, with its fibre washer, and undo the clip 7 to separate the cover from the body. Remove the element 8 and either clean it by tapping and light brushing or discard it.

Wipe out the inside of the body and cover, reassemble and refit the parts in the reverse order of dismantling and removal.

The fuel filter:

The fuel pump top and filter are shown in **FIG 2:5**. Disconnect the fuel pipe 1 from the cover. Remove the three screws 2 and take off the cover so that the filter and its seal 3 can be removed. Wash the filter in clean fuel and dry it with compressed air. Renew the filter if the gauze is torn or cannot be effectively cleaned. Brush out any dirt or sediment from the top of the fuel pump. Refit the parts in the reverse order of removal, renewing the seal 3 if it is defective, and make sure that the cover is squarely seated on the pump and that the screws 2 are evenly tightened. Start the engine and check for fuel leaks after reconnecting the pipe 1.

If water or dirt are found frequently in the fuel pump or carburetter it is advisable to drain out the fuel from the tank, by taking out the drain plug underneath it, and refill with clean fuel. Before refilling, disconnect the flexible hoses from either end of the metal fuel line and blow through the fuel line in a reverse direction using compressed air to clean out dirt. The flexible hoses are secured by spring clips which can be opened and released by squeezing their legs together with a pair of pliers. **Compressed air must not be blown through the pump.**

In extreme cases, remove the fuel tank and swill it out with clean fuel and if the tank is found to be internally corroded fit a new tank (see **Section 2:9**).

2:3 The fuel pump

Testing:

As a quick roadside test, disconnect the fuel line from the carburetter float chamber and point it well away from the engine. Crank the engine on the starter motor and if the pump is supplying fuel there should be a good spurt from the pipe at every other revolution of the engine.

A more sophisticated version of this test is shown in **FIG 2:6**. Disconnect the fuel line 1 from the carburetter float chamber and insert the end into a suitable glass container. Disconnect the white lead 2 from the ignition coil, **keeping the free end well away from any metal parts to prevent shortcircuits,** so that the engine will not start on the fuel in the float chamber.

Crank the engine over on the starter and check the flow. If there are good spurts of fuel and the container fills up rapidly then the pump is operating satisfactorily. If the flow starts off well but then dies away, check the vent system of the fuel tank as it may be blocked, causing a vacuum to form in the tank. If it is suspected that the vent is blocked, remove the filler cap. The pump flow should speed up immediately and the inrush of air into the tank can be heard. Other causes of the flow dying are blocked filters (note that some models are fitted with a filter on the inlet in the tank unit) or a partially blocked fuel line. If air bubbles keep emerging with the fuel then there is a leak on the suction side. If there is no flow, remove the pump from the engine and dry test. If the pump is satisfactory then the fuel lines are completely blocked, but do remember to check that there is fuel in the tank as fuel gauges can go wrong.

Dry testing:

Remove the pump from the engine by disconnecting the fuel lines from it and taking off the two nuts that secure it to the crankcase.

For accurate checks a vacuum gauge and pressure gauge are required though a rough check can be made without them.

Connect the vacuum gauge to the inlet nozzle and operate the pump rocker through three full strokes. The minimum vacuum reading should not drop by more than 2 inch (50 mm) mercury in 15 seconds. If a vacuum is not available, block the inlet with a thumb and after the three strokes release the thumb and an inrush of air should be heard.

Connect the pressure gauge to the outlet nozzle and operate the pump rocker through two full strokes. The minimum pressure should not drop by more than .5 lb/sq inch (.04 kg/sq cm) in 15 seconds. If a gauge is not available, press in the pump rocker fully and hold it there with a thumb over the outlet. Pressure should hold up for a minimum of 15 seconds.

Refit the pump in the reverse order of removal. Note that two gaskets and a heat insulator are fitted between the pump and crankcase. If the gaskets on either side of the insulator are damaged fit new ones.

Servicing the pump:

The pump components are shown in **FIG 2:7**. Remove the pump from the engine as just described.

1 Wash and brush down the outside of the unit. Lightly file aligning marks 1 on the body flanges to assist in reassembly. Remove the cover, seal and filter 2.

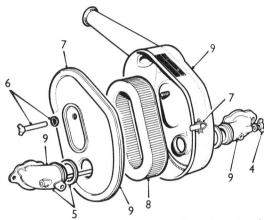

FIG 2:4   The components of the twin carburetter air cleaner

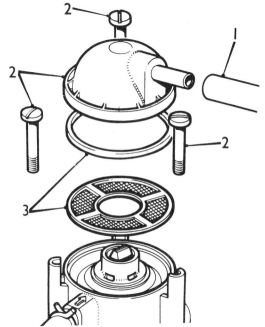

FIG 2:5   The fuel pump filter

FIG 2:6   Testing the fuel pump

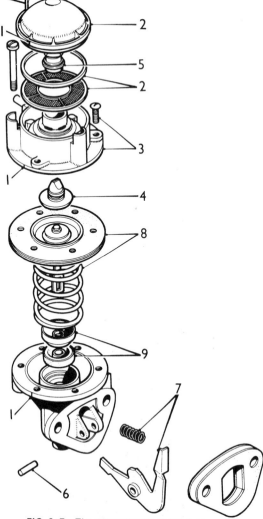

FIG 2:7 The components of the fuel pump

of a fine file. Check the valve assembly for damage and renew it if it is defective. Check the diaphragm for cracks, splits, pin holes or hardening of the rubber, and renew it if defective. Check the springs and renew them if they are weak, broken or corroded. If the pump is generally worn and in poor condition, consider fitting a new or reconditioned unit.

6 The pump is reassembled in the reverse order of dis-dismantling. When fitting together the upper and lower parts of the body, align the diaphragm holes and press in the rocker until the diaphragm is flat and then fit the upper body with the screws 3 finger tight only. Finally tighten all the screws evenly after the filter and cover parts have been refitted.

7 Dry test the pump before refitting it to the car.

2:4 Operation of an SU carburetter

A sectioned view of an HS4 carburetter is shown in FIG 2:8. The carburetters fitted to the other models are very similar in construction.

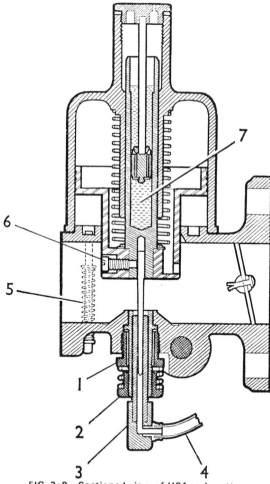

FIG 2:8 Sectioned view of HS4 carburetter

Key to Fig 2:8   1 Jet locking nut   2 Jet adjusting nut   3 Jet head   4 Feed tube from float chamber   5 Piston lifting pin   6 Needle securing screw   7 Oil damper reservoir

2 Take out the screws 3 and separate the upper body from the lower. Carefully remove the combined inlet and outlet valve assembly 4, **noting that it is a press fit and taking care not to damage the fine edge of the inlet valve.** Withdraw the insert 5 from the cover.

3 Lightly press down the diaphragm against the spring 8 and hold the rocker against its spring 7. Drive out the pivot 6 using a suitable drift. Remove the rocker and spring 7. Put a few drops of oil on the seal 9, to protect it from damage, and remove the diaphragm and its spring 8.

4 The oil seal and its retainer 9 should only be removed if they are defective.

5 Wash the parts in fuel and brush out any sediment or dirt, loosening it carefully with a small screwdriver. Check the castings for damage or hairline cracks. If the flanges are distorted, true them up by careful use

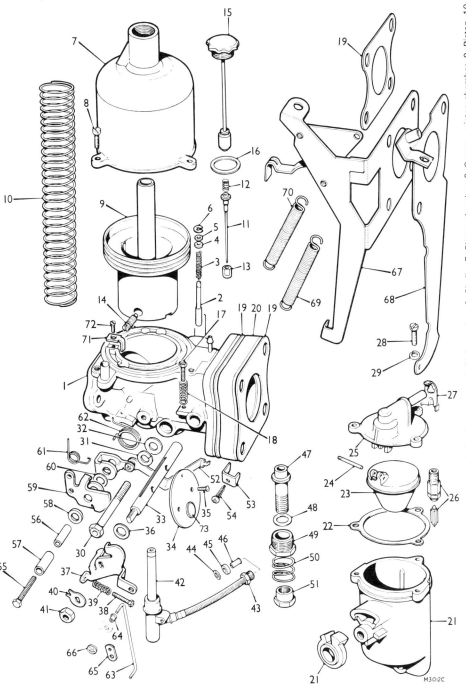

Key to Fig 2:9 1 Body 2 Piston lifting pin 3 Support guide—needle 4 Sealing washer 5 Plain washer 6 Circlip 7 Piston chamber 8 Screw—piston chamber 9 Piston 10 Spring
11 Needle 12 Spring—needle 13 Support guide—needle 14 Locking screw—needle support guide 15 Piston damper 16 Sealing washer—damper
17 Throttle adjusting screw 18 Spring for screw 19 Joint washers 20 Insulator block 21 Float chamber and spacer 22 Joint washer—chamber 23 Float
24 Hinge pin—float 25 Lid—float chamber 26 Needle and seat 27 Baffle plate 28 Screw—float chamber lid 29 Spring washer 30 Bolt—float chamber 31 Spring washer
32 Plain washer 33 Throttle spindle 34 Butterfly valve 35 Screw—securing disc assembly 36 Washer—throttle spindle 37 Throttle return lever 38 Fast-idle screw
39 Spring 40 Lockwasher—throttle spindle nut 41 Nut—throttle spindle 42 Jet assembly 43 Sleeve nut—jet flexible pipe 44 Washer 45 Gland 46 Ferrule 47 Jet bearing
48 Sealing washer 49 Jet locating nut 50 Spring 51 Jet adjusting nut 52 Pickup lever 53 Link—pickup lever (1.8 engine) 54 Screw—securing lever to jet 55 Pivot bolt
56 Pivot bolt tube—inner 57 Pivot bolt tube—outer 58 Distance washer 59 Cam lever 60 Washer 61 S ring—cam lever 62 Spring—pickup lever 63 Throttle lever rod
64 Bush 65 Anchor tag 66 Lockwasher—throttle lever rod 67 Progressive throttle linkage bracket 68 Throttle cable abutment bracket (1.3 engine) 69 Throttle return spring
70 Tensioning 71 Guide—suction chamber position 72 Screw—securing guide 73 Limit valve

FIG 2:9 The components of the carburetter

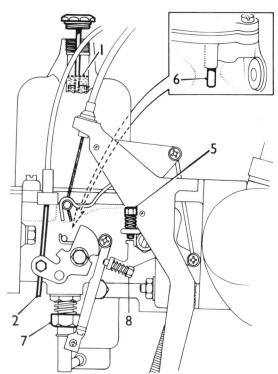

FIG 2:10 Adjustment points on a single carburetter

The throttle butterfly valve on the right is connected to the accelerator pedal by a mecanical linkage and cable. The feed tube 4 is connected to a conventional type float chamber, where the action of the float on the needle valve keeps the fuel level within limits.

When the engine is running, all the air for combustion is drawn through the carburetter. As airflow speeds up there is a reduction in pressure and the bridge below the air valve forms a reduction in the throat area, causing the flow to speed up and the static pressure to drop. This reduction in pressure draws fuel from the jet so that the fuel is mixed with the air. The pressure reduction is also transferred (by ports in the air valve piston) to the suction chamber above the air valve. The air valve will then rise to a position where the suction is balanced by the weight of the piston and the pressure of the return spring. If the throttle is opened, allowing more air to pass to the engine and speed it up, the increased airflow will first cause a further reduction in static pressure by the bridge and this will raise the air valve to a new point of balance. Conversely if the throttle is closed and the airflow reduced the static pressure will rise allowing the air valve to drop until normal suction is again restored.

As the weight of the piston and pressure of the return spring are virtually constant, the vacuum across the bridge will also be kept constant under all running conditions of the engine, with the air valve rising as the airflow increases. The jet area is fixed but the needle attached to the air valve slides up and down in the jet. The needle is tapered so that as it is withdrawn the effective area of the jet is increased. The vacuum being kept constant, the fuel flow through the jet will be proportional to the effective area. The jet effective area is governed by the position of the needle and therefore the height of the air valve and, as the height of the air valve is in turn proportional to the airflow, then the fuel flow will be proportional to the air flow. When the airflow is small, the air valve will be low down and only small mounts of fuel will be drawn through the jet. The mixture strength is therefore kept within limits for all running conditions of the engine.

For cold starts, the jet head 3 can be drawn downwards so that the jet operates on a thinner portion of the needle and the effective area of the jet will be increased, allowing more fuel to be drawn through to make the mixture richer. The mixture strength throughout the range can be altered by limiting the maximum height of the jet using the adjusting screw 2.

An oil filled damper assembly 7 is fitted to the air valve piston. The damper serves the dual function of an accelerator pump and preventing rapid fluctuations of the air valve. When the throttle valve is opened for acceleration, the damper causes the air valve to lag. The suction increases temporarily beyond its normal value and excess fuel for acceleration is then drawn through the jet.

A piston lifting pin 5 is usually fitted to allow the piston to be raised slightly, when adjusting the carburetter without having to remove the air cleaner.

The components of a carburetter are shown in **FIG 2:9.**

2:5 Single carburetter tuning and adjustment

Before attempting to tune the carburetter, make sure that the ignition system is in good working order and correctly set. Leaking manifold gaskets or an engine that is in poor condition will also make it difficult or impossible to tune the carburetter satisfactorily.

The idling speeds can be set roughly by ear but for the best results use a tachometer. Electronic test tachometers which can be clipped into the ignition system are available.

The adjustment points on the carburetter are shown in **FIG 2:10.**

1 Start the engine and run it until it has reached its normal operating temperature, with the choke fully returned. When the engine is hot give it a short burst at 2500 rev/min to clear the plugs. The engine should be run up to 2500 rev/min after every three minute period at idling to keep the plugs clear.
2 Check that the throttle cable operates smoothly and make sure that the choke 2 has $\frac{1}{16}$ inch (1.6 mm) of free movement when the control is fully returned. Make sure that the oil in the damper 1 is at the correct level of $\frac{1}{2}$ inch (13 mm) above the hollow piston rod. Make sure that the fast-idle screw on the interconnecting linkage is set so that it is clear of its stop and not affecting the slow-running speed.
3 With the engine running, check the slow-running speed. The idle speed for 1.8 models should be 800 rev/min and that for 1.1 and 1.3 models 650 rev/min. If the slow-running speed is incorrect adjust it using the screw 5, clockwise to increase and anticlockwise to decrease. If a smooth idle cannot be obtained check the mixture strength.
4 Stop the engine and use the pin 6 to raise the air valve piston, after having unscrewed the damper plunger. Release the pin and check that the air valve falls freely

under its own weight and hits the bridge in the intake with a distinct click. If the valve does not appear to fall freely, remove the air cleaner and raise the piston with a small tool through the air intake. Release the piston and check that it falls freely. If the piston does not fall freely there is an internal defect. Instructions for rectifying are given in **Section 2:8.**

5 If the piston falls satisfactorily, refit the damper plunger (and air cleaner if it has been removed) and start the engine. Turn the jet adjusting nut 7 up or down, one flat at a time, until the fastest idling speed is obtained, consistent with smooth running. Screwing the nut up weakens the mixture and down enriches it. When the fastest idling speed has been obtained, making sure that the jet head is pressed firmly up against the adjusting nut, slowly turn the nut 7 upwards until the idling speed just begins to fall. Readjust the idling speed to the correct value.

6 When the mixture is correct, the exhaust beat should be regular and even. If the exhaust is irregular with a splashy type of misfire and colourless then the mixture is too weak. A rich mixture will cause a regular misfire with a blackish exhaust smoke. Check the adjustment by lifting the piston with the pin 6 by $\frac{1}{32}$ inch (.75 mm). If the engine speed increases and stays faster then the mixture is too rich. If the speed immediately decreases or the engine stops, the mixture is too weak. If the engine momentarily increases speed slightly then the mixture is correct.

7 Switch off the engine and operate the choke several times, making sure that the jet head returns fully against the adjusting nut every time. If the jet head sticks, the parts will have to be dismantled and cleaned.

Note that if the carburetter mixture adjustment has been completely lost a rough setting for starting the engine can still be made. Remove the air cleaner and use the adjusting nut 7 to set the jet so that its top end is flush with the bridge in the air intake—or as far as it will go. Turn the adjusting nut 7 down from this position by 12 flats (two complete turns) and this will give a mixture setting enabling the engine to be run.

The slow-running adjustment screw 5 can also be roughly set to give sufficient idling speed for the engine to run and warm up. Turn the screw in until it just contacts its stop, with the throttle valve fully closed, and then screw it in a further $1\frac{1}{2}$ turns to open the throttle valve.

When all adjustment and tuning have been completed, adjust the fast-idle screw 8 on the interconnecting linkage until the engine is running at 1000 to 1100 rev/min when the choke is operated but without sufficient choke to move the jet head.

2:6 Twin carburetter tuning and adjustment

As the carburetter is of the same manufacture, many of the instructions for single carburetter installations are relevant (see previous Section). The engine, ignition system and manifolds must all be in good order otherwise the carburetters cannot be synchronized accurately. The rough starting settings for each of the twin carburetters are the same as for a single carburetter.

An electronic tachometer will be more accurate than the one fitted to the car, provided a special test one is

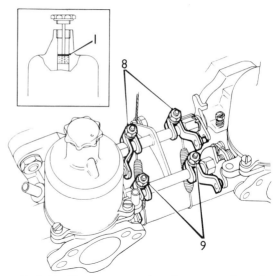

FIG 2:11   The interconnection clamps on twin carburetters

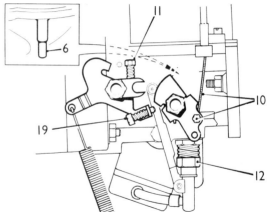

FIG 2:12   The adjustment points for twin carburetters

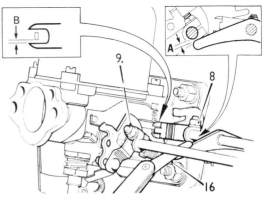

FIG 2:13   Setting the linkage on twin carburetters

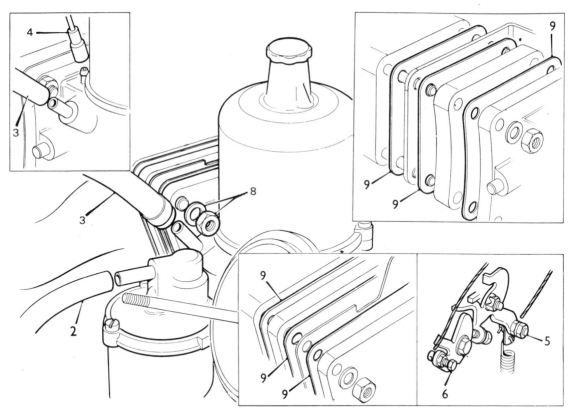

FIG 2:14   Removing a single carburetter

used, and it will also be easier to see. Some form of balance meter will make the adjustments more accurate and easier to carry out, though it is not essential.

1 Remove the air cleaner so that the carburetter intakes are accessible. Take out the damper plungers, shown in the inset in **FIG 2:11,** and check that the air valve pistons fall freely and fully under their own weight after they have been lifted and released. If either piston sticks, refer to **Section 2:8.** Make sure that the oil level is approximately $\frac{1}{2}$ inch (13 mm) above the top of the hollow piston rod and refit the damper plungers. Check that the accelerator and choke linkages move freely, that there is $\frac{1}{16}$ inch of free movement when the choke control is fully returned and that both jet heads return fully against the adjusting nuts when the choke is released.

2 Start the engine and run it until it has reached its normal operating temperature. Run the engine up to 2500 rev/min to clear the plugs and after every three minutes at idling during the adjustments run it up to this speed again to keep the plugs clear. Slacken the clamp nuts 8 and 9, shown in **FIG 2:11,** to make the carburetters independent of each other.

3 Refer to **FIG 2:12.** Slacken the nut that secures the inner cable 10 of the choke control. Adjust the slow-running stop screws 11 on both carburetters until the correct idling speed of 800 rev/min is attained and the airflow is the same through both carburetters. A

balance meter will make this task easier. If a meter is not available use a short piece of hose to listen to the 'hiss' at each intake and adjust the screws 11 until the hiss is the same in each carburetter intake.

4 Check the mixture strength at each carburetter and if necessary adjust it as described in operations 5 and 6 in **Section 2:5** for single carburetters. Note that the references to the damper plunger and air cleaner must be ignored and the adjusting nut given as 7 is the same as the adjusting nut 12 shown in **FIG 2:12.** If the original static setting of 12 flats down is used as a starting point, the two carburetters may well have a different number of flats alteration from this point after they have been adjusted and on worn carburetters there may be as much as two complete turns of the nut variation between the two. Once the mixture has been correctly set, readjust the idling speed using the two screws 11 and keeping the carburetter air flows in balance.

5 Set the throttle interconnecting clamping levers, (see items 8 in **FIGS 2:13** and **2:11**), until the lever pins rest on the lower arm of the forks. Insert a .020 inch (.5 mm) feeler gauge 16 between the throttle shaft operating lever and the choke control interconnecting rod at A. Tighten the nuts and bolts 8, making sure that the interconnecting rod has an end float of approximately $\frac{1}{32}$ inch (.8 mm). Remove the feeler gauge. The clearance B should now be equal

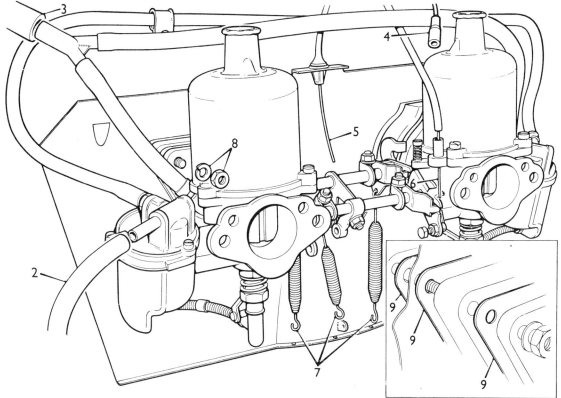

FIG 2:15   Removing twin carburetters

on both sides between each lever pin and the bottom of the fork on both carburetters, and the clearance should be .012 inch (.3 mm).

6 Position the choke control interconnecting rod so that it has an end float of approximately $\frac{1}{32}$ inch (.8 mm) and tighten the clamp nuts 9, after making sure that both jet heads are fully up against their adjusting nuts. Set the choke control cable 10 to a free movement of $\frac{1}{16}$ inch (1.6 mm) and make sure that the cable operates freely with the jets returning fully. Start the engine and pull out the choke control for approximately $\frac{1}{2}$ inch (13 mm) until the linkage is just about to move the jets. Adjust the fast-idle speed to 1000 to 1100 rev/min with the engine hot by turning both screws 19 on the carburetters.

7 Disconnect and remove the tachometer and refit the air cleaner assembly.

2:7 Removing the carburetter

The single carburetter installation is shown in **FIG 2:14** and that for the twin carburetters in **FIG 2:15**. Removal and refitting are very similar on both installations.

1 Remove the air cleaner, as described in **Section 2:2**. Disconnect the fuel pipe 2 from the carburetter float chamber inlet. Disconnect the crankcase breather pipe 3 at the point shown. Disconnect the vacuum pipe 4 for the distributor.

2 Disconnect the accelerator cable 5 and choke cable 6 by slackening the trunnion screws and pulling the inner and outer cables out of their attachments. Free the return springs 7 from the heat shield on the twin-carburetter installations.

3 Remove the attachment nuts and washers 8 and pull the carburetter(s) off the inlet manifold flange(s), collecting the gaskets, spacer and insulator. If the nuts 8 are trapped by flanges as they are unscrewed, slacken them as far as possible and remove the remainder of the nuts so that the carburetter can be eased out further while the trapped nut is being unscrewed. Do not forget to fit these awkward nuts first when refitting the carburetter.

Before refitting the carburetter(s) check the mounting flanges on the carburetter and manifold. If they are distorted or damaged, true them up with a fine file or by lapping with fine-grade emerycloth or grinding paste spread over plate glass.

Refitting the parts is the reverse order of the removal procedure. Use new joint washers 9 as shown in the figures. Jointing compound should not be necessary but if the parts are so badly distorted as to cause air leaks then jointing compound is a cure. **Do not overtighten the attachment nuts 8 as this is a main cause of flange distortion.**

When the installation is complete refit and adjust the accelerator and choke cables.

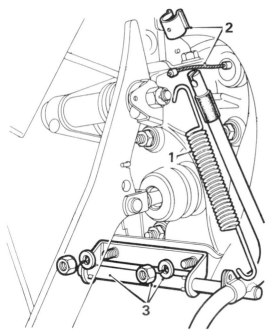

FIG 2:16 Later type throttle pedal assembly, early cars do not have the return spring shown

Accelerator cable:

The attachments of the throttle pedal are shown in **FIG 2:16** and the figure is self-explanatory. The removal of the cable is shown in **FIG 2:17**. Disconnect the cable at the trunnion 1, press in the retainers on the plastic abutment 2 and ease the cable out through the trunnion and bracket. Unhook the cable from the pedal lever 3 and draw it out into the engine compartment so that it can be removed.

The cable is refitted in the reverse order of removal. To adjust the cable refer to **FIG 2:18**. Pull down on the inner cable 5 until all free movement of the throttle pedal is eliminated. Hold the inner cable tight and raise the cam operating lever 6 until it contacts the cam. Tighten the

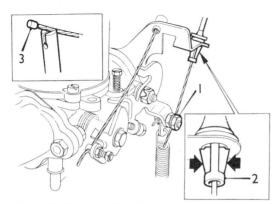

FIG 2:17 The throttle cable attachments at the carburetter

trunnion 7 with the parts in position and check that the cable has a free movement of $\frac{1}{16}$ inch (1.6 mm) before the cam operating lever begins to move when the throttle pedal is pressed.

Twin carburetter controls:

Stiffness in the throttle operation on twin carburetter models may often be due to incorrect assembly of the components making up the throttle cable trunnion, particularly if it has been dismantled for any reason. These components are shown clearly in **FIG 2:18A** and it is most important that they should be assembled in that order.

Insert a .02 inch (.5 mm) feeler gauge between the throttle shaft operating lever and the choke control interconnecting rod. Feed the cable through the trunnion, fit the copper washer and then tighten the nut.

Remove the feeler gauge and check for full and free movement of the throttle control.

Choke cable:

This is secured to its cam by a trunnion and the end of the outer cover is located in the bracket on the carburetter. Once the trunnion has been released the cable can be freed from the carburetter. The dash control is secured by a nut and lockwasher behind the dash. Undo the nut and the cable can be pulled out from the dash.

Refit the cable in the reverse order of removal and adjust it so that there is $\frac{1}{16}$ inch (1.6 mm) free movement.

Pull out the control knob about $\frac{1}{2}$ inch (13 mm) until the linkage is about to move the jet. Start the engine and adjust the fast-idle screw to give an engine speed of 1000 to 1100 rev/min.

Push the control fully-in and check that there is a small clearance between the cam and the fast-idle screw.

Later cars:

Some series 2 cars have a warning light switch mounted on the control, access to these is obtained by removing the two halves of the steering column cowl. When refitting, note that the large locating pip on the switch body locates in the hole nearest the control knob.

The free movement on these controls should be .06 inch (2.0 mm).

2:8 Carburetter faults

Instructions for completely dismantling the carburetter will not be given as a separate section, but dismantling of the various parts to cure the faults will be given in this section. The faults are laid out in such an order that if the dismantling in each part is carried out in turn the complete carburetter will be dismantled at the end.

The components of the carburetter are shown in **FIG 2:9**.

Sticking or defective air valve:

When the damper plunger 15 has been removed from the top of the piston chamber 7, the piston 9 must fall fully and freely so that it hits the bridge in the air intake with a metallic click, after it has been raised and released. The piston can be raised using a thin tool through the air intake or it can be raised using the piston lifting pin 2.

If the piston does stick, remove it and the suction chamber. Scribe light marks across the suction chamber 8 and body 1 to assist in reassembly. Take out the three securing screws 8 and carefully lift off the suction chamber 7. Remove the spring 10 and withdraw the piston 9 complete with the needle parts. **Take very great care of these parts, as the piston and suction chamber are machined to very close tolerances and the needle 11 may get bent if weight is allowed to rest on it.** A little oil will spill when the suction chamber is removed and the remainder of the oil should be poured out of the hollow piston rod.

Clean the suction chamber and piston by washing them in clean fuel or methylated spirits. **Do not use any form of abrasive as it will alter the carefully machined clearance between the piston and inside of the suction chamber.** Very lightly oil the piston rod but keep oil away from the inside of the suction chamber or lands of the piston. Insert the piston back into suction chamber and check that it slides in and out freely. **There must be no metal to metal contact.** If the piston sticks, try cleaning the parts again in case a speck of dirt is causing the fault. If the piston sticks or there is metal to metal contact between piston lands and the inside of the suction chamber the parts must be renewed as a matched set.

Refer to **FIG 2:19**. Fit a washer, screw and nut as shown at B to prevent the piston from falling out of the suction chamber. Plug the ports in the piston C with two small rubber bungs A, or pieces of plasticine. Invert the assembly as shown and pull the piston up until it is stopped by the washer B. Release the piston and time how long it takes to complete its travel. The time taken should be between 5 and 7 seconds. If the time taken is outside the limits, wash the parts again in clean methylated spirits, recheck for any physical damage and use a little light oil on the outside of the piston rod. Repeat the test and if the time taken is still outside the limits, a new matched piston and suction chamber assembly must be fitted. **Note that dropping the suction chamber will cause a dent deep enough to make the piston stick.**

If the piston and suction chamber assembly are satisfactory but the air valve sticks when fitted then the cause is a bent needle 11. To remove or renew the needle, unscrew and discard the locking screw 14, also shown in **FIG 2:20**. Withdraw the needle, taking great care not to bend or damage it if it is to be used again. A sticking needle can sometimes be freed by lightly tapping it into the piston first and then withdrawing it. Remove the needle 11 from the guide 13 and remove the spring 12. Refit the spring and guide to the needle and carefully push the assembly back into the piston, so that the guide is flush with the face of the piston and the flat on the guide faces squarely towards the threaded hole for the locking screw. Secure the needle assembly in place using a new locking screw 14.

Refit the parts in the reverse order of removal, checking that the guide 71 is securely in place. Correctly fill the damper with oil.

Jet sticking, leaking or blocked:

The jet parts are shown in **FIG 2:21**. Take out the screw 54 that secures the lever to the plastic base of the jet 42. Unscrew the sleeve nut 43 from the float chamber 21 and withdraw the flexible hose, carefully collecting washer 44, gland 45 and ferrule 46. Withdraw the jet

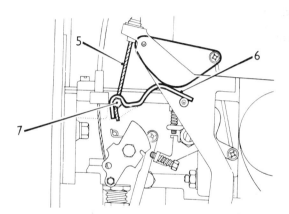

FIG 2:18   Adjusting the throttle cable

assembly 42 out from the carburetter. Unscrew the adjusting nut 51 and remove the spring 50. Unscrew the locating nut 49 from the body 1 and remove the seal 48 and jet bearing 47.

Blow through the jet to remove any dirt. Wash the parts in clean fuel or methylated spirits. A little petroleum jelly (vaseline) may be used on the outside of the jet 42 as a lubricant.

Refit the bearing 47 and a new seal 48 then screw the locating nut 49 back into position. Fit the spring 50 onto the jet bearing and screw on the adjusting nut 51 as far as it will go. Raise the air valve as high as possible and

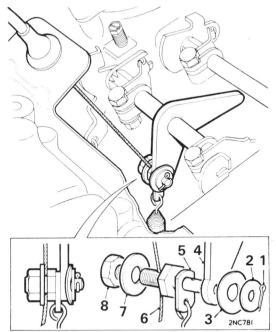

FIG 2:18A   Showing the correct assembly of the throttle cable on twin carburetter models

Key to Fig 2:18A   1 Splitpin   2 Plain washer   3 Curved washer   4 Throttle shaft operating lever   5 Spring and anchor tag   6 Throttle cable   7 Copper washer   8 Nut

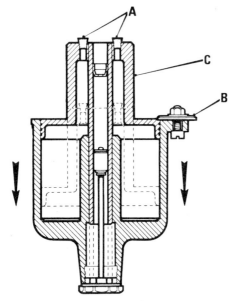

FIG 2:19 Checking the piston and suction chamber

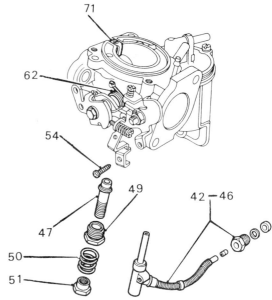

FIG 2:21 The jet parts

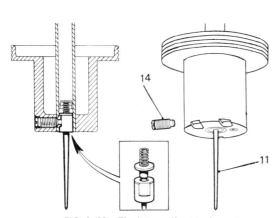

FIG 2:20 The jet needle attachment

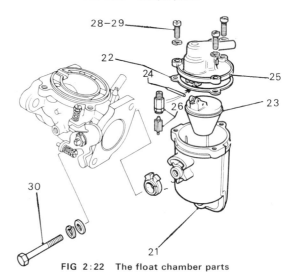

FIG 2:22 The float chamber parts

slide the jet 42 up through the bearing. **Take great care to ensure that the needle 11 enters the jet and does not catch on the end.** The safest method is to refit the jet with the air valve and suction chamber removed.

Refit the parts 43 to 46 to the end of the flexible tube, noting that the ferrule 46 must project a minimum of $\frac{3}{16}$ inch (4.8 mm) beyond the gland 45. Screw the brass sleeve nut 43 back into the float chamber 21 until the gland 45 is compressed. **Do not overtighten as this will cause leaks.**

Flooding or starvation:

If there is flooding check that it is not caused by loose attachments or defective gaskets. Starvation can be caused by a faulty fuel pump or blocked fuel lines so check for these faults if the carburetter is satisfactory.

Either fault can be caused by a defective float chamber. The parts of the float chamber are also shown in **FIG 2:22**. The float chamber can be removed from the carburetter by disconnecting the jet feed tube (undo sleeve nut 43) and taking out the bolt 30, though this is not necessary other than for full dismantling of the carburetter.

Disconnect the fuel line from the float chamber cover 25. Take out the three screws 28, lightly scribe across the cover 25 and body 21 to assist in reassembly, and remove the cover 25 complete with the float and needle valve. Collect the gasket 22. Remove the pin 24 so that the float 23 can be taken off, taking care not to lose the needle of the valve 26. Discard the float and fit a new one in its place if it is damaged, leaks or contains fuel.

Unscrew the seat of the valve 26 from the cover. Blow through the inlet tube of the cover to clear out any dirt and wash the valve assembly 26 in clean fuel. Check the tapered end of the needle for signs of wear and renew the complete valve 26 if the needle is worn or the valve leaks when blown through with the needle held closed on its seat.

Refit the parts to the cover in the reverse order of removal. Do not overtighten the seat of the valve 26. The fuel level on SU carburetters is not particularly critical but it should be checked as shown in **FIG 2:23**. Invert the cover, omitting the gasket, and lay a drill shank or test bar

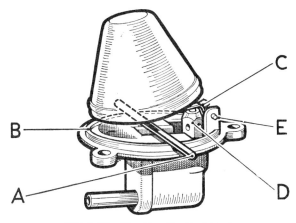

FIG 2:23 Checking the float level

Key to Fig 2:23 **A** Test bar ($\frac{1}{8}$ to $\frac{3}{16}$ inch) **B** Machined lip
C Float lever resetting point **D** Needle valve assembly
E Hinge pin

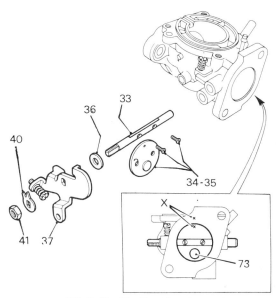

FIG 2:24 The throttle valve parts

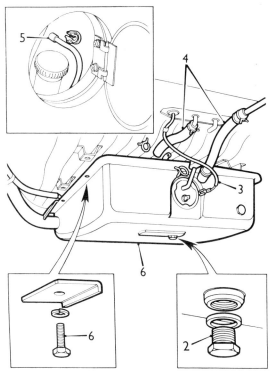

FIG 2:25 The fuel tank attachments. It should be noted that the filler cap on Van models is of the vented type, those fitted to Saloon and Estate cars are not vented

A of $\frac{1}{8}$ to $\frac{3}{16}$ inch (3.18 to 4.76 mm) diameter across the machined flange B. Carefully bend the float arm at C so that the angle between the straight portion and its hinge allows the float just to rest on the test bar when the needle D is fully closed.

Blow and brush out any sediment from inside the float chamber. Refit the cover assembly in the reverse order of removal and reconnect the fuel line.

Air leaks:

Defective flanges or joint washers can be one cause of air leaks. A worn throttle spindle or butterfly valve will also allow air to leak in and in all these cases the slow-running will be erratic and uneven. The flanges and joint washers have already been covered in **Section 2:7**.

The spindle and valve parts are shown in **FIG 2:24**. The parts will be accessible only after the carburetter has been removed from the manifold. Disconnect the linkage, remove the nut 41, lockwasher 40, throttle return lever 37 and the washer 36. Mark the butterfly 34 and body at X, so that the marks are on the opposite side to the limit valve 73. Take out the screws 35, noting that they are split to lock them. Slide out the butterfly valve 34 from its slot in the spindle 33 and withdraw the spindle from the body.

Try fitting a new spindle but if this does not take up the wear a new carburetter must be fitted. Renew the butterfly valve 34 if it is worn or damaged.

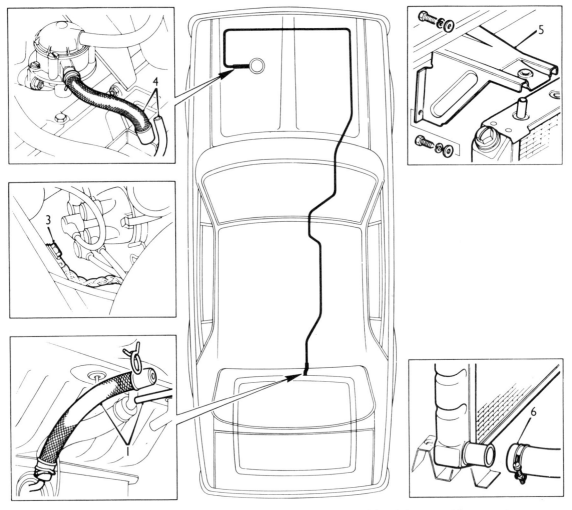

FIG 2:26 The fuel lines, showing the points to be disconnected for their removal (early cars)

The parts are refitted in the reverse order of removal. Fit the spindle first and then manoeuvre the valve into the slot, so that the marks align and the limit valve is at the bottom with the head towards the engine. Snap the throttle open and closed to centralize the valve and loosely secure it with new screws, just tight. Adjust the position of the butterfly valve so that it is central in the bore and the throttle can close fully. Tighten the screws 35 and open the splits to lock them.

2:9 The fuel tank and fuel lines

There have been a few modifications to the fuel tank installation and the associated pipes and hoses since the Marina was introduced, but the following description should enable the home operator to remove and refit them without difficulty. Note that later fuel tanks do not have a drain plug. A typical fuel tank installation is shown in **FIG 2:25**.

Tank removal:

Raise the rear of the car and place it securely on axle stands. Remove the drain plug 2 and drain the fuel into a suitable container. If the fuel is contaminated or dirty it can be used for cleaning operations. Disconnect the lead 3 from the tank unit. Disconnect the vent and fuel pipes 4, using pliers to squeeze the legs of the clips open. Release the vent pipe 5 by the filler cap. On Vans, release the filler pipe grommet from the cut-out in the body panel. Support the tank and remove the securing bolts and plates. Lower the tank down and out of the car.

If the tank unit is removed from the tank, **take great care not to damage or bend the float arm.**

The fuel tank is refitted in the reverse order of removal, but note that on Vans it may be desirable to fit a new grommet and anti-rattle pad. The filler vent pipe is routed over the rear chassis member.

Fuel line:

The run of the metal line, its attachments and the points to disconnect for removing it are shown in **FIG 2:26**. Disconnect the flexible hose at the fuel tank end 1, plugging the hose if the tank is full. Release the clips that secure the metal pipe to the body. Disconnect the engine earth strap 3 and disconnect the pipe from the hose to the fuel pump at 4. Free the radiator support brackets 5 and disconnect the bottom radiator hose 6, catching the coolant as it drains in a clean container. The metal pipe can now be withdrawn through the engine compartment. On the 1.3 models withdraw the pipe from between the radiator and grille but on the 1.8 models withdraw it from between the radiator and engine.

The pipe is refitted in the reverse order of removal and the cooling system must be refilled.

If the pipe is blocked, disconnect it at points 1 and 4 and blow through with compressed air from the point 4. If this does not clear a blocked pipe then it must be removed and a new one fitted in its place.

On vans, estate cars and later saloons the layout of the pipes is different and a typical removal procedure is as follows.

Disconnect the pipe from the tank flexible hose, bend back the clips on the body to release the pipe and then remove the pipe protective grommet.

Unclip the pipe from the plastic supports and disconnect the pipes from the flexible portion of hose at the crossmember. Remove the flexible hose.

Disconnect the pipe from the fuel pump flexible hose, unclip it from the plastic supports and pull the front end of the pipe through the body grommet in the wheel arch. Remove the pipe by pulling it forward through the crossmember and long member grommets.

Refit in the reverse order, using new grommets as necessary.

2:10 Fault diagnosis

(a) Leakage or insufficient fuel delivered

1 Fuel tank vent restricted
2 Fuel pipes obstructed
3 Air leaks at pipe connections
4 Filters obstructed
5 Pump gaskets faulty
6 Pump diaphragm defective
7 Pump valves sticking or damaged
8 Fuel vaporizing in lines due to heat

(b) Excessive fuel consumption

1 Carburetter(s) require adjusting
2 Fuel leakage
3 Sticking controls or choke linkage
4 Dirty air cleaner
5 Excessive engine temperature
6 Brakes binding
7 Tyres under-inflated
8 Car overloaded

(c) Idling speed too high

1 Rich fuel mixture
2 Carburetter controls sticking
3 Slow-running incorrectly adjusted
4 Worn carburetter butterfly valve

(d) Noisy fuel pump

1 Loose mountings
2 Air leaks on suction side and at diaphragm
3 Clogged pump filter

(e) No fuel delivery

1 Float needle stuck
2 Fuel tank vent blocked
3 Pipe line blocked
4 Fuel pump defective
5 Bad air leak on suction side of pump
6 Fuel tank empty

NOTES

CHAPTER 3

THE IGNITION SYSTEM

3:1 Description

On early models in the range covered in this manual the distributor is a Lucas 23.D4 or 25.D4. Both types include a centrifugal mechanism for automatic advancement of the ignition with increasing engine speed, and some have also a hand operated vernier adjustment for fine setting of the timing. Only the 25.D4 incorporates a vacuum operated timing mechanism.

On later cars a 43.D4 or 45.D4 distributor may be fitted. These are very similar to the earlier types, but do not have a vernier adjuster. There is a one-piece contact set for easy replacement.

The earlier type will be discussed first and any important points of difference in the later type will be given in **Section 3:7**.

The centrifugal advance mechanism is incorporated between the distributor cam and distributor shaft. As the engine speed increases, two small spring-loaded weights are thrown outwards by centrifugal force and turn the cam so as to advance the ignition. The vacuum unit (if fitted) is connected to the carburetter by a small-bore pipe so that the unit senses manifold depression. As the manifold suction drops at high loads and wide throttle openings, such as hill-climbing, the unit rotates the base plate of the contact breakers about the cam so as to retard the ignition.

The distributor is synchronized to the engine and the contact breakers open and close under the action of the cam. As the contacts open the current flow through the ignition coil is sharply cut off, assisted by the action of the capacitor, and the rapid collapse of the magnetic field around the primary coils induces a very high voltage in the secondary turns of the coil. The HT voltage is fed back to the distributor cap centre electrode and the rotor arm leads the high voltage to the correct side electrode which is connected to the sparking plug of the cylinder that is at the firing point. Heavily insulated HT leads are used to carry the high voltage. The HT voltage jumping across the electrodes of the sparking plug ignites the air/fuel mixture in the cylinder.

3:2 Maintenance

The components of the distributor are shown in **FIG 3:1**. Free the two side clips and lift off the distributor cap 23. Carefully pull the rotor arm 1 off the end of the cam 16.

When maintenance is complete, press the rotor arm fully and squarely back onto the cam (making sure that its lug aligns with the slot in the cam) and refit the distributor cap so that it is correctly aligned by its lugs. Always wipe the rotor arm and distributor cap clean with a soft piece of cloth before refitting them. Periodically wipe over the HT leads to remove any oil or grease from them.

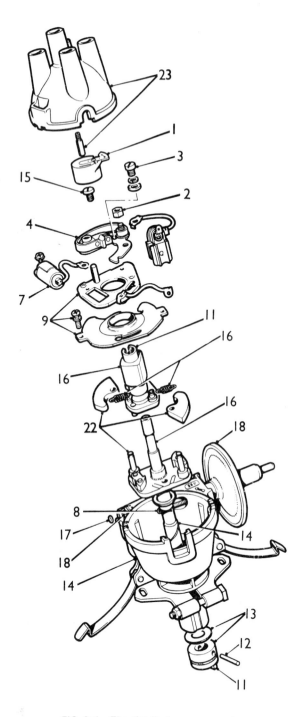

FIG 3:1   The distributor components

Key to Fig 3:1   1 Rotor arm   2 Nut   3 Screw
4 Contact points   7 Capacitor   8 Vacuum control link
9 Baseplate assembly   11 Slot and drive dog offset relation
12 Parallel pin   13 Drive dog and thrust washer   14 Shaft
15 Cam retaining screw   16 Cam and springs   17 Circlip
18 Vacuum unit and knurled nut   22 Control weights and
pivots   23 Cap and carbon brush

Lubrication:

The lubrication points are shown in **FIG 3:2. Over-lubrication is even more harmful than slightly neglected lubrication,** as excess oil or grease will reach the contact points causing them to have a high resistance, as well as covering the inside of the distributor cap so that dirt can collect and form a leakage path for the HT voltage.

1 Pour a few drops of oil into the recess on top of the cam at 1. There is no need to remove the screw as there is a clearance provided around it for the passage of the oil.

2 Put a single drop of oil onto the moving contact pivot at 2.

3 Lightly spread a thin film of grease around the cams at 3. Engine oil may be used if grease is not available.

4 Pour a few drops of oil through the hole in the contact breaker plate through which the camshaft passes.

Take great care not to allow any lubricant onto the contact points themselves and wipe away all surplus lubricant with a piece of cloth.

Setting the points gap:

Before setting the gap, make sure that the points are clean and meet squarely. Renew the points if they are excessively worn or pitted. If the moving contact sticks, check the spring tension with a modified spring balance and renew the points if the spring is weak. If the spring is satisfactory, remove the moving contact and lightly polish the pivot with a piece of fine emerycloth and lubricate it with a single drop of oil before refitting the moving contact. The method of adjustment is shown in **FIG 3:3.**

1 Turn the engine so that a lobe of the cam is directly under the foot of the moving contact and the contacts are at their widest gap.

2 Slightly slacken the screw arrowed so that the fixed contact can be moved by inserting a screwdriver between the slots in the fixed contact and base plate and turning the screwdriver. The screw arrowed should be slackened enough to allow the contacts to move under slight pressure but not so slack that they float on their own.

3 Insert a feeler gauge of the correct thickness between the contacts, as shown. The gap should be between the limits of .014 to .016 inch (.35 to .40mm). When fitting new contacts set them to the widest limit to allow for bedding in of the contact foot. If the points are slightly pitted, as is normal after use, make sure that the feeler gauge fits between the unworn portions of the contacts and does not bridge the pit to give a false reading.

4 Rotate the screwdriver to alter the gap until the feeler gauge is just nipped between the contacts and slight drag is felt on it as it is moved. **Make sure that the feeler gauge has been wiped clean before using it.** Tighten the screw in this position and check that the gap has not altered.

Cleaning or renewing the contact points:

1 Refer to **FIG 3:1.** Unscrew the nut 2 from the fixed contact post and remove the two leads. The moving contact can now be lifted off from the fixed contact, carefully collecting and noting the positions of the

insulating washers. The fixed contact can be lifted out after taking out its securing screw 3 (arrowed in **FIG 3:3**).

2 Clean the points using a fine file or oil stone. The points must be cleaned so that they meet squarely and the surfaces are left very slightly rough and matt-grey in colour. The most effective way of cleaning is to use garage equipment to grind them. If they are worn or deeply pitted, discard them and fit a new set. Wash the points in methylated spirits to remove any oil or dirt, noting that new points should also be washed to remove any preservative.

3 Refit the points in the reverse order of removal, making sure that the insulating washers and bush are correctly refitted between the contacts. Check that the moving contact pivots freely about its post. One-piece contact sets are now available and if they are used they will be found much easier to remove and refit, both contacts being removed and refitted together without the owner having to separate them or worry about the insulating washers between them.

4 Set the contact gap.

3:3 Ignition faults

It is recommended that the car is taken to an agent who has electronic test equipment (such as Sun or Crypton) for fairly regular checks. All adjustments and settings can then be checked, faults pin-pointed, and weak points found before they develop into a fault. This applies not only to the ignition but to the whole engine and fuel system as well.

Before carrying out checks on the ignition system make sure that the carburetter(s) are correctly adjusted, the contact points clean and at the correct gap, and the ignition timing correctly set. Fouled or defective sparking plugs will also cause ignition faults.

If there is a persistent misfire that cannot be traced, check the sparking plugs and ignition circuits. Start the engine and run it until it has reached its normal operating temperature. Use the choke control to increase the idling-speed to fast-idle but do not pull the control out so far that the carburetter jets move.

Disconnect each HT lead from its sparking plug in turn. **Use insulated tongs, thick gloves or dry rags as an insulator to prevent getting electrical shocks from a defective HT lead.** If the rough running or mis-firing becomes more pronounced as the lead is disconnected that cylinder is firing satisfactorily. If there is no difference in the engine note as the lead is disconnected then that cylinder is not firing. Check all four cylinders in turn.

Having identified the faulty cylinder, stop the engine. Remove the insulating shroud from the end of the HT lead and restart the engine so that it runs on three cylinders. Hold the end of the HT lead, using insulation, approximately $\frac{3}{16}$ inch (5 mm) away from a convenient earthed metal part of the car, but **well away from the fuel system.** There should be a fat, blue, regular spark. If the spark is good then it is likely that the sparking plug is defective. Remove the sparking plug and clean and test it, or fit a new sparking plug in its place. If the misfire is not cured then the fault lies in the engine, such as a defective or sticking valve.

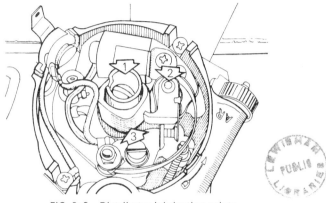

FIG 3:2 Distributor lubrication points

If the spark is poor, irregular, thin and reddish in colour the fault lies in the ignition system. Stop the engine and check the HT lead. Renew the lead (using the correct resistive type) if it is cracked, perished or shows burn spots. HT leads can be checked with a resistance meter (see **Section 3:6**).

If there is no improvement after renewing the HT lead, check the distributor and ignition coil. The coil can be checked by disconnecting the HT lead from the centre electrode of the distributor cap and holding it $\frac{3}{16}$ inch away from a metal part while cranking the engine on the starter motor. The sparks should be much faster than when testing an individual cylinder lead and if they are weak or irregular suspect the HT lead or ignition coil.

Remove the distributor cap and rotor arm. Wipe them both clean all over using a soft piece of cloth and washing with methylated spirits, paying particular attention to the crevices between the electrodes inside the cap and those between the HT leads on the outside of the cap. Check that the carbon brush in the centre of the distributor cap is not broken or excessively worn and that it moves freely against the pressure of its spring. Renew brush and spring

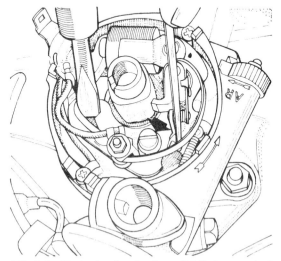

FIG 3:3 Method of adjusting distributor contact points

if they are defective. Check the distributor cap very carefully for hairline cracks or signs of tracking, and renew the cap if either of these are found. Tracking will show up as thin black lines between electrodes inside the cap or from an electrode to the edge of the cap.

Testing the low-tension circuit:

As a quick field test, switch on the ignition and remove the distributor cap. Turn the engine until the contact points are closed and then flick them apart with a fingernail. Current flowing through the distributor will then show as a small low-voltage spark across the contact points. If no spark is present, further investigation must be made.

Disconnect the lead from between the ignition coil and distributor and reconnect it with a low-wattage test lamp in series. Remove the distributor cap so that the action of the points can be seen. Switch on the ignition and slowly rotate the engine by hand. If the circuit is satisfactory, the lamp will light as the contacts close and go out as they open.

If the lamp does not light at all, trace back through the wiring until the fault is found and can be repaired. Use the test lamp, or 0-20 voltmeter, between terminals and a good earth on the car to check which parts of the circuit are live and which are dead.

If the lamp stays on continuously, there is a short-circuit in the distributor. Disconnect the capacitor, and any radio suppressors fitted, and repeat the test. If the lamp now lights and goes out correctly then the capacitor is at fault. The fault is more likely to be in frayed insulation of the internal wires or incorrect reassembly with the insulating washers and bushes incorrectly fitted.

Capacitor:

The capacitor is not usually prone to failure and short-circuits in it are unlikely. The unit is made up of foil wrapped with paper as insulation and if the insulation fails the spark usually erodes away the foil in that area to make the capacitor self-healing. A shortcircuit can be found as described just previously.

An open-circuit capacitor is more difficult to detect without special test equipment. It may be suspected if starting is difficult and the points are excessively burned or 'blued'. The best check is to fit a new capacitor and see whether this cures the faults.

3:4 Servicing the distributor

Removal:

The attachments of the distributor are shown in **FIG 3:4,** as well as the ignition timing marks.

Disconnect the battery. Remove the distributor cap 3 and turn the engine until the timing marks align and the brass end of the rotor arm 2 is pointing towards the position of the electrode in the cap 3 connected to the sparking plug of No. 1 (front cylinder).

Provided that the bolt and nut that secure the clamp to the base of the distributor are not slackened or the clamp rotated about the distributor, the distributor can be removed and refitted without losing the ignition timing. Before removing the distributor, make aligning marks across the clamp 6 and crankcase and refit the distributor so that these marks again align accurately. If there is any

doubt, correctly set the ignition timing as described in the next section.

Disconnect the lead 4 from the low-tension terminal on the side of the distributor. Disconnect the vacuum pipe 5 to the vacuum unit, noting that it is not fitted on standard 1.3 engines.

Remove the two bolts that secure the clamp 6 and withdraw the distributor 7 from the engine.

Refit the distributor in the reverse order of removal, turning the shaft until the rotor arm is approximately in the right position and then making slight adjustments to its position so that the offset on the driving dog slips into the slot in the drive shaft. Align the marks and tighten the bolts to a torque of 8 to 10 lb ft (1.1 to 1.4 kg m).

Dismantling:

Remove the distributor from the engine and take off the distributor cap and rotor arm. Refer to **FIG 3:1.**

1 Take out the screw 3 and nut 2 so that the contact points 4 can be removed. Slide out the low-tension terminal assembly from its slot in the body. Remove the securing screw and take out the capacitor 7.

2 Release the end 8 of the vacuum unit 18 (if fitted) from the post of the moving plate 9. Take out the two screws and remove the base plate assembly 9. The moving plate can be separated from the base plate by holding the moving plate and turning the base plate clockwise, collecting any spring washers fitted between them.

3 Carefully note the relation of the slot in the cam 16 to the offset of the drive dog 13, shown at 11 in both parts. Drive out the pin 12 and pull off the drive dog 13 with its thrust washer. Make sure that the end of the shaft 14 is perfectly free from burrs or high spots, polishing with emerycloth if required, and slide the shaft assembly up and out of the body, noting the nylon washer fitted on the shaft.

4 Take out the screw 15 and very carefully free the return springs 16. **Take great care not to bend or distort these springs as they control the centrifugal advance.** If one spring appears too long and loose no action need be taken as the springs on some models are designed to be of different rates and come into operation at different times. Once the springs have been freed the cam and weights 22 can be separated from the shaft.

5 Remove the circlip 17 and unscrew the knurled adjusting nut 18, after noting its position on the vernier so that it can be reassembled to the same position, and remove the vacuum unit 18, taking care not to lose any ratchet springs fitted to the body.

Reassembly:

The distributor is reassembled in the reverse order of dismantling, after cleaning all the parts and checking for wear. Lubricate all bearing and pivot points with engine oil. **Make sure that the relation 11 is reassembled correctly otherwise the timing will be 180 deg. out.**

Check that the end float of the shaft 14 does not exceed $\frac{1}{32}$ inch (.8 mm) in the body. If the end float is excessive, fit a new nylon washer to the shaft and a new thrust washer 13 under the drive dog.

Bearing:

The wear on the bush in the body should be checked using a new distributor shaft or a mandrel of .490 inch (12.45 mm) diameter.

1 Drive out the old bush, downwards from the inside of the body.

2 Soak the new bush in engine oil for at least 24 hours. In an emergency the bush can be soaked in oil heated to 100°C over a bath of boiling water for 2 hours and then taken out and fitted after the oil has cooled.

3 Insert the smaller diameter of the bush into the bottom of the distributor body and press it in as far as possible by hand. Squeeze the bush fully into place, so that its end is flush with the end of the body, between the padded jaws of a vice. **Do not machine or bore the bush.**

4 Drill a new drain hole through the bush, using the shank hole as a guide. Remove all metal particles and deburr the hole thoroughly inside the bush.

5 Make sure that the shaft 14 is free from burrs or high spots, polishing it with fine emerycloth if required. Wipe the shaft clean and lubricate it with engine oil. Slide the shaft back into position and check that it rotates freely. **The shaft must rotate freely** and if it is tight, remove it and polish it with a very fine grade of emerycloth. Clean and lubricate the shaft every time and keep polishing until the shaft does rotate freely. Use a test rig, lathe or electric drill to spin the shaft in the bush for 15 minutes. Remove the shaft, clean it and relubricate it with fresh oil before reassembling the distributor.

3:5 Setting the ignition timing

1 Remove the sparking plugs and turn the engine over by hand until No. 1 (front) piston is at the timing point on the compression stroke. The timing marks are shown in **FIG 3:4.** The correct timing points are as follows:

1.1 engine	8 deg. BTDC
1.3 engine	9 deg. BTDC.
1.8 engine (SC)	10 deg. BTDC.
1.8 TC	7 deg. BTDC
1.8 engine (1975 on) HC and	
LC	3 deg. BTDC
1.8 engine, GT and HL ..	7 deg. BTDC

As the engine is being turned over, place a thumb over the hole for No. 1 sparking plug and the pressure inside the cylinder will be felt to rise as the piston comes up on the compression stroke. Turn the engine until the correct timing point is reached. If the mark is overshot, turn the engine well back and then turn it forwards to the point, otherwise the backlash in the system will not be taken up. The position can also be found if the rocker cover is off, as the valves on No. 4 (rear) cylinder will be at the point of balance when the No. 1 piston is near the correct point.

2 Remove the distributor cap and disconnect the low-tension lead from the terminal on the distributor. Reconnect the lead with a low-wattage test lamp fitted in series and switch on the ignition.

3 Set the vernier adjustment to the middle of its scale and slacken the pinch bolt that secures the clamp to the distributor body. Press the rotor arm lightly in a

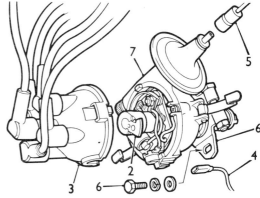

FIG 3:4 The distributor attachments and ignition timing marks. The last pointer in the direction of rotation indicates TDC, each of the other pointers represents a 5 deg. interval BTDC

clockwise direction to take up any backlash and turn the distributor body slightly either side of its position until the point is found where the light has just gone out, indicating that the points have just opened. Tighten the pinch bolt on the clamp.

4 Rotate the engine in a forward direction for two full turns. Towards the end of the second revolution slow down the rate of turning and stop immediately after the test lamp goes out. If the timing is correct the timing marks will again be in exact alignment. Fine adjustments can be set on the distributor vernier.

5 Remove the test lamp, after switching off the ignition, and correctly reconnect the distributor lead. Refit the distributor cap and sparking plugs. Reconnect the HT leads. If the leads were not marked on removal, No. 1 lead is connected to the electrode in the cap opposite to the rotor arm and the remainder of the leads are connected anticlockwise around the cap in the firing order (1-3-4-2).

Stroboscopic timing:

This method may be used as an accurate setting and checking, but the static setting must be made with reasonable accuracy to allow the engine to run safely. Some form of scale will have to be fitted to the timing cover to give accurate readings and the main points, as well as the notch in the pulley, should be marked with thin white lines to make reading easier. Connect the light as instructed by the makers of the instrument. **Take great care to keep tools, hands or clothes out of the moving fan belt and cooling fan.** The range of advance is given in Technical Data.

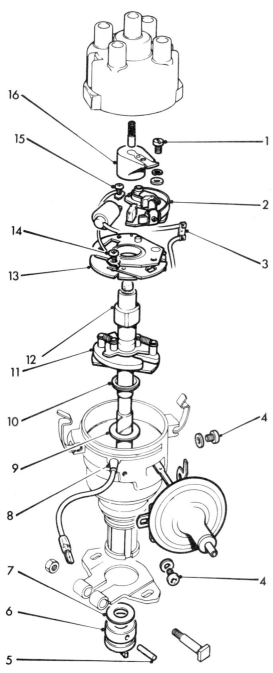

3:6 The sparking plugs

The recommended sparking plugs for all versions are Champion N-9Y and they should be gapped between .024 and .026 inch (.625 and .660 mm). Service the plugs at 6000 miles and renew them at 12,000 miles.

Removal:

Slacken the sparking plug by one or two turns, using a well fitting box spanner or plug wrench. Blow away loose dirt from the base of the plug using an air-line or tyre pump. Unscrew the sparking plug fully by hand.

If the sparking plug is stiff to remove, slacken it as far as possible with a box spanner and then wind it in and out a few times to this point before trying to unscrew it further. In really difficult cases wrap the base of the plug with a piece of rag soaked in paraffin, penetrating oil or hydraulic fluid and leave it overnight.

Store the plugs in their correct order for later examination.

Examination:

The condition of the firing end will give a good guide to the conditions inside the combustion chamber. After examination, throw away any sparking plugs which have badly burnt electrodes or cracked insulators without bothering to clean and test them.

A light powdery deposit ranging in colour from brown to greyish tan coupled with light wear on the electrodes, shows that the conditions are the ones expected from normal driving. Long periods of constant-speed or much city driving will leave the deposits white or yellowish. Cleaning and testing the sparking plugs is all that is required in these cases.

If the deposits are wet and black they are caused by oil entering the combustion chamber. An engine overhaul is the only cure but fitting a hotter-running grade of sparking plug may help to alleviate the problem.

Black fluffy deposits are caused by incomplete combustion. This may be caused by excessive idling but it may also be caused by defective ignition, a defective sparking plug or running with too rich a mixture.

Overheated sparking plugs will have a white blistered look about the central electrode and there may be glints of metal on the central insulator from the lead in the fuel. The electrodes will be excessively burnt away. Some possible causes are; engine overheating, very weak mixture, incorrectly set ignition timing, incorrect grade of sparking plug or running at high-speeds with the car overloaded.

Cleaning, adjusting and testing:

Wash oily sparking plugs with fuel. Have the plugs cleaned on an abrasive blasting machine and pressure tested after attention to the electrodes. A stiff wire brush can be used to clean the plugs but this will not be so effective as it cannot penetrate deep inside. Never use a brush made with soft-metal bristles as they will leave metal deposited on the central insulator.

Trim the electrodes square using a fine file. Adjust to the correct gap by bending the side electrode only, using feeler gauges to check the gap. Never bend the central electrode as this will crack the insulator.

FIG 3:5 The components of the Lucas distributor type 45.D4

Key to Fig 3:5 1 Fixed contact retaining screw   2 Spring   3 LT lead   4 Vacuum unit retaining screws   5 Pin   6 Drive dog   7 Thrust washer   8 LT lead grommet   9 Steel washer   10 Nylon spacer   11 Weights   12 Camshaft   13 Baseplate   14 Baseplate retaining screw .   15 Earth lead and capacitor screw   16 Rotor

Clean the external portion of the insulator with methylated spirits and keep it free from oil or grease when refitting the sparking plug. Clean the threads of the plug with a wire brush.

Refitting:

If the threads in the cylinder head are dirty, clean them out using a well-greased tap. Failing a tap use an old sparking plug with cross-cuts down the threads.

Only graphite grease may be used on the threads of the sparking plug as any other grease will bake hard and lock the plug in place.

Fit a new sealing ring to the plug if the old one is compressed to less than half its original thickness.

Screw the plugs in by hand and use a box spanner or torque wrench for the final tightening. Half a turn beyond the handtight position is quite adequate and over-tightening can cause damage to the sparking plug.

HT leads:

Special resistive leads are fitted and the old type of lead with a copper wire core must not be fitted in their place. When removing or refitting leads, pull or push on the connector and not on the lead itself. The leads use a nylon core coated with carbon granules and stretching can easily break this core causing it to fail later.

The leads can be checked with an ohmmeter as they have a resistance of approximately 420 ohms per inch.

The leads should be marked for order. If the order is lost, set the engine to the TDC position on the compression stroke of No. 1 piston (as described in **Section 3:5**) and the electrode in the distributor cap by the brass end of the rotor arm is connected to No. 1 sparking plug. The remainder of the leads are then connected around the cap in an anticlockwise direction in the firing order (1-3-4-2).

3:7 Lucas distributors, 43.D4 and 45.D4

The components of this later type distributor are shown in **FIG 3:5** and after removal from the engine (see **Section 3:4**) it may be dismantled in a similar manner to the earlier type.

Clean and examine all the parts and renew any which show signs of excessive wear or damage. Reassembly is a reversal of the dismantling procedure but note carefully the following points.

Refer to **FIG 3:6**. The thrust washer must be fitted with its raised pips towards the drive dog and the drive dog must have the tongues parallel to the rotor arm and to the left of the centre line as shown. Secure the pin by staking the holes. If a new drive spindle is fitted, tap the drive end of the dog to flatten the pips on the washer and ensure the correct amount of end float.

Refer to **FIG 3:7**. Locate the base plate assembly with the two prongs A straddling the screw hole below the cap clip and press it into the body register with the chamfered edge engaging the undercut.

Carefully measure across the distributor cap register B at right angles to the slot C in the base plate. Tighten the securing screw D and remeasure the distance across the body. Unless this dimension has increased by at least .006 inch (.152 mm) the contact breaker base plate must be renewed.

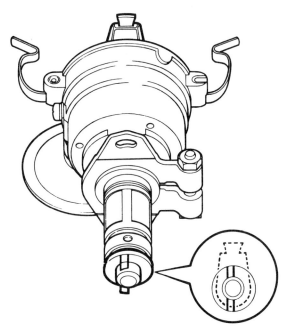

FIG 3:6 Showing the alignment of the driving dog and rotor arm

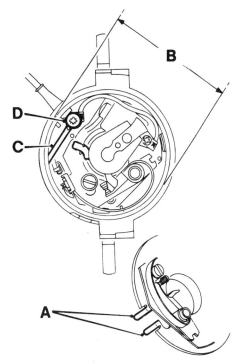

FIG 3:7 Fitting the baseplate assembly

Ensure that the two prongs are still correctly positioned and refit the vacuum unit, engaging the arm with the pin on the moving plate.

The contact points gap must be set to .014 to .016 inch (.36 to .40 mm). If equipment is available, the dwell angle is 51 deg. ± 5 deg.

3:8 Fault diagnosis

(a) Engine will not fire

1 Battery discharged or terminals dirty
2 Distributor points dirty or incorrectly adjusted
3 Distributor cap dirty, cracked or tracking
4 Carbon brush inside distributor cap defective
5 Faulty or loose connections in low-tension circuit
6 Distributor rotor arm cracked, or omitted on reassembly
7 Faulty coil
8 HT coil lead defective
9 Broken contact spring
10 Contacts stuck open
11 Internal shortcircuit in distributor
12 Damp or dirt on HT leads, distributor cap and ignition coil

(b) Engine misfires

1 Check 2, 3, 5 and 7 in (a)
2 Weak contact breaker spring
3 Defective HT lead
4 Sparking plug(s) loose
5 Sparking plug insulation cracked
6 Sparking plug gap incorrectly set
7 Ignition timing too far advanced

CHAPTER 4

THE COOLING SYSTEM

4:1 Description

Coolant passes through the internal passages in the crankcase and cylinder head, collecting excess heat from the engine. The coolant then passes through the radiator where it is cooled by the passage of air over the fins before returning to the engine. A natural thermo-syphon action is set up and the coolant would circulate unassisted. To ensure that there is a positive flow at all times and that the coolant circulates rapidly a centrifugal pump is fitted into the system. The pump is driven by a belt from the crank-shaft pulley. To assist the airflow through the radiator, particularly when the car is stationary or travelling slowly, a cooling fan is fitted to the water pump.

A thermostat valve is fitted into the outlet from the cylinder head to ensure that the engine temperature stays reasonably constant and to give a shorter warming-up period from cold. When the coolant is cold the valve stays closed, preventing the coolant from passing through into the radiator. The coolant recirculates directly back to the engine through a bypass hose and the warming-up period is considerably reduced because the amount of coolant to be heated is reduced and there are no heat losses through the radiator. When the coolant reaches its normal temperature, the valve opens and allows the coolant to pass through the radiator.

The radiator is fitted with a plug that can be removed for filling the system and it is connected by a hose to an expansion tank. The expansion tank is fitted with a pressure cap which allows the pressure in the cooling system to rise to 15 lb/sq inch (1.05 kg/sq cm) before it opens and allows surplus air to escape. The cap is also fitted with a vacuum relief valve to ensure that air can return into the expansion tank when the system cools. **Never remove the radiator filler cap when the system is hot.** If the system is overheated or boiling, allow it to cool before taking off the filler cap on the expansion chamber. If the cap is removed the sudden reduction in pressure will cause the coolant to boil and force scalding water over the operator's hand, while air in the expansion tank will force out coolant if the radiator filler cap is removed. The system is pressurized as this raises the boiling point of the coolant and allows the engine to be run hotter without danger of boiling at localized hot spots.

4:2 Routine maintenance

There are no lubrication points in the system. Periodically check the level of the coolant in the expansion tank. The correct level is marked on the outside of the tank and it should be topped up to this mark. If water only is used for topping up, have the specific gravity of the coolant

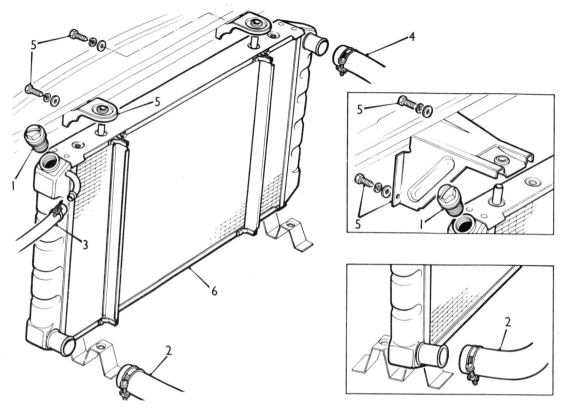

FIG 4:1   The radiator and its attachments

checked before winter to ensure that it still contains sufficient antifreeze to protect the system down to the lowest temperatures expected.

Regularly check the fan belt tension and adjust if it is slack (see **Section 4:4**).

Antifreeze has a life of approximately two years, after which the corrosion inhibitors lose their effect, so the system should be drained, flushed and refilled with fresh coolant every two years.

Draining:

The radiator and its attachments are shown in **FIG 4:1**. If the system is being drained for any reason other than renewing the coolant, the coolant in the system should be drained into clean containers so that it can be used again.

If the system is hot, the filler cap on the expansion tank should be carefully undone to its first unlock position so that the pressure in the system can escape. Do not attempt this if the engine is very hot, but allow it to cool and as a safety precaution swathe the hand in rags.

Remove the radiator filler cap 1 and the filler cap from the expansion tank. Remove the cylinder block drain plug and then disconnect the bottom radiator hose 2 from the radiator 6. To drain the coolant from the expansion tank, disconnect the hose 3 from the radiator and allow the coolant to run out.

Flushing:

Proprietary compounds may be used, in which case the instructions on the tin should be followed accurately.

Water alone can be used for flushing. Reconnect the bottom hose 2 to the radiator. Remove the thermostat valve and refit the water outlet to the cylinder head, after disconnecting the top radiator hose 4 from it. Refit the radiator filler plug 1. Insert a hosepipe into the water outlet on the cylinder head and use rags to make the joint reasonably tight. Turn on the hose and let water run through until it comes out clean through the radiator top hose 4 and engine drain hole. In extreme cases it may be necessary to remove the radiator, invert it and flush through so that the water carries out any scale or dirt from the water passages. Refit the thermostat valve and water outlet to the cylinder head and reconnect the top hose.

Filling:

Make sure that all the hoses are correctly connected and that the cylinder block drain plug is fitted. Fill the system through the filler 1 on the radiator and top up the expansion tank to the level marked on its side. Refit the radiator filler cap and the expansion tank cap. Start the engine and run it at a fast-idle for 30 seconds. Stop the engine and remove the radiator filler cap 1 again. Fill the radiator right up and refit the filler plug. Start the engine

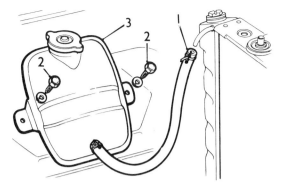

FIG 4:2 The expansion tank and its attachments

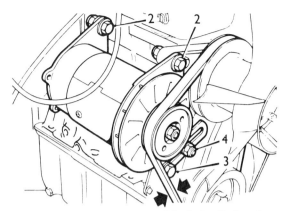

FIG 4:3 The generator and fan belt adjustment

and run it until it has reached its normal operating temperature. Stop the engine and allow it to cool before finally topping up the expansion tank to the correct level.

Clean soft water should be used in the system as this helps to prevent corrosion and the formation of scale. It is advisable to use a mixture of antifreeze and water as the antifreeze contains corrosion inhibitors and will raise the boiling point as well as lowering the freezing point.

4:3 The radiator and expansion tank

Radiator removal:

The attachments of the radiator are shown in **FIG 4:1**. Drain the cooling system by removing the filler 1, and disconnecting the bottom radiator hose 2. Full draining will not be required and the cylinder block drain plug can be left in place. Disconnect the hose 3 to the expansion tank and the top radiator hose 4.

Remove the screws 5 retaining each radiator side shroud panel to the radiator bracket (when fitted) and the screws retaining the brackets to the body.

Remove (when fitted) the nuts and washers and the shroud top panel. Lift out the radiator and the radiator shroud (if fitted).

Refit the radiator in the reverse order of removal and fill the cooling system.

It should be noted that dust and insects will gradually block the air passages through the radiator. Occasionally blow through the radiator fins from the rear, using an airline or hosepipe to remove the accumulation. In extreme cases remove the radiator so that it can be soaked and scrubbed in a hot weak detergent solution.

The expansion tank:

The attachments of the tank are shown in **FIG 4:2** and the figure is self-explanatory.

4:4 The fan belt

The adjustment point at the generator is shown in **FIG 4:3**. When the belt is correctly tensioned there should be a total movement of approximately $\frac{1}{2}$ inch (13 mm) when the belt is moved using moderate hand pressure at the centre of the run shown by the two arrows. Over-tensioning the belt will damage the bearings of the generator and water pump while if the belt is slack it will slip.

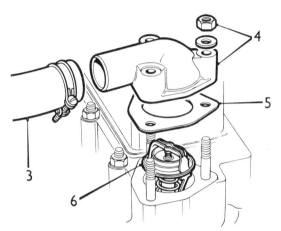

FIG 4:4 The thermostat and its attachments

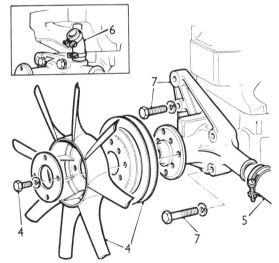

FIG 4:5 The water pump attachments

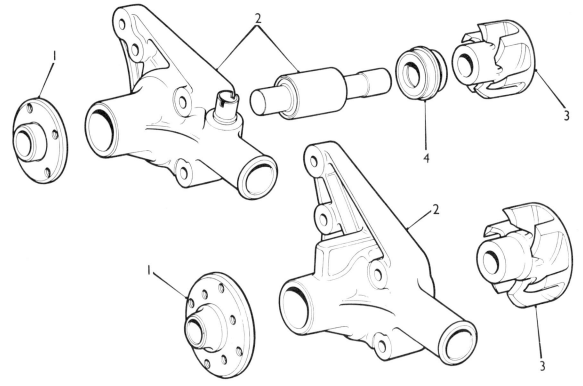

FIG 4:6   The water pump components

To adjust the belt, slacken the nuts and bolts 2, 3 and 4 slightly so that the generator can be moved under pressure. Lever the generator gently upwards using a wooden tool until the tension is correct. Tighten all the nuts and bolts to hold the generator in place.

The fan belt can be removed after slackening all the generator attachments. Press the generator down to relieve as much tension as possible. Work the belt off the generator pulley in the normal direction of rotation. If the belt sticks or is too tight then it can be helped off by turning the fan in its normal direction of rotation. Free the belt from the crankshaft pulley and lift it off over the fan blades. Refit the belt in the reverse order of removal, turning the fan to help it on if need be.

4:5   The thermostat

The attachments of the thermostat are shown in **FIG 4:4**. Drain the cooling system by removing the radiator filler plug and disconnecting the radiator bottom hose. Remove the nuts and lift off the cover 4. Usually the top radiator hose 3 is sufficiently flexible for the cover to be lifted off without having to disconnect the hose from it. Remove the gasket 5 and withdraw the thermostat 6.

The parts are refitted in the reverse order of removal, noting that the thermostat 6 is refitted first followed by the gasket 5. Renew the gasket if it is torn or damaged.

The thermostat can be tested by suspending it in a container of water and heating the water. The valve should start to open at the temperature stamped on it and open fully when the water is heated further. If the valve does not open, or sticks in the open position, reject the thermostat and fit a new one in its place.

Note that three different grades of thermostat can be fitted.

4:6   The water pump

The water pump attachments are shown in **FIG 4:5**. The inset shows the bypass hose fitted on the 1.3 models only.

Removal:

1 Drain the cooling system and remove the radiator (see **Section 4:3**).
2 Disconnect the battery. Refer to **FIG 4:3**, and disconnect the leads from the generator as well as removing the fan belt. Take out the bolts 2, 3 and 4 so that the generator can be removed.
3 Take out the bolts and remove the fan blades, spacer if fitted and pulley 4 from the water pump. Disconnect the bottom hose 5 and the bypass hose 6 (fitted only to 1.3 models).
4 Remove the bolts 7 and detach the water pump from the cylinder block.

The water pump is refitted in the reverse order of removal. Fill the cooling system, make sure that the generator leads are correctly connected and set the fan belt tension.

Dismantling:

The components of the water pump are shown in **FIG 4:6**. A press will be required to dismantle and reassemble the water pump.

1 Press off the hub 1 from the spindle or use a suitable two-legged extractor.
2 Support the pump body and press the spindle 2 out of the body so that the spindle is removed complete with the impeller 3 and seal 4.
3 Press the impeller off from the spindle and remove the seal.
4 The bearings are sealed onto the spindle and if they are defective or worn the complete spindle assembly must be renewed.

Reassembly:

Check the parts for damage or wear and renew any that are defective. Brush and wash out any sediment from the castings. Remove any scale or dirt from the spindle assembly using fine-grade emerycloth, but taking care not to allow dirt into the bearings. Both the hub 1 and impeller 3 must be an interference fit on the spindle, and if they are slack parts must be renewed to cure. Renew the impeller if its blades are eroded away.

The complete pump must be renewed if the bore in the body for the bearings is worn or pitted.

Reassemble the pump in the reverse order of dismantling, preferably using a new seal 4. As the parts are pressed together they must be positioned so that the dimensions shown in **FIG 4:7** are correct for the 1.3 pumps and those shown in **FIG 4:8** for the 1.8 pumps. Before fitting the impeller, smear the face adjacent to the seal with a silicone grease.

4:7 Frost precautions

The only adequate frost precaution is to add antifreeze. In extremely cold weather the water can freeze in the radiator even with the engine running, if antifreeze is not added. **Draining the system over night is not an adequate precaution as some water will remain in the heater.**

Unipart Frostbeat or Bluecol Antifreeze are recommended but any antifreeze used must be ethylene-glycol-based and must conform to specification BS.3151 or BS.3152.

The amounts of antifreeze to use and the mixture strength are given in the following table:

Antifreeze required		Mixture strength	
		$33\frac{1}{3}\%$	50%
1.3 Car and all Vans	pint	$2\frac{1}{2}$	$3\frac{3}{4}$
	litres	1.5	2
	US pints	3	4
1.8 Car and Estate	pints	3	$4\frac{1}{8}$
	litres	1.7	2.5
	US pints	$3\frac{1}{2}$	5
Commences to freeze	°C	—19	—36
	°F	—2	—33
Frozen solid	°C	—36	—48
	°F	—33	—53

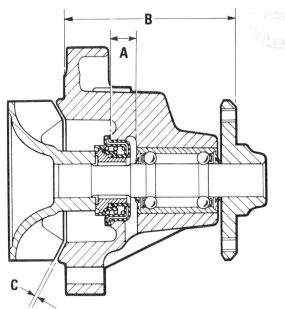

FIG 4:7 The assembly dimensions of the 1.3 engine water pump

Key to Fig 4:7   **A** .533 to .543 inch (13.54 to 13.79 mm) **B** 3.712 to 3.732 inch (94.305 to 94.8 mm)   **C** .02 to .03 inch (.508 to .762 mm)

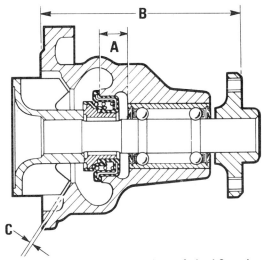

FIG 4:8 The assembly dimensions of the 1.8 engine water pump

Key to Fig 4:8   **A** .527 to .537 inch (13.39 to 13.64 mm) **B** 3.244 to 3.264 inch (82.4 to 82.9 mm)   **C** .02 to .03 inch (.508 to .762 mm)

4:8 Fault diagnosis

(a) Internal water leakage

1 Cracked cylinder wall
2 Cracked cylinder head
3 Cracked tappet chest wall
4 Loose cylinder head nuts
5 Defective cylinder head gasket

(b) Poor circulation

1 Radiator core blocked
2 Engine water passages restricted
3 Low coolant level
4 Loose fan belt
5 Defective thermostat
6 Perished or collapsed hoses

(c) Corrosion

1 Impurities in the water
2 Neglected draining and flushing

(d) Overheating

1 Check (b)
2 Sludge in crankcase
3 Incorrect ignition timing
4 Low oil level in sump
5 Tight engine
6 Choked exhaust
7 Binding brakes
8 Slipping clutch
9 Incorrect valve timing
10 Mixture too weak

CHAPTER 5

THE CLUTCH

5:1 Description

A hydraulically operated clutch is fitted to all versions of the Marina. When the clutch pedal is depressed a pushrod moves the piston into the master cylinder and the pressure generated is fed to the slave cylinder by a fluid hose, shown in **FIG 5:1**.

The clutch consists of a cover assembly, which cannot be dismantled, and a driven plate assembly. The clutch cover contains a diaphragm spring which acts between the cover and a pressure plate to force the pressure plate forwards. The cover is bolted to, and revolves with, the engine flywheel. The driven plate is splined to the input shaft of the gearbox. The forward pressure of the pressure plate grips the driven plate, by its friction linings, between the faces of the pressure plate and flywheel so that the driven plate is forced to rotate with the flywheel. Drive is therefore transmitted from the engine to the gearbox.

When the pedal is pressed down the slave cylinder piston is forced out to act on a release lever and this release lever presses forward the release bearing against the fingers in the centre of the diaphragm spring. As the fingers move forwards the outside of the spring bows backwards and draws the pressure plate with it. The driven plate is released and allowed to rotate independently so that there is no longer drive between engine and gearbox.

5:2 Maintenance

A hydrostatic type slave cylinder is fitted so there are no adjustments required on the system.

At regular intervals check the fluid level in the master cylinder reservoir. The brake and clutch master cylinders are shown in **FIG 5:2. Wipe the top and filler cap clean before removing the cap,** to prevent dirt from falling into the reservoir. If the fluid is low, top up to the correct level shown on the side of the reservoir. **Use only approved fluids as the incorrect type can be dangerous.** On models fitted with disc brakes to the front use Unipart 550 or a fluid that meets specification SAE.J.1703c. On models with drum brakes at the front, use Unipart 410 or a fluid that meets specification SAE.J.1703c.

On models fitted with disc brakes, the level will steadily fall in the brake master cylinder reservoir as the pads wear. If there is a sudden drop in the level then the system must be carefully examined for leaks and if any are found they must have immediate attention.

Before refitting the filler caps, make sure that the small vent holes arrowed are clear.

5:3 The clutch master cylinder

Removal:

The attachments are shown in **FIG 5:3**. From inside the car, extract the splitpin and remove the clevis pin 1 to free the master cylinder pushrod from the pedal.

Syphon out or drain the fluid from the reservoir and disconnect the pipe 2, **using rags to catch any spillage as hydraulic fluid quickly removes paint.** Take off the two nuts 3 and remove the master cylinder.

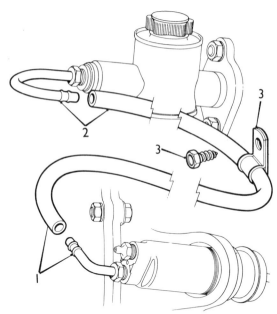

FIG 5:1 The fluid hose attachments

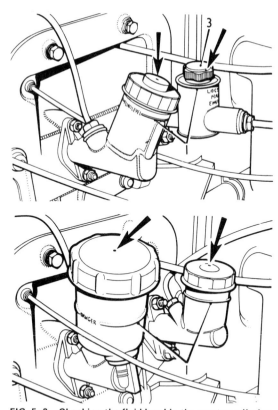

FIG 5:2 Checking the fluid level in the master cylinder reservoirs. The master cylinder with the smaller reservoir is the one for the clutch

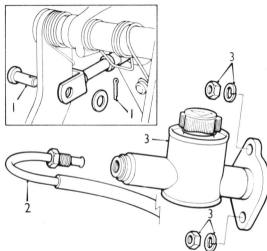

FIG 5:3 The master cylinder attachments

Refit the master cylinder in the reverse order of removal. Fill and bleed the hydraulic system as described in **Section 5:5**.

Dismantling:

The components of the master cylinder are shown in **FIG 5:4**. Pull back the dust cover 2 and extract the circlip 3 from the bore of the unit. The pushrod 4 and its integral stopwasher can now be removed.

Tap the open end of the master cylinder onto the palm of the hand to shake out the piston and its seal 5. Separate the seal from the piston, and remove the piston washer 6. Extract the main cup seal 7, spring retainer 8 and spring 9.

Examination:

Wash all the parts in methylated spirits or hydraulic fluid. **No other solvent may be allowed to come into contact with the seals otherwise they will swell and perish.**

It is most advisable to renew the seals, available in service kits, and only if the old seals are in perfect condition should they be used again. Do not turn the seals inside out as this will damage them.

Examine the bore of the cylinder and renew the complete unit if the bore is at all pitted, scored or worn.

Check that all the ports are clear.

Reassembly:

The unit is reassembled in the reverse order of dismantling. Wet the seals in clean hydraulic fluid before refitting them. The piston washer 5 should be refitted using only the fingers. Dip the internal parts into clean hydraulic fluid and slide them back into position while they are wet. **Take great care not to damage or bend back the lips of the seals as they enter the bore.** Refit the pushrod and secure the parts with the circlip. Check that the piston returns freely under the action of the return spring, after it has been pushed down the bore.

5:4 The slave cylinder

The slave cylinder can only be removed after the gearbox has been taken out of the car. The instructions for

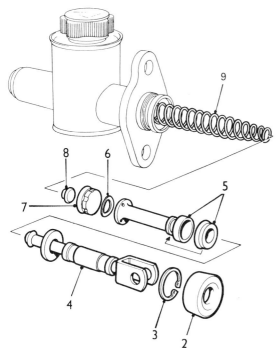

FIG 5:4   The master cylinder components

removing and refitting the gearbox are given in **Chapter 6, Section 6:2**.

The attachment of the slave cylinder is shown in **FIG 5:5** and, once the gearbox is out, the slave cylinder can be withdrawn as shown.

When refitting the slave cylinder, make sure that the bleed screw is uppermost and apply some Laminoid 'O' grease to the spherical end of the operating rod. When the gearbox has been refitted, reconnect the hydraulic pipe then fill and bleed the hydraulic system as instructed in **Section 5:5**.

The components of the slave cylinder are shown in **FIG 5:6**. To dismantle the unit, pull back the dust cover and remove the pushrod 2. The internal parts (piston 3, seal 4 and cup filler 5) can be removed by tapping the open end of the cylinder onto the palm of the hand or by gently blowing down the inlet port.

Wash the parts in methylated spirits and renew the cup seal 4. Renew the complete unit if the bore of the cylinder is scored, worn or damaged.

Wet the internal parts with hydraulic fluid before refitting them. Fit the spring 6 with its larger diameter end leading, followed by the cup seal spreader 5. Carefully insert the seal 4, lips leading, taking great care not to damage or bend back the lips. Slide in the piston, flat face leading. Smear both ends of the pushrod 2 with Girling rubber grease and refit it, holding it in place with the dust cover.

5:5   Bleeding the hydraulic system

The method is shown in **FIG 5:7**. Bleeding is only required when air has entered the system after dismantling and reassembly or by allowing the fluid level in the reservoir to fall so low that air is drawn into the master cylinder.

Before starting the operation, fill the master cylinder up as far as it will go without spilling and then keep a constant check on the level as bleeding progresses, topping up as required.

Discard fluid that has been bled through the system unless it is perfectly clean. If the fluid is clean, **do not return it directly to the reservoir** but allow it to stand in a sealed clean container for at least 24 hours to allow all the air to disperse. Use only Unipart 550 or Unipart 410 fluid.

Attach a length of small-bore plastic or rubber tube 2 to the bleed screw 3 on the slave cylinder and dip the free end of the tube into a little clean fluid in a clean glass container.

Open the bleed screw approximately $\frac{3}{4}$ turn and have an assistant press the clutch pedal down. Close the bleed screw when the pedal reaches the end of its travel and allow the pedal to return. Again open the bleed screw and repeat the cycle of operations until the fluid coming out of the bleed tube is completely clear and free from air bubbles.

Top up the master cylinder reservoir to the correct level and remove the bleed tube from the slave cylinder, making sure that the bleed screw is closed.

5:6   The release bearing assembly

The parts are shown in **FIG 5:8**. Before they can be removed, the gearbox must be taken out of the car (see **Chapter 6, Section 6:2**).

Release the operating lever from its ballpin 4 and the lugs from the release bearing 3. Slide off the release bearing and remove the operating lever.

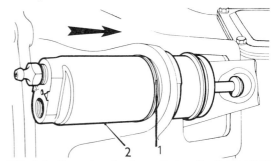

FIG 5:5   Removing the slave cylinder after the gearbox has been removed. The circlip 1 must be removed

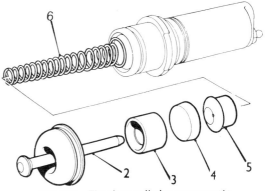

FIG 5:6   The slave cylinder components

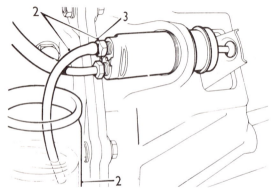

FIG 5:7 Bleeding the hydraulic system

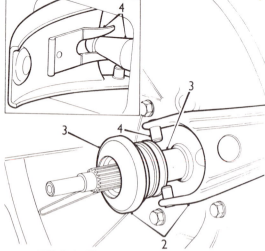

FIG 5:8 The release bearing and lever

Renew the release bearing 3 if it is worn or operates noisily. The parts are refitted in the reverse order of removal, but first apply some Laminoid 'O' grease to the groove in the release bearing, the spherical face of the gearbox fulcrum pin and the rubbing surface of the first motion shaft front end cover.

5:7 Servicing the clutch

The removal of the clutch from the flywheel, after the gearbox has been removed, is dealt with in **Chapter 1, Section 1:8**, and the instructions for refitting it are also given in this section.

If either the cover assembly or the driven plate is defective, the parts cannot be repaired and new items must be fitted in their place.

Cover assembly:

The unit must not be washed in any solvent, as this will remove the lubricant from the pivot points in the cover. Loose dust and dirt should be removed using an airline, or tyre pump, and brush. If there is oil on the pressure plate face or cover, wipe it off with a cloth moistened in fuel or suitable solvent that will evaporate completely.

Check the pressure plate face for burn or score marks as well as hairline cracks. Check the cover for cracks or distortion, paying particular attention to the areas around the attachment holes and any rivets.

Driven plate:

The driven plate must be renewed if the linings are worn down nearly to the rivet heads, the linings are contaminated with oil or grease or the assembly is mechanically defective. **Do not attempt to rivet new linings into place.**

Check the driven plate for loose or pulled rivets as well as for loose or broken damper springs. Slide it back onto the gearbox input shaft and check that it slides freely without excessive rotational play.

The linings are at their maximum efficiency when they have an even, polished finish through which the grain of the friction material is clearly visible. Small amounts of oil will leave dark coloured smears on the linings, while larger amounts will leave a dark glaze which hides the grain of the friction material. Large amounts of oil will be obvious from the oil-soaked appearance of the linings and the free oil in the housing. Provided that the grain of the friction material can be seen, and the unit is mechanically satisfactory, it can be used again. Do not forget to find and cure the source of the oil leak before reassembling the parts.

5:8 Fault diagnosis

(a) Drag or spin

1 Oil or grease on the driven plate linings
2 Air leak in the hydraulic system
3 Leaking master cylinder, pipe or slave cylinder
4 Driven plate hub binding on input shaft splines
5 Distorted driven plate
6 Warped or damaged pressure plate
7 Broken driven plate linings

(b) Fierceness or snatch

1 Check 1 in (a)
2 Worn driven plate linings

(c) Slip

1 Check 1 in (a) and 2 in (b)
2 Weak diaphragm spring
3 Seized piston in slave cylinder

(d) Judder

1 Check 1, 5, 6 and 7 in (a)
2 Pressure plate not parallel with flywheel
3 Contact area on friction linings not evenly distributed
4 Bent input shaft in gearbox
5 Faulty engine or gearbox mountings
6 Worn suspension shackles
7 Weak rear springs
8 Loose propeller shaft bolts

(e) Rattle

1 Broken springs in driven plate
2 Worn release mechanism
3 Excessive backlash in transmission
4 Wear in transmission bearings
5 Release bearing loose on lever

(f) Tick or knock

1 Worn crankshaft spigot bearing
2 Badly worn splines on driven plate hub
3 Loose flywheel

CHAPTER 6

THE GEARBOX

6:1 Description

The manually operated gearbox is fitted with four forward speeds, with synchromesh engagement for each speed, and a reverse gear. The gearlever is mounted on the rear extension housing and is connected by a shaft to the selector mechanism in the gearbox top extension. Moving the gearlever sideways rotates the shaft so that pins on the shaft fit into the appropriate selector fork. Pushing the gearlever forwards or pulling it back moves the selector fork to shift the outer sleeve of the appropriate synchromesh unit so that gear is selected, for the forward speeds. For reverse gear, a pin on the selector shaft engages with a lever and movement of the gearlever then operates the reverse lever to slide an idler gear into mesh between the countershaft and mainshaft so that the direction of drive is reversed.

The input shaft of the gearbox is splined to the hub of clutch so that they rotate together. The input shaft meshes with a gear on the countershaft cluster and the remaining gears of the cluster in turn mesh with the gears on the mainshaft. The mainshaft gears are free to revolve about the mainshaft so that when the gearbox is in neutral the mainshaft does not revolve. When the outer sleeve of the synchromesh unit is moved by the selector fork, the synchromesh cup (baulk ring) first takes the drive by the friction of the conical surfaces and when the mainshaft and gear are rotating at the same speed the sleeve can slide over onto the dog teeth of the gear to make the drive positive. The inner hub of the synchromesh unit is splined to the mainshaft and the outer sleeve is splined to the hub so drive is then transmitted to the mainshaft.

A sectioned view of the gearbox is shown in **FIG 6:1**.

Lubrication:

The casing of the gearbox is filled with oil up to the level of the filler plug. The gears, shafts and their bearings rotate in the oil bath and the remainder of the parts are lubricated by splash thrown from the revolving gears. A drain plug is fitted under the gearbox so that the oil can be drained out. Routine or seasonal oil changes are not required and the only time that the oil does need to be changed is after a new gearbox has been run-in. The drain and filler plugs are shown in **FIG 6:2**. Hypoid SAE.90 oil should be used in normal climates but if the temperature regularly drops below −5°C (20°F) then Hypoid SAE.80 oil should be used instead. Try to avoid mixing brands, even though each different brand is recommended, as additives in different brands may not always be compatible.

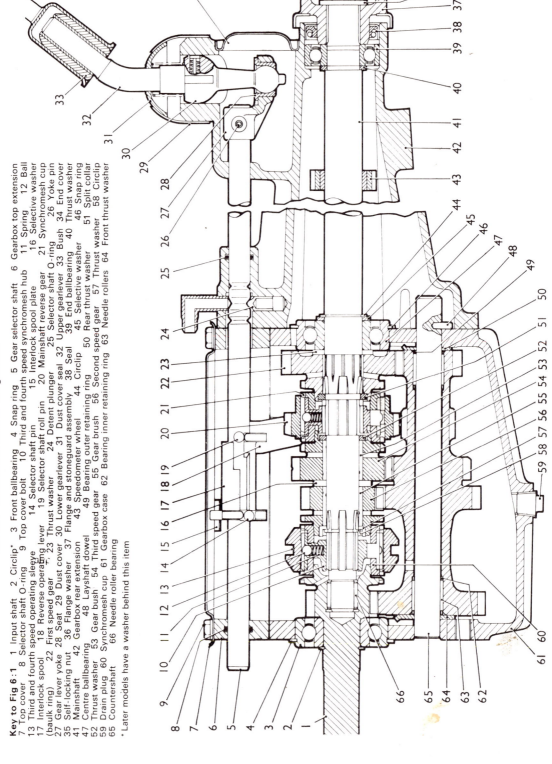

FIG 6:1   A sectioned view of the gearbox

Key to Fig 6:1 1 Input shaft 2 Circlip* 3 Front ballbearing 4 Snap ring 5 Gear selector shaft 6 Gearbox top extension
7 Top cover 8 Selector shaft O-ring 9 Top cover bolt 10 Third and fourth speed synchromesh hub 11 Spring 12 Ball
13 Third and fourth speed operating sleeve 14 Selector shaft pin 15 Interlock spool plate 16 Selective washer
17 Interlock spool 18 Reverse operating lever 19 Selector shaft roll pin 20 Mainshaft reverse gear 21 Synchromesh cup
(baulk ring) 22 First speed gear 23 Thrust washer 24 Detent plunger 25 Selector shaft O-ring 26 Yoke pin
27 Gear lever yoke 28 Seat 29 Dust cover 30 Lower gearlever 31 Dust cover seal 32 Upper gearlever 33 Bush 34 End cover
35 Self-locking nut 36 Flange washer 37 Flange and stoneguard assembly 38 Seal 39 End ballbearing 40 Thrust washer
41 Mainshaft 42 Gearbox rear extension 43 Speedometer wheel 44 Circlip 45 Selective washer 46 Snap ring
47 Centre ballbearing 48 Layshaft dowel 49 Bearing outer retaining ring 50 Rear thrust washer 51 Split collar
52 Thrust washer 53 Gear bush 54 Third speed gear 55 Second speed gear 56 Second speed gear 57 Thrust washer 58 Circlip
59 Drain plug 60 Synchromesh cup 61 Gearbox case 62 Bearing inner retaining ring 63 Needle rollers 64 Front thrust washer
65 Countershaft 66 Needle roller bearing

* Later models have a washer behind this item

The level in the gearbox should be checked at intervals of 6000 miles (10,000 kilometres). Stand the car on level ground, preferably checking when the engine has not been run for some time. Unscrew the filler plug 1 and check that the oil level reaches the bottom of the aperture. Top up, if required, using a squeeze bottle and plastic hose and allow any surplus oil to drain out before refitting the filler plug. **Wipe the area clean before removing the filler plug and wipe away surplus oil after the plug has been refitted.**

6:2 Removing the gearbox

The gearbox is removed from underneath the car and the work can best be carried out using a pit or garage hoist. If neither of these is available, make sure that the car is firmly and safely raised off the ground on secure supports. Before removing the gearbox, take off the gearlever assembly.

Gearlever assembly:

The parts are shown in **FIG 6:3**. Remove the front carpet and unscrew the gearlever knob 2. Take out the screws 3 and slide the draught excluder and its retaining plate 4 up and off the gearlever. Set the gears to neutral and undo the bayonet fitting of the gearlever retainer 5, by pressing it down and turning it anticlockwise. **Carefully collect the anti-rattle plunger and spring 6.**

The parts are refitted in the reverse order of removal, making sure that the ball joint on the end of the gearlever fits into its socket and remembering to refit the spring and plunger 6.

Note that the gearlever is made in two parts joined by a bush, as this helps to damp out vibrations of the assembly.

Removing the gearbox:

Drain out the oil by removing the drain plug and, from inside the car, remove the gearlever assembly. The attachments of the gearbox are shown in **FIG 6:4**. Disconnect the battery before starting work.

1 Disconnect the exhaust pipe(s) from the exhaust manifold. On the SC versions the pipe is secured to the manifold by a clamp but on the TC versions take off the three nuts and washers that secure each exhaust pipe flange to the manifold. Remove the carburetter(s) (see **Chapter 2, Section 2:7**). Disconnect the translucent plastic hose 3 from the slave cylinder junction pipe and remove the clip that secures the hose to the bulkhead. When disconnecting the hose, have a container handy to catch the fluid as it drains out. **Do not allow the hydraulic fluid to run onto paintwork otherwise the paint will be rapidly removed.**

2 Make marks 5 on the gearbox and propeller shaft flanges so that they will be reassembled back into the same relative positions. Take out the nuts and bolts 6 to disconnect the propeller shaft and tie the propeller shaft safely out of the way to a torsion bar of the front suspension.

3 Disconnect the speedometer drive cable by taking out the clip 7 that secures it. Remove the two bolts 8 that secure the starter motor and move the motor out of the way into the engine compartment (note that the earth strap is secured to the lower starter motor attachment bolt on the 1.3 models).

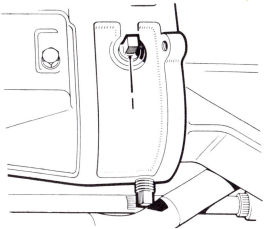

FIG 6:2 The gearbox drain and filler plugs

4 On the 1.3 models, free the exhaust pipe clip and remove the supporting bracket shown in inset 9. On the 1.8 models free the exhaust pipe and remove the bracket shown in inset 10.

5 Support the engine and gearbox with a jack placed as far as possible to the rear under the engine sump, using a pad of wood between the jack and sump to prevent damage to the sump. Remove the two bolts 12 that secure the sump connecting plate to the flywheel housing. Take off the bolts 13 that secure the crossmember to the frame and then free the crossmember from the gearbox mounting by taking off the nut 14.

6 On 1.8 models, remove the two sets of nuts, washers and bolts 15 that secure the top of the flywheel

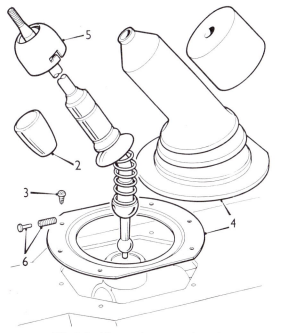

FIG 6:3 The gearlever attachments

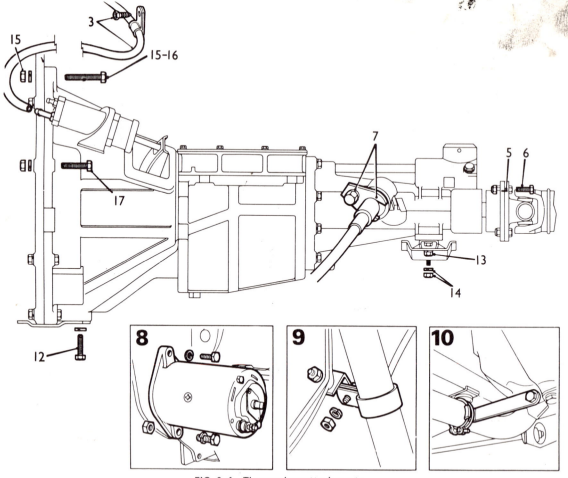

FIG 6:4   The gearbox attachments

housing to the gearbox adaptor plate on the engine. On the 1.3 models remove the two bolts and washers 16 that secure the top of the flywheel housing.

7 Support the gearbox and remove the five remaining sets of nuts, washers and bolts that secure the housing to the adaptor plate. Lower the jack under the engine, still supporting the weight of the gearbox, until the flywheel housing is clear, and draw the gearbox rearwards until the input shaft is well clear of the clutch so that the gearbox can be removed. **Do not allow the weight of the gearbox to hang on the input shaft otherwise the clutch may be seriously damaged.**

The gearbox is refitted in the reverse order of removal. If the clutch has been removed from the flywheel, it is essential that the driven plate is centralized with a mandrel while refitting the clutch. **Do not allow the weight of the gearbox to hang on the input shaft in the clutch.**

On the 1.8 engines, the longest flywheel housing bolt is for the upper starter motor mounting flange, and the bottom lefthand bolt secures the exhaust pipe clamp. The engine earth strap is secured by the bolt immediately

below the starter motor. Nuts and bolts are fitted to the top housing attachments.

On the 1.3 engines, the earth strap is secured by the longest bolt which also passes through the lower starter motor flange. The second bolt from the bottom on the lefthand side secures the exhaust pipe bracket while bolts and washers only secure the top of the flywheel housing.

When the gearbox is in place, set the carburetter control adjustments (see **Chapter 2, Section 2:7**). Fill and bleed the clutch hydraulic system (see **Chapter 5, Section 5:5**). Refill the gearbox with fresh Hypoid oil.

6:3 Dismantling the gearbox

The components of the gearbox are shown in **FIG 6:5**.

Rear extension:

The dismantling of the parts is shown in **FIG 6:6**.

1 Pull firmly on the speedometer drive pinion 21 so that it and its housing 23 are withdrawn from the rear extension housing 12 and then withdraw the pinion from its housing and take off the seals 22 and 24 (see **FIG 6:5**).

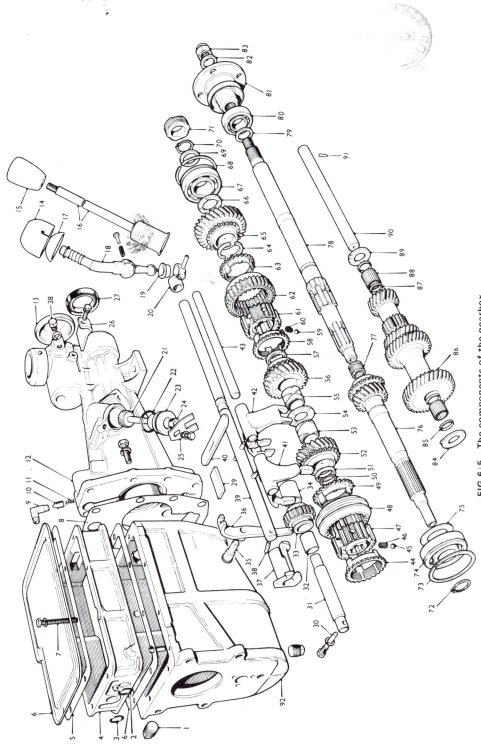

FIG 6:5 The components of the gearbox

Key to Fig 6:5 1 Filler plug 2 and 3 O-ring 4 Top extension 5 Gasket 6 Cover 7 Bolt 8 Gasket 9 Plug 10 Detent plunger 11 Detent spring 12 Rear extension 13 End cover 14 Dust cover 15 Gear knob 16 Upper gearlever 17 Dust cover 18 Lower gearlever 19 Seat 20 Yoke 21 Speedometer drive pinion 22 O-ring 23 Housing 24 Seal 25 Clip 26 Reverse lift plate 27 Oil seal 28 Screw for reverse light switch 29 Magnet 30 Dowel bolt 31 Spindle 32 Bush 33 Reverse idler gear 34 Pin for lever 35 Reverse operating pin 36 Reverse operating lever 37 Interlock spool 38 Roll pin 39 Selector shaft 40 Interlock spool plate 41 Third/fourth selector fork 42 First/second selector fork 43 Selector fork shaft 44 Synchromesh cup (baulk ring) 45 Ball 46 Spring 47 Third/fourth synchromesh sleeve 48 Third/fourth synchromesh hub 49 Synchromesh cup 50 Mainshaft circlip 51 Third speed gear thrust washer 52 Third speed gear 53 Bush 54 Selective washer 55 Bush 56 Second speed gear 57 Thrust washer 58 Synchromesh cup 59 Ball 60 Spring 61 First/second synchromesh hub 62 Mainshaft reverse gear and first/second synchromesh sleeve 63 Synchromesh cup 64 Split collar 65 First speed gear 66 Thrust washer 67 Centre bearing 68 Snap ring 69 Selective washer 70 Circlip 71 Speedometer drive 72 Circlip 73 Snap ring 74 Ballbearing 75 Oil flinger 76 Input shaft 77 Needle roller bearing 78 Mainshaft 79 Washer 80 Ballbearing 81 Drive flange 82 Washer 83 Nut 84 Thrust washer 84 and 87 Bearing retaining rings 86 Countershaft gears 88 Needle roller bearing 89 Needle roller bearing 90 Thrust washer 91 Pin 92 Gearbox casing

MARINA

75

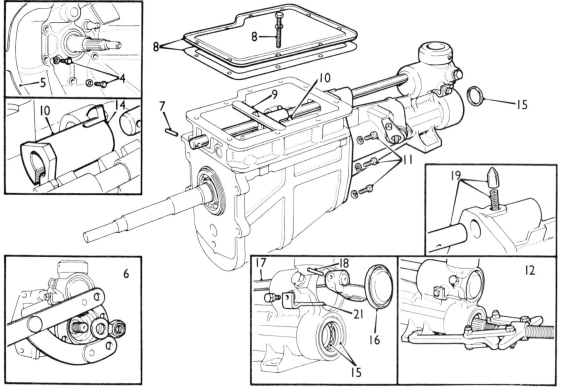

FIG 6:6 Removing the rear extension

2 Support the gearbox in a vice, by clamping onto the drain plug so that the gearbox is upright. Use wood or lead packing to prevent damage to the drain plug. Take out the bolts 4, noting that there is a sealing washer fitted under the bottom bolt 4, and remove the clutch housing 5 from the gearbox. Extract the oil seal and remove the O-ring from behind the flange of the front end cover.

3 Hold the drive flange, preferably with the special spanner 18G.1205, and remove the nut and washer that secures the flange, as shown in the inset 6. If the special tool is not available, the gearbox can be locked

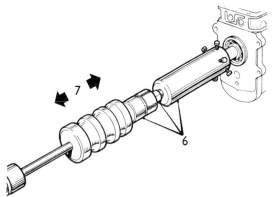

FIG 6:7 Withdrawing the input shaft assembly

after removal of the top extension by selecting two gears at once so that the mainshaft cannot turn.

4 Remove the rollpin 7 from the end of the selector rod. Take out the nine bolts and spring washers so that the cover 8 and its gasket can be removed. Lift out the interlock spool plate 9. Turn the selector shaft until the reverse gear position is reached and make sure that the selector shaft pins will clear the interlock spool and gear selector forks. Remove the bolts and washers 11 that secure the rear extension to the main casing and use the extractor 18G.2, as shown in inset 12, to draw off the rear extension, **making sure that the selector shaft pins do not foul as the shaft is withdrawn.** If the special extractor is not available use a hide-faced hammer to tap gently and carefully on the mounting lugs to drive the rear extension off. Remove the gaskets for the rear extension.

5 Remove the interlock spool 14 and take out the distance washer 15 from the mainshaft. Remove the cover 16 by gently tapping the selector shaft 17 rearwards and then push the shaft further out to expose the gearlever seating yoke. Lightly scribe marks across the end of the shaft and yoke so that they will be correctly reassembled in the right alignment. Drive out the rollpin 18 and remove the socket from the shaft. Withdraw the selector shaft and collect the spring and plunger 19. Take out the bolt and remove the reverse gear lift plate 21.

6 If necessary, extract the oil seal and bearing from the rear end of the extension housing.

Input shaft assembly:

Refer to **FIG 6 : 5**.

1 Remove the rear extension as just described. Drive out the rollpin 91 that secures the countershaft 90. Use the dummy countershaft 18G.1208 to press out the countershaft 90 from the gearbox. The dummy shaft is shorter than the actual one and of the same diameter. When pressing out the countershaft, keep the dummy shaft in contact with it until the dummy is fully in the countershaft gear cluster 86 and its bearings, and the countershaft cluster can slide to the bottom of the main casing, with the dummy shaft still in it.

2 Use the special impact hammer 18G.284 with adaptors 18G.284.AW and 18G.284.AAA located and secured to the input shaft, as shown in **FIG 6 : 7**, and draw the input shaft out of the case by sliding the handle 7 firmly against the end of the tool.

3 Remove the mainshaft spigot roller bearing 77 from the end of the input shaft 76. Remove the securing circlip 72 as well as the locating snap ring 73 and the backing washer between them on later models. Use a press and suitable tools to draw the bearing 74 off the input shaft. Remove the oil flinger 75.

Main case parts:

The method of removing the parts is shown in **FIG 6 : 8**, after the rear extension and input shaft have been removed.

1 Fit the special tool 18G.47.BG to the front of the gearbox using two of the flywheel housing retaining bolts and washers, as shown in the inset 4, making sure that the bolt 5 is screwed right out. When the tool is in position, screw in the bolt 5 and guide it so that it supports and locates the end of the mainshaft. Tighten the locknut to hold the bolt in this position.

2 Remove the locating snap ring 6 from around the centre bearing and release the circlip 7 from its groove in the mainshaft. Unscrew the dowel bolt 8 so that the reverse idler spindle and bush 9 can be removed.

3 Use a suitable puller, as shown in inset 10, and remove the bearing, selective washer, circlip and speedometer drive gear 11 from the mainshaft.

4 Remove the special tool 18G.47.BG from the front of the gearbox, **without slackening the locknut or altering the position of the central bolt.** Tilt the mainshaft assembly 13 and remove it from the case. Lift out the countershaft gear cluster 14 from the bottom of the case and collect the thrust washers. Lift out the reverse idler gear 15 and remove the reverse operating lever 16 as well as its pin 17. Remove the magnet 18.

5 If need be, refer to **FIG 6 : 5** and drive out the bush 32 from the reverse idler 33. Also if need be, take out the dummy countershaft from the countershaft gear cluster 86 and remove the twenty-five rollers 88 and their retainers 85 and 87.

Mainshaft assembly:

The parts of the mainshaft are shown in **FIG 6 : 9**. The parts are removed in the numerical order shown in the figure. The circlip 24 is removed using the special tool 18G.1199, as shown in the inset, with the three long splines inserted between the splines and the thrust washer tabs. **It is advisable to discard the circlip 24 and use a new one on reassembly.**

The synchromesh units 22 and 31 should be removed as an assembly, without sliding the sleeve off the hub. The synchromesh cups (baulk rings) 20, 23 and 29 are very similar in appearance but they should not be interchanged (as they have bedded-in) and they should be stored so that they will be refitted into their original positions.

If the synchromesh units are to be dismantled, mark them across the faces so that the hub and sleeve will be refitted together in their original positions. **Wrap the unit completely in cloth before pushing the inner hub out of the outer sleeve.** If this precaution is not taken the balls and springs will shoot out and be lost.

6 : 4 Reassembling the gearbox

Wash all the parts in clean fuel and examine them for wear or damage. Check all splines for wear. Examine all the teeth on the gears for chipping, wear or fractures. Check the cones on the synchromesh cups (baulk rings) and gears for wear or scoring. Wash the bearings separately in clean fuel to make sure that they do not pick up dirt and examine them for damage or wear, making sure that they rotate smoothly when lubricated with light oil.

The bushes and shafts should not show signs of wear, chatter or fretting. Make sure that the mating faces of all the castings are true and undamaged. Small burrs can be cleaned off by careful use of a fine file. Reject any damaged parts and fit new ones in their place.

Discard all old seals and gaskets, using new ones on reassembly. The reassembling of the gearbox is generally the reverse of the dismantling operations (see previous section) but all end floats should be checked and adjusted as the parts are reassembled. The settings, and the washers available to alter them, are given in **Technical Data**. Washers must be selectively fitted to give the correct end floats. Lubricate the parts with Hypoid oil as they are refitted.

Mainshaft assembly:

The parts are shown in **FIG 6 : 5** but refer to **FIG 6 : 9**. The parts are refitted in the reverse numerical order shown in the figure. The third gear circlip 24 should be refitted as shown in the inset 39, using the tool 18G.1198.

If the synchromesh units 22 and 31 have been dismantled, identify the parts and markings made on dismantling. Refit the balls and springs to the hub, holding them in place with grease. Use a large worm-driven hose-clip to compress them into place. Slide the sleeve back onto the hub, so that the previously made marks align, allowing the hoseclip to slide off as the balls all enter the sleeve. Press the sleeve on until the balls click into the detent groove.

Before refitting all the parts check the end floats, shown in **FIG 6 : 10**. The end float of the gears on their bushes (26 and 28) 37 should be .002 to .006 inch (.05 to .152 mm) and the bushes must be renewed if the end float is outside the limits.

Fit the second gear washer 30 to the mainshaft with its oil groove face away from the shoulder. Fit the gears to their bushes (28 and 26) and slide them back onto the shaft, with the selective washer (27) between them. Slide on the third gear thrust washer (with its oil groove towards the bush as shown) and secure the parts with a broken half of the old circlip (24). Breaking the old circlip

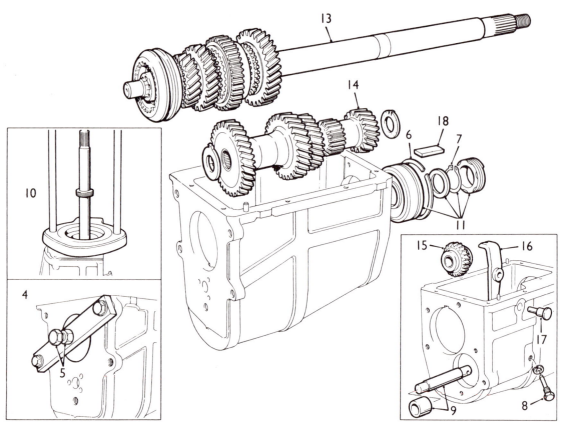

FIG 6:8   Removing the parts from the main case

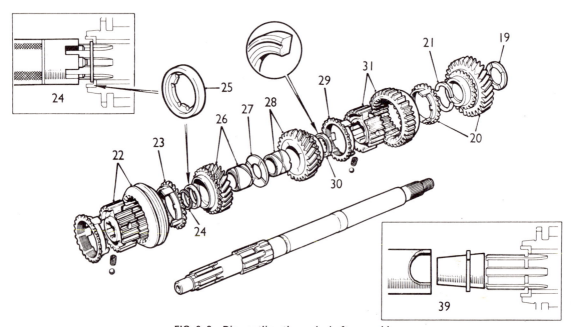

FIG 6:9   Dismantling the mainshaft assembly

and using it this way will make the task easier, rather than trying to fit and remove the new circlip. Measure the clearance 36 with feeler gauges. The end float should be .004 to .006 inch (.101 to .152 mm) and if it is incorrect then the washer (27) must be selectively fitted to bring the end float within limits. In some gearboxes the split collars 21 are marked with orange dye on one side. This side must face away from the first speed gear.

Main case parts:

If the roller bearings have been removed from the countershaft gear cluster, refit them making sure that the retaining rings are pressed in to the correct distances. A special drift 18G.1209 is made for driving in the retaining rings. Hold the rollers in with grease and slide in the dummy countershaft. Fit new thrust washers on either side of the cluster if the old washers are worn. Lower the assembly to the bottom of the casing.

Check the fitting of the reverse idler gear on its bush, noting that it should be flush at one end and the bush should be .010 inch (.254 mm) below the gear face. Place the idler into position and refit the lever and its pivot. Refit the magnet into its location. Fit the mainshaft assembly back into place through the top aperture. Locate the mainshaft with the special tool 18G.47BG by screwing the tool back onto the case, **leaving its centre bolt locked at the position found on dismantling.** Refit the locating snap ring to the centre bearing and press the bearing back into place until the snap ring is tight against the case. Fit the selective washer that was removed and secure it with the circlip (items 11 in **FIG 6:8**). Measure the gap between the selective washer and circlip with feeler gauges. Selectively fit a washer until the gap is correct at .000 to .002 inch (.00 to .05 mm).

Input shaft assembly:

Reassemble the parts in the reverse order of dismantling, using grease to keep the oil flinger in place when refitting the bearing.

Refit the spindle and distance piece for the reverse gear idler and secure them in place with the dowel bolt. Remove the mainshaft locating tool and press the input shaft assembly back into position so that the locating flange on the bearing is tight against the casing. **Do not forget to refit the roller bearing for the spigot of the mainshaft into the input shaft before refitting the input shaft.**

Lift the countershaft cluster assembly up into alignment, making sure that the thrust washers are in place, and press out the dummy countershaft using the countershaft, keeping both shafts in constant contact. Secure the countershaft with its rollpin.

Rear extension:

This is refitted in the reverse order of removal. Make sure that the rollpin for the selector shaft is fitted with an equal protrusion on either side of the shaft, otherwise there may be difficulty in refitting the clutch housing. Make sure that the selector forks are correctly fitted to the outer sleeves of the synchromesh units and that the

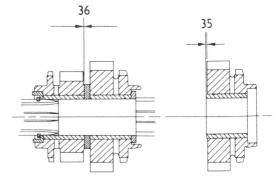

FIG 6:10   Checking the end float on the bushes of the mainshaft

reverse operating lever engages correctly with the idler. **Do not forget to fit a sealing washer to the bottom bolt that secures the clutch housing.**

Oil seals:

It should be noted that the oil seal on the rear extension and those on the speedometer drive can be renewed without having to remove the gearbox from the car, or remove the rear extension from the gearbox.

Renewal of the speedometer drive oil seals is the same as if the gearbox is on the bench, as the parts can be pulled out once the speedometer cable has been disconnected.

To renew the rear oil seal, disconnect the propeller shaft and remove the gearbox drive flange. The old seal can then be extracted and the new one pressed in using a suitable tube. If the face, on which the seal operates, of the drive flange is damaged or scored then a new drive flange should be fitted. Reconnect the propeller shaft after the flange is in place and check the oil level in the gearbox.

6:5 Fault diagnosis

(a) Jumping out of gear

1 Broken or weak detent spring for selector shaft
2 Excessively worn grooves in selector shaft
3 Wear in appropriate driven gear, bush or synchromesh unit
4 Worn or loose pin in selector shaft

(b) Noisy gearbox

1 Incorrect or insufficient oil
2 Excessive end float
3 Worn or damaged bearings
4 Worn or damaged gear teeth

(c) Difficulty in engaging gear

1 Worn baulk rings
2 Defective clutch release mechanism

(d) Oil leaks

1 Excessively high oil level
2 Damaged joint faces or gaskets
3 Worn or damaged oil seals

NOTES

CHAPTER 7

AUTOMATIC TRANSMISSION

7:1 Description

A Borg-Warner automatic transmission unit can be fitted in place of the conventional manually operated gearbox and clutch. Once engaged, the unit automatically selects the correct gear for the road conditions and load on the engine, changing up or down as required with no effort on the part of the driver. The car can be slowed to a stop on the brakes and then driven away again, using the throttle pedal, without the driver having to make any change of selection.

A floor-mounted selector lever is fitted to allow the driver to select the direction of drive, whether neutral or partially overriding the action of the transmission. A conventional throttle pedal and brake pedal are fitted but there is no clutch pedal.

A torque converter takes the place of the clutch. The unit is filled with oil as a drive transmitting medium and it gives a smooth take-up of drive (with torque multiplication) from rest, and then acts as a fluid flywheel to transmit direct drive at speed.

An epicyclic gearbox is used instead of the conventional gears in mesh rotating on shafts. The various selections are made by holding the parts of the epicyclic gear train.

The parts are held and driven by a combination of brake bands and clutches operated from the hydraulic control system integral in the assembly.

A sectioned view of the automatic transmission is shown is shown in **FIG 7:1**.

Torque converter:

A schematic view of the torque converter is shown in **FIG 7:2**. The unit is filled with fluid and there is a constant flow through it, from and to the gearbox, to take away heat from friction losses. The unit is sealed on manufacture and cannot be dismantled for repairs, so a defective torque converter must be renewed. The impeller **D** is made up of vanes attached inside the casing of the unit and therefore revolves with the engine, as the casing is bolted to the drive plate of the engine. As the vanes rotate they drag the fluid around with it and the fluid acts on the vanes of the turbine **A** to make it rotate in the same direction. Centrifugal force acts on the coil causing it to have a slightly higher pressure at the outside of the impeller blades than the inside. This difference in pressure sets up a circulatory flow in the cross-sectional plane, so that the combination of this circulation and drag of the

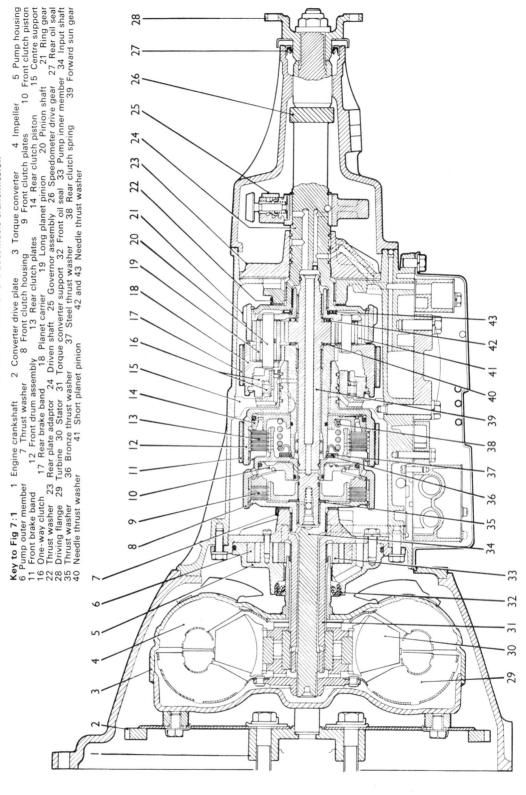

FIG 7:1   Sectioned view of the automatic transmission

Key to Fig 7:1   1 Engine crankshaft   2 Converter drive plate   3 Torque converter   4 Impeller   5 Pump housing
6 Pump outer member   7 Thrust washer   8 Front clutch housing   9 Front clutch plates   10 Front clutch piston
11 Front brake band   12 Front drum assembly   13 Rear clutch plates   14 Rear clutch piston   15 Centre support
16 One-way clutch   17 Rear brake band   18 Planet carrier   19 Long planet pinion   20 Pinion shaft   21 Ring gear
22 Thrust washer   23 Rear plate adaptor   24 Driven shaft   25 Governor assembly   26 Speedometer drive gear   27 Rear oil seal
28 Driving flange   29 Turbine   30 Stator   31 Torque converter support   32 Front oil seal   33 Pump inner member   34 Input shaft
35 Thrust washer   36 Bronze thrust washer   37 Steel thrust washer   38 Rear clutch spring   39 Forward sun gear
40 Needle thrust washer   41 Short planet pinion   42 and 43 Needle thrust washer

fluid makes it follow the path of an imaginary spiral spring laid concentrically into the unit. The stator **B** guides the fluid flow from the inside of the turbine blades so that it impinges on the inside of the blades of the impeller, assisting it to rotate. The turbine will therefore be driven by the fluid flow and because of the stator there will be a torque multiplication effect of up to approximately 2.2:1. As the impeller and turbine speed up, the fluid flow starts to impinge on the back of the stator blades and this would normally cause power losses. The stator is fitted onto a one-way clutch **C** which allows it to freewheel under the action of the fluid impinging on the back of the stator blades, so that the power losses are minimized. At this point the torque converter acts as a fluid flywheel with a 1:1 drive. Because of the frictional losses the turbine will never rotate at the full speed of impeller and the actual speed is approximately 98 per cent of the impeller speed. The 2 per cent losses are wasted as heat.

The greater the slip, the greater will be the heat produced by churning. In normal driving this does not matter as the heat produced will be radiated and conducted away from the automatic transmission, and a flow of air around the converter (through the stone guards) further assists in cooling. An oil cooler is also fitted to some models so that the fluid is passed through it and cooled by the passage of air. If the car is held stationary with drive selected and the engine speeded up then there will be large amounts of slip and a great deal of heat produced. **This condition should only be used as a test and even then the amount of time taken for the test must be strictly limited.**

Epicyclic gearbox:

The unit consists of an epicyclic gear train and the various ratios are selected by hydraulic pressure acting on internal clutches and brake bands. The actual selection is carried out by a complex valve system which uses both the position of the throttle (through the downshift cable) and a pressure proportional to the road speed. A governor assembly is fitted to the output shaft of the gearbox and it is this unit which supplies the pressure proportional to the road speed of the car. A manually operated selector mechanism overrides the valve assembly as required and also selects the direction of drive.

Oil pressure to lubricate the parts, and to supply the hydraulic pressure for the operation of the unit, is supplied by an oil pump mounted on the input shaft of the gearbox. An oil strainer is fitted to the valve assembly, accessible after the sump has been removed, to ensure that the oil passing through the pump and into the unit is kept clean and free from particles.

The external parts of the automatic transmission are shown in **FIG 7:3**. The internal parts and valve system are not shown as most of them are beyond the powers of the owner to service or dismantle. An inhibiting switch 53 is fitted to the case. This switch prevents the stator from operating when a drive gear is selected, thus ensuring that the car cannot move off accidentally when the engine is started, and it also operates the reverse light when reverse is selected.

A parking pawl is fitted to the output shaft. When the selector is placed to the **P** position this pawl engages and locks the gearbox. The pawl should and will hold the car

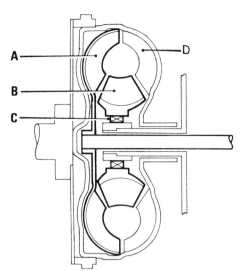

FIG 7:2   A schematic section of the torque converter

on hills but it should always be used in conjunction with the handbrake, as a safety precaution and to ensure that the pawl can easily be disengaged when selecting drive.

The car cannot be tow-started or pushed to start. However, the car can be towed, provided that the automatic transmission is in a satisfactory condition and correctly filled, but the distance of tow must not exceed 40 miles (64km) and the speed must not exceed 30 mile/hr (48km/hr). If these conditions cannot be complied with, disconnect the propeller shaft from the rear axle and tie it safely out of the way, or tow the car with the rear wheels on a dolly or hoisted clear of the ground and the steering locked or tied into the straight-ahead position.

The unit is very complicated, requiring many special tools for servicing, and fitters at garages are specially trained for working on automatic transmissions. **If faults cannot be corrected by carrying out the work outlined in this chapter then the car should be taken to an agent specializing in automatic transmissions. Under no circumstances attempt to dismantle the epicyclic gearing parts or valve assembly.**

7:2 Routine maintenance

The level of the fluid in the unit can be checked when the unit is cold or when it has reached its normal operation temperature. Stand the car on level ground and allow the engine to idle for at least two minutes to ensure that the torque converter is full. Select **P** and withdraw the dipstick 3 from its tube, shown in **FIG 7:4**. Leave the engine idling, wipe the dipstick and reinsert it. Immediately withdraw the dipstick and check the level against the marks. The difference between the upper and lower marks represents 1 Imperial pint (1.2 US pint, .57 Litre). If the level is low, top up to the upper mark **using a transmission fluid Type F. Absolute cleanliness is essential. Do not overfill the unit as this will cause frothing of the oil and possible faulty operation.**

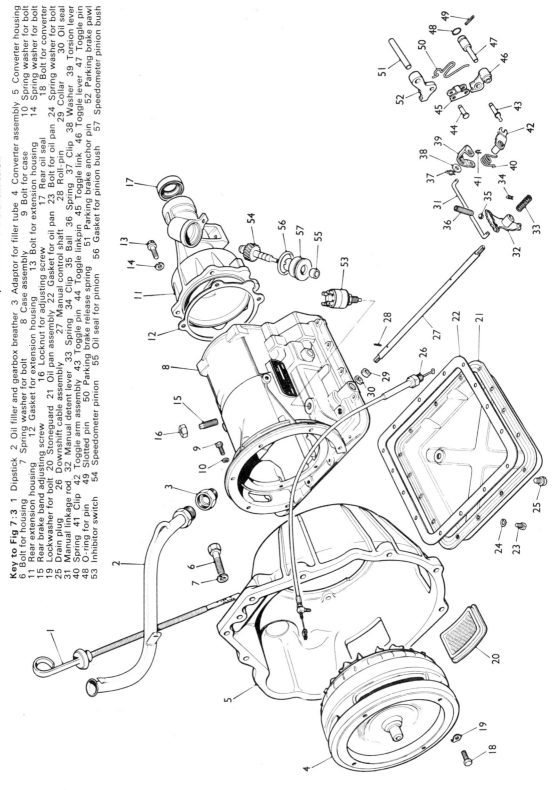

FIG 7:3 The external components of the transmission

Key to Fig 7:3 1 Dipstick 2 Oil filler and gearbox breather 3 Adaptor for filler tube 4 Converter assembly 5 Converter housing 6 Bolt for housing 7 Spring washer for bolt 8 Bolt for case 9 Bolt for case 10 Spring washer for bolt 11 Rear extension housing 12 Gasket for extension housing 13 Bolt for extension housing 14 Spring washer for bolt 15 Rear brake band adjusting screw 16 Locknut for adjusting screw 17 Rear oil seal 18 Bolt for converter 19 Lockwasher for bolt 20 Stoneguard 21 Oil pan assembly 22 Gasket for oil pan 23 Bolt for oil pan 24 Spring washer for bolt 25 Drain plug 26 Downshift cable assembly 27 Manual control shaft 28 Roll-pin 29 Collar 30 Oil seal 31 Manual linkage rod 32 Manual detent lever 33 Spring 34 Clip 35 Ball 36 Spring 37 Clip 38 Washer 39 Torsion lever 40 Spring 41 Clip 42 Toggle arm assembly 43 Toggle pin 44 Toggle linkpin 45 Toggle link 46 Toggle lever 47 Toggle pin 48 O-ring for pin 49 Slotted pin 50 Parking brake release spring 51 Parking brake anchor pin 52 Parking brake pawl 53 Inhibitor switch 54 Speedometer pinion 55 Oil seal for pinion 56 Gasket for pinion bush 57 Speedometer pinion bush

84

Draining:

The sump attachments are shown in **FIG 7:5**. If the unit is drained after the car has been used, **take great care as the fluid will be hot enough to cause serious scalding.** Unscrew the drain plug and allow the fluid to drain out into a suitable container. Note that the unit will not empty completely as some fluid will remain in the torque converter, and oil cooler if one is fitted.

When the fluid has stopped draining, the sump can be removed by taking out the bolts 2. The oil strainer will then be found secured by four bolts. Remove the strainer and wash it thoroughly in clean fuel. Make sure that it is dry and refit the parts in the reverse order of removal, after wiping out and washing the sump. Clean the magnet to remove any metal particles. It is advisable to use a new sump gasket and the drain plug should be sealed with a little Locktite Hydraulic Seal.

Fill the unit with slightly less fluid than is required and run the engine to fill the torque converter. Check the level on the dipstick and add more fluid as required to bring the level to the upper mark. **Do not overfill, and if the unit is accidentally overfilled the surplus should be drained or syphoned out.**

The quantities required to refill the unit are as follows:
Normal draining only, 5 Imp pint (6.5 US pint, 3 Litres)
Torque converter emptied, 9.5 Imp pint (10.7 US pint, 5.4 Litres)
Torque converter and oil cooler emptied, 11 Imp pints (13.2 US pint, 6.2 Litres)

If the oil is black and evil smelling or particles of lining or metal are found in the sump, take the car to an agent for further checks.

Cleanliness:

All operations carried out on the automatic transmission must be done with absolute cleanliness, as even a speck of dirt can block a valve and cause faulty operation. For this reason always use fresh fluid to top up or fill the unit as well as wiping the top of the filler tube clean.

External cleanliness is also important. Periodically wash off the accumulations of mud and road dirt that gather on the casing and make sure that the stone guards in the converter housing are clear and free from mud or stones. If an oil cooler is fitted, blow through the fins with an air-line or hosepipe to remove the accumulations of mud and insects. The automatic transmission produces quite a considerable amount of heat and if dirt is left on the outside it will act as an insulator, causing the unit to overheat.

7:3 Adjustments

The correct procedures must be adhered to and if the special tools required are not available then the car must be taken to a properly equipped agent for the adjustments to be carried out.

It should be noted that service parts are only available from British Leyland (AustinMorris) Limited Service Division through authorized dealers and distributors and that Borg-Warner do not supply parts direct

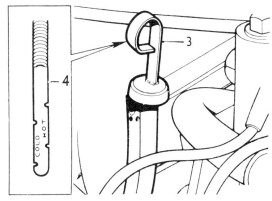

FIG 7:4   The automatic transmission dipstick and filler tube

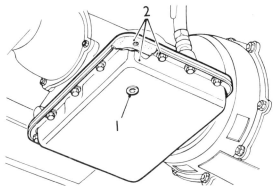

FIG 7:5   The sump and drain plug

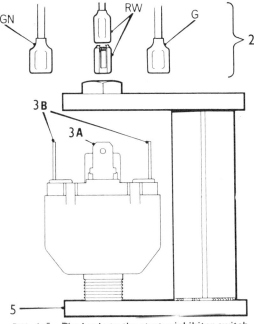

FIG 7:6   The leads to the starter inhibitor switch

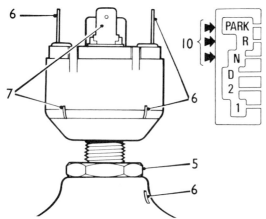

FIG 7:7 Adjusting the starter inhibitor switch

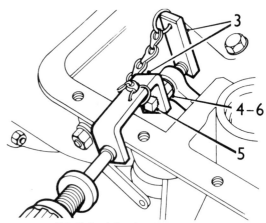

FIG 7:8 Adjusting the front brake band

Inhibitor switch:

The attachments and leads to the switch are shown in **FIG 7:6**. Before checking the action of the switch, chock the rear wheels to prevent the car from moving off. As a further safety precaution, the lead between the distributor and ignition coil can be disconnected at the ignition coil, ensuring that the engine cannot start, but be sure to reconnect the lead when the tests and adjustments are complete.

Disconnect the leads from the switch, **making sure that none of them accidentally earth against a metal part of the car.** Use a separate supply and test lamp to test the switch (12-volt). Connect the test lamp and battery across the starter terminals 3A and move the selector in the car to each position in turn. The test lamp should only light when the selector is in the **P** and **N** selections. Connect the test lamp and battery across the reverse light terminals (wide) 3B and check the test lamp with the selector in each position in turn. The lamp should only light when the selector is in the **R** selection. If the lamp never lights, either the adjustment is completely wrong or the switch is defective.

Refer to **FIG 7:7** for adjusting the switch. Slacken the locknut 5, preferably using the special spanner 18G.679, shown at 5 in **FIG 7:6**. Connect the test lamp and battery across the terminals 6 for the reverse light and select '1'. If the light is out, unscrew the switch until the light comes on. Screw the switch back in again until the light has just

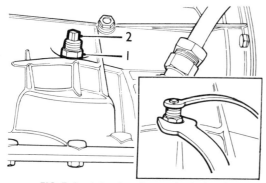

FIG 7:9 Adjusting the rear brake band

gone out and make aligning marks 6 on both the switch and case.

Disconnect the test lamp and battery from the terminals 6 and reconnect them across the starter terminals 7, when the lamp should be off. Screw in the switch until the light comes on, noting that approximately three quarters of a turn will be required. Make a mark 7 on the switch in line with the previously made mark 6 on the case. Remove the test lamp and battery. Turn the switch until it is midway between the two marks and retighten the locknut 5 without allowing the switch to turn.

Recheck, using the test lamp as described earlier, and then reconnect the leads to the switch. Check that the starter motor only operates in Park and **N** selections and that the reversing lights come on when **R** is selected.

Some inhibitor switches are non-adjustable for position and are marked SC on the body. The exposed length of the plunger is however adjustable and this must be $\frac{9}{16}$ inch (14.28 mm).

Front brake band:

The method of adjustment is shown in **FIG 7:8**. Drain the fluid out of the unit and remove the sump (see **Section 7:2**). Move the servo lever outwards and fit the gauge block of the special tool 18G.678 between the adjuster and the servo body, as shown at 3. Slacken the locknut 4 and tighten the adjusting screw to a torque load of 10 lb in (.115 kg m). The best tool to use is the torque screwdriver 18G.681. Hold the adjusting screw in position and retighten the locknut 4. Refit the sump, tightening its attachment bolts to a torque of 9 to 12 lb ft (1.2 to 1.7 kg m). Refill the unit to the correct level with fresh fluid. Note that if the oil appears black and evil smelling or particles of metal or lining are found in the sump, the car should be taken to an agent for further checks.

Rear brake band:

The method of adjustment is shown in **FIG 7:9**. It will be easier to carry out the adjustment if the transmission is supported on a jack, the rear crossmember freed from the frame and the transmission lowered slightly. A special extension spanner, 18G.701, is made for adjusting the brake band when the transmission is fitted to the car, as a torque spanner cannot be applied directly. Slacken the locknut 1. Tighten the adjusting screw 2 to the correct torque load. If a torque spanner is applied directly to the adjuster then it should be tightened to 10 lb ft (1.4 kg m). If the extension spanner 18G.701 is used between the torque spanner and adjuster, the adjuster must only be tightened to a torque of 7 lb ft (1.0 kg m), to allow for the leverage of the extension spanner. Slacken back the adjuster by two complete turns and then tighten the lock-nut 1 while holding the adjuster 2.

Selector rod:

The method of checking and the adjustment point are shown in **FIG 7:10**.

Set the manual selector to the **N** position but allow it to be positioned by the detent in the manual control valve on the gearbox. Check that the lever aligns with the **N** mark on the selector. Move the manual selector to the Park position and check that the gearbox has locked by trying to rock the car backwards and forwards.

If the adjustment of the rod is incorrect, disconnect the rod from the base of the manual selector lever. Push the manual selector lever right forward and pull it back by three clicks until it is accurately in the **N** position of the selector. Set the selector lever on the gearbox to the **N** position. Slacken the locknut 8 and adjust the turnbuckle 7 until the end of the selector rod freely enters the hole in the bottom of the manual selector lever. Reconnect the selector rod after tightening the locknut 8 on the turn-buckle.

Check the selector in all positions and make sure that the valve on the gearbox is not overriden.

Downshift cable:

A special service tool No. 18G.677.Z is made for check-ing the pressure and engine speed. The unit contains an accurate electronic tachometer which is connected into the ignition system and a pressure gauge which is connected by an adaptor 3 in place of the plug 2, as shown in **FIG 7:11**. An accurate tachometer and pressure gauge reading to at least 200 lb/sq inch can be used in place of the special service tool. **The service tool or gauges are essential for accurately setting the length of the cable.**

Chock the rear wheels and apply the handbrake firmly.

Refer to **FIG 7:12**. Pull down the inner cable by hand and make sure that it is rotating the down-shift cam. If it is not rotating the cam, remove the sump 3a and make sure that the cable and nipple are correctly in place as shown in 3b. Check the cam in the idling position 3c. Have an assistant open the throttle fully and make sure that the down-shift valve enters the kick-down position of the cam, as shown in 3d, adjusting the cable if neces-sary. Refit the sump and refill with fluid to the correct level. Note that the checks 3 need only be carried out if the cable is not rotating the down-shift cam and need not be carried out if the cam is rotating.

Start the engine and allow it to idle at 750 rev/min. Check that the crimped stop on the inner cable is $\frac{1}{16}$ inch (1.6 mm) from the outer cable collar 5 and that the trunnion is free to swivel, adjusting as required, by slackening the locknut and turning the adjuster 6. This

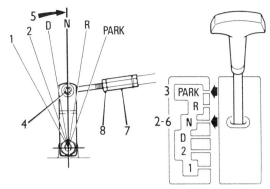

FIG 7:10   Adjusting the selector rod

will give an initial setting for the cable, but the final adjustments should be made with the pressure gauge and tachometer.

Use the car until the transmission has reached its normal operating temperature. Stop the engine and connect the instruments as shown in **FIG 7:11**. **Make sure that the wheels are chocked and the hand-brake firmly applied.** Start the engine, apply the foot-brake to make absolutely sure that the car does not move, and select **D** with the engine idling between 700 to 750 rev/min. The pressure reading at idling should be 50 to 60 lb/sq inch (3.5 to 4.2 kg/sq cm). Increase the engine speed to 1000 rev/min and if the cable adjustment is correct, the pressure will rise by 20 lb/sq inch (1.4 kg/sq cm). If the pressure rise is not correct, stop the engine. If the pressure rise is less than 20 lb/sq inch increase the effective length of the outer cable at the adjuster 6, and if the pressure rise is less then decrease the effective length of the cable.

Restart the engine and repeat the test, making further adjustments to the outer cable length as required until

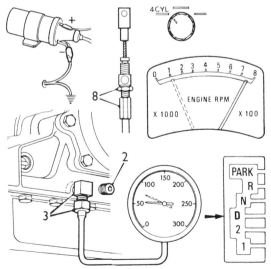

FIG 7:11   **Checking the adjustment of the downshift cable**

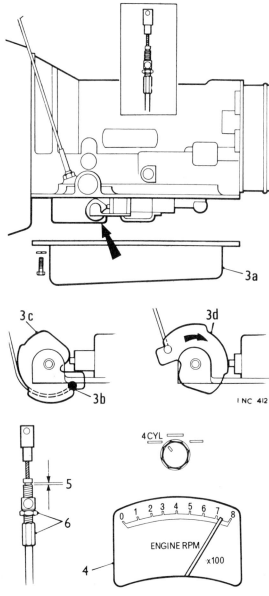

FIG 7:12 Preliminary setting of the downshift cable

churning the fluid in the torque converter and as the energy must be dispersed it is converted into heat. **If the heat is prolonged then the unit will very rapidly overheat and become damaged. For this reason a stall test should not last longer than 10 seconds and if the test has to be repeated, sufficient time must be allowed between tests to allow the unit to cool down.** Allow the unit to cool down by running the engine at idle with **N** selected as this will ensure oil circulation.

Before carrying out the test, make sure that the unit is filled with fluid to the upper mark on the dipstick. Connect an accurate tachometer into the ignition circuit so that it can be seen from the driver's seat. Use the car until the transmission has reached its normal operating temperature.

Chock the wheels and firmly apply the handbrake, using the footbrake as well to prevent the car from moving. Select either '1' or **R** positions and floor the accelerator pedal, **for a maximum of 10 seconds,** noting the reading on the tachometer. If everything is in order, the maximum speed that the engine will reach is 1600 to 1900 rev/min for 1.3 engines and 1800 to 2100 rev/min for 1.8 engines.

If the maximum speed obtainable is only 1350 to 1600 rev/min for 1.3 engines or 1500 to 1800 rev/min for 1.8 engines then the engine is not producing its full power.

A very low maximum speed, below 1250 rev/min for 1.3 engines and below 1300 rev/min for 1.8 engines indicates stator slip in the torque converter. The one-way clutch in the torque converter is defective, allowing the stator to slip so that the torque multiplication effect cannot take place. The fault will be confirmed by the car having poor acceleration from standstill and having difficulty driving away on steep hills. The only cure is to fit a new torque converter.

If a high maximum engine speed is obtained, over 2200 rev/min for both models, the gearbox is slipping. If the fault is apparent in both '1' and **R** selections then it is most likely caused by low oil pressure or oil starvation. Remove the sump and check the oil strainer for blockage, after making sure that the fluid level in the unit is correct. If the fault occurs in only one selection then it is caused by either a brake band slipping (try adjustment) or a defective clutch.

Road test:

This should be carried out by a qualified mechanic trained on automatic transmissions. The shift speeds should be checked and undue noises listened for. Make sure that the starter motor only operates in Park and **N** selections and check that the reversing lights come on in **R** selection. Ensure that the transmission only will hold the car in Park when facing up or down a hill (apply the brake before releasing the selection). Hold the car on the handbrake and see that it attempts to move off in the correct direction in all the drive selections.

It should be noted that the stator clutch can be defective even if the stall speed is correct. If the maximum speed in the gears, particularly top, is reduced and the transmission tends to overheat rapidly and severely then it is likely that the one-way clutch on the stator has seized. This is a rare fault. Usually if the clutch does fail it slips in both directions, but seizing is a fault to be borne in mind.

the pressure rises by 20 lb/sq inch when the speed is raised from idle to 1000 rev/min.

Stop the engine and remove the test equipment, making sure that the blanking plug is refitted and that the locknut on the adjuster is tight.

7:4 Stall speed test

This test provides a quick and accurate guide to the condition of the automatic transmission, and to some degree the condition of the engine. The test, as the name implies, is carried out with the car stationary and the turbine stalled. All the power from the engine goes into

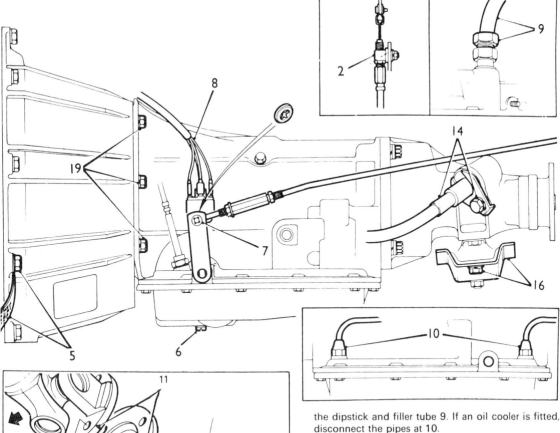

FIG 7:13   Removing the transmission

7:5 Removing the automatic transmission

The attachments of the unit are shown in **FIG 7:13**.

1 Disconnect the battery, Disconnect the down-shift cable 2 from the throttle linkage. Remove the transmission dipstick. Free the exhaust pipe(s) from the exhaust manifold and the clips on the steady bracket under the car. Disconnect the engine earth cable 5 and drain the transmission by removing the drain plug 6.

2 Disconnect the selector rod from the lever on the transmission by removing the spring washer 7. Disconnect the leads to the starter inhibitor switch 8. Hold the adaptor and unscrew the union nut to remove

the dipstick and filler tube 9. If an oil cooler is fitted, disconnect the pipes at 10.

3 Make aligning marks 11 on the drive flange and propeller shaft flange and take out the nuts and bolts 12 which secure them together. Move the propeller shaft to one side and tie it out of the way to a front suspension torque bar. Disconnect the speedometer drive cable by removing the clip 14.

4 Support the engine using a jack and pad of wood under the sump or using a sling and hoist attached with lifting eyes to the rocker cover attachment bolts. Support the transmission on a trolley jack. Remove the bolts 16 that secure the crossmember to the frame and lower the power unit to gain access to six bolts 19. Remove the bolts and draw the transmission rearwards until the input shaft is well clear of the torque converter. **Do not allow the weight of the transmission to hang on the input shaft in the torque converter.** Remove the transmission from under the car.

Refit the unit in the reverse order of removal, making sure that the converter and front pump driving dogs are horizontal and aligned as the transmission is refitted. Tighten the bolts 19 to a torque of 8 to 13 lb ft (1.1 to 1.8 kg mm).

Torque converter:

Remove the transmission as just described. Remove the starter motor. The attachments are shown in **FIG 7:14**. Take out the two bolts 3 which secure the engine

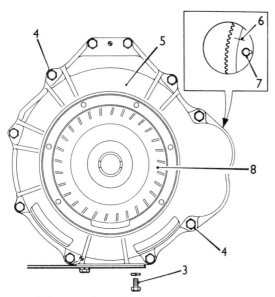

FIG 7:14 Removing the torque converter

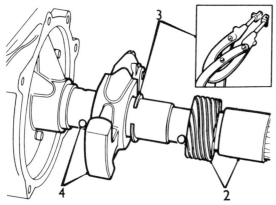

FIG 7:15 The governor attachments

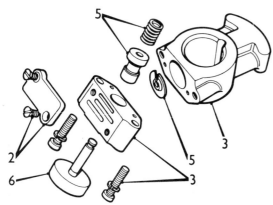

FIG 7:16 The governor components

sump connecting plate. Raise the engine slightly on its support and remove the bolts 4 which secure the housing to the engine, and then lower the engine so that the housing 5 can be removed. Make alignment marks 6 across the engine drive plate and torque converter. Free and slacken the bolts 7 that secure the torque converter to the drive plate through the aperture for the starter motor, turning the engine to gain access. Support the torque converter, noting that it will contain fluid, and remove the four bolts 7 so that the torque converter can be removed.

The torque converter is refitted in the reverse order of removal. Tighten the bolts 7 progressively to a load of 25 to 30 lb ft (3.4 to 4.1 kg m) and lock them with new lock-washers. Tighten the bolts 4 to a torque of 8 to 13 lb ft (1.1 to 1.8 kg m).

7:6 The rear extension

The rear extension can be removed without having to take the transmission out of the car.

The oil seal at the rear end of the extension can be renewed without having to remove the extension. Disconnect the propeller shaft, take off the nut that secures the drive flange and remove the drive flange using a suitable extractor. Prise out the old oil seal and press a new one back into place. Refit the drive flange, checking that its operating surface is not scored or damaged, and reconnect the propeller shaft.

The seals for the speedometer drive pinion parts can also be renewed without having to remove the rear extension. Disconnect the speedometer cable by removing its securing clip and pull out the drive pinion and housing. Renew the O-ring and seal. Refit the parts in the reverse order of removal.

Removing rear extension:

The procedure is very similar to removing the transmission unit (see previous section). Carry out the removal operations 1 to 3 inclusive but do not remove the dipstick tube or, disconnect the down-shift cable or the oil cooler pipes. If the rear of the car is raised for access there is no need to drain the transmission, though a little fluid may be spilt. Support the power unit with a jack under the transmission sump, using a pad of wood to protect the sump. Remove the drive flange from the rear of the extension. Take out the bolts that secure the mounting crossmember to the frame and lower the rear of the power unit for access room. Remove the four bolts which secure the extension to the main case and withdraw the extension rearwards to remove it.

The rear extension is refitted in the reverse order of removal.

7:7 The governor

The governor is accessible after the rear extension has been removed, and its attachments are shown in **FIG 7:15**.

To remove the unit, withdraw the speedometer drive gear 2. Remove the circlip 3 and slide off the governor, collecting the drive ball 4.

The governor is refitted in the reverse order of removal. Turn the output shaft until the detent is uppermost and the drive ball can be held in place with a little petroleum jelly (vaseline) and slide on the governor so that the coverplate is away from the gearbox.

The components of the unit are shown in **FIG 7:16**. Take out the screws and remove the coverplate 2. Remove the screws 3 to separate the valve body from the counterweight. Pull off the retainer so that the valve and spring 5 can be removed and the weight 6 withdrawn.

Wash the parts in clean fuel and examine them for scoring or wear. Renew worn or damaged parts.

The unit is reassembled in the reverse order of dismantling. The screws 3 must be tightened to a torque of 4 to 5 lb ft (.6 to .7 kgm) and the screws 2 to a torque of 20 to 48 lb in (.23 to .55 kgm) **otherwise there is a danger of the unit leaking in use.**

7:8 Fault diagnosis

This section does not cover all the faults that can be found but only the more common ones that can be cured by the owner. If the fault persists after adjustment or repairs, take the car to a qualified agent.

(a) Transmission overheats

1 Stone guards on converter housing blocked
2 Unit covered in dirt
3 Stator one-way clutch seized (rare fault)
4 Rear brake band incorrectly adjusted
5 Front brake band incorrectly adjusted
6 Oil cooler defective

(b) Noisy operation

1 Incorrect fluid level
2 Incorrectly adjusted selector rod
3 Incorrectly adjusted downshift cable
4 Defective oil pump (screech or whine increasing with engine speed)

(c) Incorrect shift speeds

1 Check 2 and 3 in (b)
2 Governor valve sticking or incorrectly assembled

(d) No drive

Check (b)

(e) Poor acceleration

1 Check 3, 4 and 5 in (a)
2 Stator clutch slipping

(f) Jumps in engagement

1 Check 4 and 5 in (a) and also check 2 and 3 in (b)
2 Incorrect engine idling speed

(g) Car does not hold in Park

1 Check 2 in (b)

(h) Incorrect stall speed

1 Check 3, 4 and 5 in (a); 2 in (e). Also check (b) and (c)

(i) Reverse slips or chatters

1 Check 4 in (a) and 2 in (b)

NOTES

CHAPTER 8

THE PROPELLER SHAFT, REAR AXLE
AND REAR SUSPENSION

8:1 The propeller shaft

The attachments of the propeller shaft are shown in
FIG 8:1.

Removal:

1 Jack up the rear of the car so that the propeller shaft
can be turned. Make marks 1 across the flanges of the
universal joints and those on the gearbox and rear axle
drive flanges. These marks should be realigned on
reassembly.

2 Take out the nuts and bolts 3 that secure the front
propeller shaft to the gearbox and lower the front end
of the propeller shaft. When carrying out work on the
transmission which requires disconnecting this point,
tie the propeller shaft safely out of the way to one of
the front suspension torsion bars.

3 Support the rear end of the propeller shaft and remove
the nuts and bolts 4 that secure it to the pinion flange
of the rear axle.

4 Take out the two sets of bolts and washers 5 that
secure the centre bearing to the frame and remove the
complete propeller shaft from the car.

Refit the propeller shaft in the reverse order of removal.
If the self-locking nuts 3 and 4 can be run up and down
the threads of their bolts, using only the fingers, the nuts
are worn and must be renewed. The nuts 3 and 4 should

be tightened to a torque of 28 lb ft (3.8 kgm) and the
bolts 5 should be tightened to 22 lb ft (3.0 kgm).

Centre bearing:

This can be renewed once the propeller shaft has been
removed from the car. Free the tabwasher 7 and remove
the bolt and C-washer 8. Remove the rear propeller shaft
from the front one.

The bearing can be pulled off from the front propeller
shaft, preferably using the special tools 18G.47.C and
18G.47.AJ. The new bearing should be driven back into
place, preferably using the special drift 18G.519.

Universal joints:

Service kits are available to repair universal joints that
are worn or defective. The complete set of parts supplied
in the kit should be used.

On later cars a grease nipple is fitted to the front joint
and should be given three or four strokes with a grease gun
every 6000 miles (10,000 km).

Sliding joint:

Further details of the propeller shaft are shown in **FIG
8:2**. The rear propeller shaft 22 is fitted with a sliding
joint which allows the length of the shaft to alter slightly
as the axle moves in its springs. Before separating the

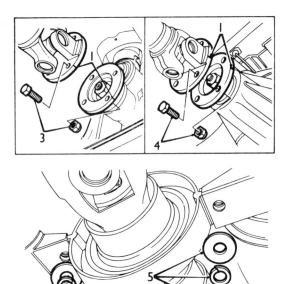

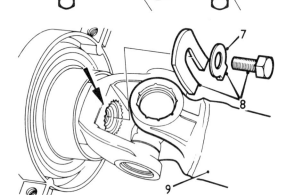

FIG 8:1 The propeller shaft attachments

halves of the rear propeller shaft mark them with aligning marks. **It is essential that these marks are again aligned on reassembly, as the two universal joints on the rear propeller shaft must be in the correct phase.** A single universal joint does not give a perfect even drive but, by having the two joints in the correct phase the angular variations in each joint are cancelled out.

Unscrew the cap 20 by hand and separate the two halves of the shaft by pulling them apart. If the splines are worn or damaged a new rear shaft must be fitted.

Lubricate the splines with grease, fit a new cork seal 18, and slide the halves together so that the previously made marks again align. Tighten the cap nut 20 handtight.

8:2 The rear axle (Saloon and Estate cars)

The components of the rear axle, including the propeller shaft, are shown in **FIG 8:2**. The removal of the axle from the car will be dealt with separately in **Section 8:5**.

Lubrication:

The rear axle combined filler and level plug is shown in **FIG 8:3**. No drain plug is fitted as seasonal oil changes are not required. If the oil has to be drained out the nuts and washers securing the differential carrier to the axle casing must be removed, allowing the oil to seep out.

The level in the rear axle should be checked at intervals of 6000 miles (10,000 kilometres) or 6 months, whichever occurs the sooner. Stand the car on level ground and clean the area around the filler plug free from dirt. Unscrew the plug and check that the oil comes level with the bottom of the aperture. If the level is low, top up using a squeeze bottle and plastic hose. Allow all surplus oil to drain out through the filler hole before refitting the plug. **Do not overfill the axle as this can cause oil to leak past the seals in the hub and contaminate the brakes.** At the same time, check that the breather (14 in **FIG 8:2**) is clear and not blocked with dirt. A blocked breather can also cause oil leaks, as pressure rises inside the case when the unit gets hot and blows oil past the seals.

Use Hypoid SAE.90 for temperate and warm climates or Hypoid SAE.80 for Arctic climates.

Hub and drive shaft:

The method of servicing the parts is shown in **FIG 8:4**.
1 Jack up the wheel and support the car securely on an axle stand. Remove the road wheel, noting that this will be easier if the wheel nuts have been slackened before jacking up the car.
2 Firmly apply the handbrake to lock the rear brake drums. Undo and remove the stub axle nut 3 with its washer. Release the handbrake and, if necessary, slacken off the brake shoe adjusters. Remove the two countersunk screws 4 that secure the brake drum and withdraw the drum from the assembly.
3 Withdraw the hub assembly from the drive shaft using the extractor 5 (S356B).
4 Disconnect the handbrake cable from the brake by extracting the splitpin and removing the clevis pin 6. Disconnect the hydraulic feed pipes 7 from the wheel cylinder. Only the righthand brake is fitted with two pipes, one of them being the bridge pipe between the brakes. Use a container to catch any fluid that spills and plug the pipe to prevent dirt from entering or fluid from leaking out.
5 Remove the nuts and bolts 8 that secure the oil catcher 9 (noting the position of the drip lip in relation to the wheel cylinder), the brake backplate 10 and the oil seal complete with its housing 11. Use a container to catch any oil spillage.
6 The oil seal in the housing 11 is best removed using the extractor 18G.1087 as shown at 12. Carefully drive out the axle key 13. Withdraw the drive shaft from the axle casing, using the impact tool 18G.284 as shown at 14. Press the bearing from the shaft. Remove the inner oil seal using the extractor 18G.1087 as shown in inset 15.

Wash all the parts in clean fuel and examine them for wear or damage. The bearing should be washed separately so that it does not pick up dirt. Renew the bearing if it rotates roughly or with noise when lubricated with light oil. It is most advisable to discard the old oil seals and fit new ones on reassembly. If it is certain that the old seals

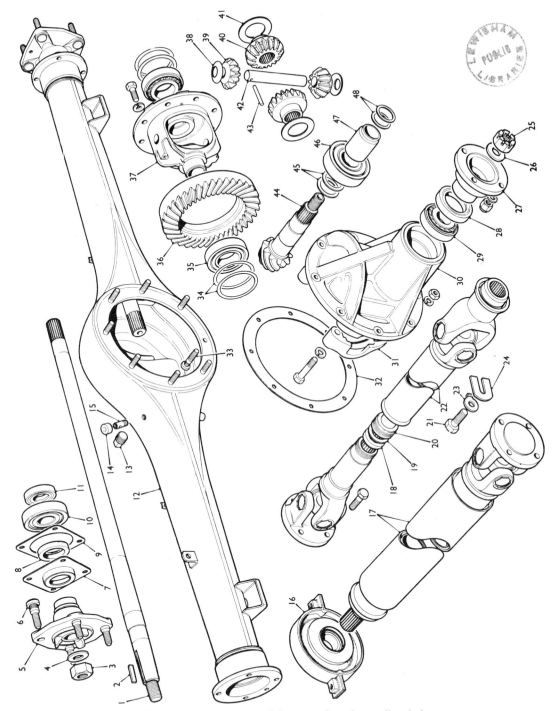

FIG 8 : 2   The components of the rear axle and propeller shaft

Key to Fig 8 : 2   1 Drive shaft   2 Key   3 Nut   4 Washer   5 Rear hub   6 Wheel stud   7 Oil seal housing   8 Oil seal
9 Gasket   10 Bearing   11 Oil seal   12 Axle casing   13 Drain plug   14 Breather cap   15 Breather stem   16 Centre bearing
mounting   17 Front propeller shaft   18 Seal   19 Seal retainer (steel)   20 Screw cap   21 Bolt   22 Rear propeller shaft
23 Tabwasher   24 C-washer   25 Pinion nut   26 Washer   27 Drive flange   28 Oil seal   29 Bearing   30 Differential carrier
31 Bearing cap   32 Gasket   33 Stud   34 Shim   35 Bearing assembly   36 Crownwheel   37 Differential case   38 Thrust
washer   39 Differential pinion   40 Differential gear   41 Thrust washer   42 Cross-pin   43 Locating pin   44 Pinion   45 Shim
46 Bearing   47 Bearing spacer   48 Shim

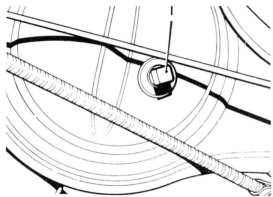

FIG 8:3 The rear axle filler and level plug. Note that no drain plug is fitted

are satisfactory then they should be left in place and not removed, but remember that they are likely to be damaged as the parts are dismantled.

Refit the oil seals using the mandrel 18G.1200 as shown at 18 and 20. The seal in the axle casing must be fitted with its lips facing inwards.

If the bearing has been removed from the drive shaft, press it back so that the dimension between the bearing and threaded end of the drive shaft is 2.84 inch (72.14 mm).

Refit the parts in the reverse order of removal. Use a new hub gasket and pack the bearing with lithium-based grease. Tighten the backplate securing bolts 8 to a torque of 32 to 38 lb ft (4.4 to 5.3 kg m). Clean the axle shaft threads and the axle shaft nut. Apply a little Loctite to the nut and tighten it to a torque of 100 to 110 lb ft (13.8 to 15.2 kg m).

Correctly reconnect the brake pipes and handbrake cable then bleed and adjust the brakes as described in **Chapter 11**. Refit the road wheel and lower the car back to the ground.

If difficulty is found in slackening or fully tightening the drive shaft nut 3 then slacken it slightly before raising the rear wheel and tighten it as far as possible with the road wheel removed, completing the tightening when the weight of the car is on the ground and the wheel can be chocked.

The differential unit:

Dismantling or servicing the unit should not be carried out by the owner. As the parts of the differential are reassembled they must be set to the correct clearances and mesh, otherwise the unit will not operate quietly and satisfactorily. Special tools, a good selection of shims, and personal skill, are all essential.

The unit can be removed from the rear axle, without having to remove the axle from the car. Jack up the rear of the car and place it securely onto axle stands, after slackening the road wheel nuts and the drive shaft nut. Remove both drive shafts as described just previously, noting that seals and bearings can be left in place. Disconnect the propeller shaft from the differential drive flange (see **Chapter 9, Section 9:1**). Refer to **FIG 8:2** and remove the ring of nuts that secure the differential carrier 30 to the axle casing 12. Have a suitable container positioned under the differential to catch the oil as it

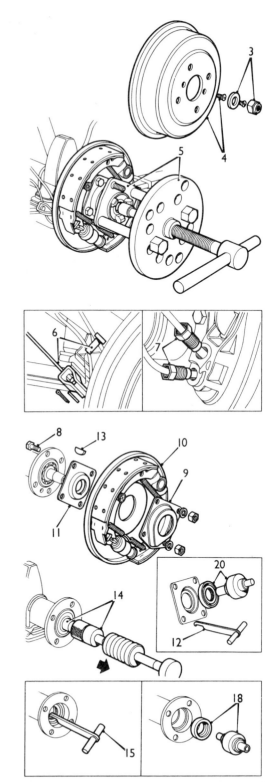

FIG 8:4 Servicing the hub and drive shaft assembly

drains out. Once the nuts have been removed the differential assembly can be withdrawn from the rear axle.

The differential assembly is refitted in the reverse order of removal, using a new gasket 32 between it and the casing. Refit the drive shafts in the reverse order of removal (see previous section).

Pinion oil seal:

The parts are shown in **FIG 8:2**. The oil seal 28 can be renewed without having to take out the rear axle or remove the differential.

Disconnect the rear propeller shaft from the drive flange 27. Hold the drive flange to prevent it from rotating, preferably using the special wrench 18G.1205, and remove the nut 25 and washer 26 after extracting the splitpin which locks the nut. Place a container under the flange to catch oil as it leaks out and withdraw the drive flange, preferably using the two-legged extractor 18G.2. Prise out the old oil seal. Soak the new seal in light oil for at least one hour before fitting it. Check the face of the drive flange onto which the seal operates for scoring or damage and renew the drive flange if it is defective. Press the new seal back into place so that its lips face into the differential. Refit the drive flange and torque load the nut to a load of 90 lb ft (12.4 kg m) before reconnecting the propeller shaft. Check the level of the oil in the rear axle and top up as necessary.

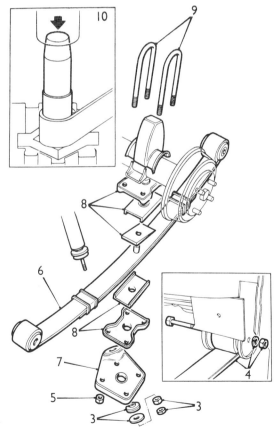

FIG 8:5 The rear suspension components. The inset shows a spring eye bush being pressed out

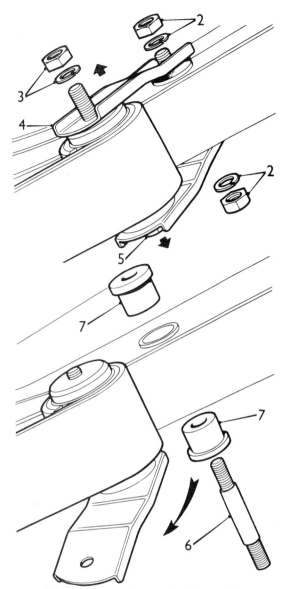

FIG 8:6 The spring rear shackle assembly

8:3 The rear suspension

Details of the rear suspension as fitted to cars up to 1975 are shown in **FIG 8:5**. Later cars, Marina 2 or Series K, have also an anti-roll bar mounted in rubber-insulated clamps on the rear axle, and bolted to the chassis side members.

Road spring:

1 The rear shackle attachment of the spring is shown in **FIG 8:6**. Raise the rear end of the car and place it securely onto stands under the chassis member. Remove the road wheel. Remove the nuts and washers 2 from either side of the shackle pin. Remove the nut and washer 3 so that the shackle plate 4 can be taken

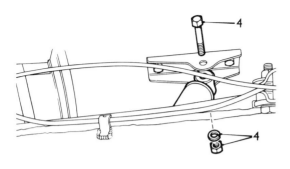

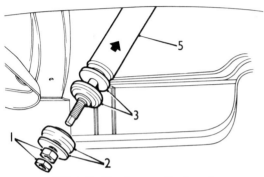

FIG 8:7 The damper attachments

Anti-roll bar:

Details of the anti-roll bar mountings are shown in **FIG 8:9** and its removal is undertaken as follows:

Remove the two pivot bolts 1 with their nuts and washers securing the anti-roll bar to the chassis then jack-up the rear of the car and support it on stands. Remove the road wheels.

Remove the lower nuts 4 from the damper mounting. Slacken the upper damper bolts 5 and push the damper to one side out of the way.

Unscrew the clamp bolts and nuts 6 and remove the anti-roll bar clamps 7. The anti-roll bar can now be withdrawn from under the car and, if desired, the mounting rubbers and end fittings removed.

Refit in the reverse order, noting the following points:

Rotate the end fittings on their threads to align the bush with the chassis bolt holes so that the pivot bolt can be inserted without distorting the rubber bush.

Tighten the bolts and lock nuts after the car has been lowered to the ground.

8:4 The dampers

The damper attachment is shown in **FIG 8:7**. The dampers are sealed telescopic units that cannot be repaired if they are defective. The damper is removed by taking off the attachments in the numerical order shown in the figure and is refitted in the reverse order of removal. Check that the rubber bushes are all in good condition before refitting the damper.

Testing:

Specialized test equipment is required to check that the dampers are acting with full efficiency. Equipment is just lately coming into use which will allow the dampers to be tested without removing them from the car, but do not expect every agent to have it and even the test equipment for checking dampers when they have been removed is not always held.

off. Support the axle with a small jack underneath it. Fit a slave nut onto the spring bolt 5, to protect the threads, and partially drift out the bolt in the direction of the arrow so that the outer shackle plate can be released from the shackle pin 6 and swivelled out of the way. Withdraw the shackle pin 6 and its two rubber bushes 7.

2 Refer to **FIG 8:5**. Disconnect the lower damper attachment by removing the nuts, washer and bush 3, carefully noting the position of the rubber bush. Remove the nut, spring washer and bolt 4 that secure the front end of the spring to the frame. Take off the U-bolt nuts 5 while supporting the spring 6. Lower the spring after removing the damper mounting plate 7 and the lower rubber mounting plate and rubber 8. The spring 6 can then be lifted out from under the car, collecting the upper mountings and noting the position of the wedge 8 if fitted. Withdraw the U-bolts 9 so that the bump rubber can be freed.

The parts are refitted in the reverse order of removal, using new rubber mounts and bushes if the old ones are worn, perished or damaged. Check the spring for cracked leaves or other damage and renew it if it is defective. Make sure that the spring wedge is correctly positioned. Old eye bushes can be pressed out as shown in inset 10 and new ones pressed back into place.

The springs fitted to the Estate versions are much stiffer than the ones fitted to the Saloon and Coupé models and possibly the dampers will have different shock absorbing characteristics. When obtaining spares quote the model type, commission number and chassis number to ensure correct replacements. Renew the springs on all models in axle pairs.

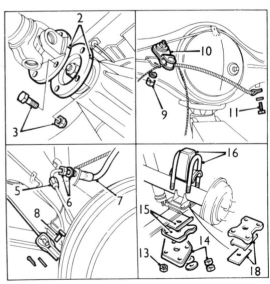

FIG 8:8 Removing the rear axle

The dampers are weak if the car keeps pitching after going over a bump in the road, and they can be roughly checked by bouncing the suspension and checking that the oscillations are damped out.

The damper must be renewed if it is mechanically damaged, such as with oil leaks, bent ram or dented body.

A check can be made to find a defective damper, though if it passes the test it is no guarantee that it is operating at its full efficiency. Mount the damper vertically in the padded jaws of a vice and pump it up and down, using short strokes about the mid-point. This will ensure that any air is expelled from the fluid and driven to the top of the damper. Gradually increase the length of the strokes until they are reaching the full travel of the damper. If the damper operates noisily, has pockets of weak or no resistance (especially when changing direction) or is too stiff to move by hand it is defective and should be renewed. A rough guide as to condition can be made by comparing the force to that required on a new damper.

Unless a damper is being changed because of mechanical damage, it is advisable to renew dampers in axle pairs.

8:5 Removing the rear axle

The method is shown in **FIG 8:8**.

1 Raise the rear of the car and support it securely on stands positioned under the body forward of the axle. Disconnect the propeller shaft, after making aligning marks 2, by taking out the nuts and bolts 3. Remove both road wheels.

2 Disconnect the brake pipe. Undo the union nut 5, while holding the flexible hose 7, then unscrew the locknut 6 so that the flexible hose can be freed from the chassis bracket. Hydraulic fluid will drain through, so plug the pipe and use a container to catch spillage. Disconnect the handbrake cables from the levers on the brakes, by removing the clevis pins 8. Remove the nut and washer 9 so that the compensating lever 10 can be freed from the axle. Remove the bolt 11 that secures the handbrake cable clip.

3 Support the rear axle, preferably with a trolley jack under the differential. Remove the U-bolt nuts 13 from both sides. The lower damper attachment 14 to the plate need not be disconnected as the damper and plate can be swung to one side. If applicable, remove the nuts and bolts securing the clamps for the anti-roll bar and remove the clamps. Remove the lower mountings 15. Remove the U-bolts and bump stops 16 from each side and lift the axle up over a spring on one side of the car and out onto the floor. Remove the upper mountings 18, noting the positions of the wedges.

The axle is refitted in the reverse order of removal. Tighten the U-bolt nuts 13 to a torque load of 15 to 18 lb ft for saloon and estate cars or 18 to 23 lb ft on vans (2 to 2.4 or 2.4 to 3.1 kg m). Renew any mounting rubbers that are worn or damaged.

Once the axle is in place and the parts reconnected, fill and bleed then adjust the braking system (see **Chapter 11**).

8:6 Rear axle and final drive—10 cwt Van

In order to handle the loads required of a commercial vehicle, a slightly different back axle assembly is used.

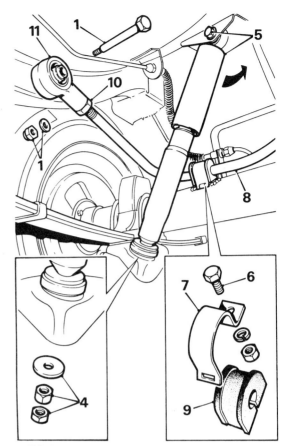

FIG 8:9   Removing the anti-roll bar (Series 2 cars)

Key to Fig 8:9   1 Pivot bolt and nuts   4 Damper lower nuts   5 Damper upper bolt   6 Clamp mounting bolt   7 Clamp   8 Anti-roll bar   9 Rubber block   10 Locknut   11 End fitting

This section includes details of those operations within the scope of the home operator which vary from those described earlier.

Axle halfshaft:

Jack-up the rear of the car and support it firmly on stands. Remove the appropriate road wheel.

Remove the two countersunk screws and pull of the brake drum, slackening off the brake shoe adjustment if they are binding on the drum.

Remove the single countersunk screw retaining the halfshaft flange and withdraw the halfshaft. Remove the gasket and the 'O' ring seal.

Refitting is a reversal of the above, but ensure that the hole for the retaining screw in the halfshaft flange is correctly aligned with the hub so that the holes for the drum retaining screws are clear. It is advisable to use a new 'O' ring and gasket.

Differential assembly:

This can be removed from the axle in a similar manner to that described in **Section 8:2** but again the owner/driver is advised not to attempt further dismantling.

Pinion oil seal:

This can be renewed by following the procedure given in **Section 8:2**, but note that there is no splitpin securing the flange nut. There is, however, a dished washer acting as a stone guard fitted between the flange and the oil seal.

On reassembly, which is a reversal of the removal procedure, the pinion flange nut must be tightened to a torque of 140 lb ft.

8:7 Rear hub assembly—10 cwt Van

Removal:

Raise the rear of the car, remove the road wheel and withdraw the halfshaft as described in **Section 8:6**.

Remove the bearing spacer, knock back the tab of the lock washer and unscrew the hub nut and keyed lock washer using tool 18G 152.

The hub assembly can now be extracted by using tools 18G 304, 304B and 304 J or other suitable pullers.

Oil seal:

The oil seal is easily removed after removing the rear hub assembly and driving the bearing from its recess.

When fitting the new seal, note that the seal lip must face towards the bearing and the thrust face of the bearing, stamped with the maker's name and reference number, towards the outside of the hub.

Pack the bearing with grease and also the space between the bearing and the oil seal.

Refitting:

This is the reverse of the above, but do not omit to pack the bearing with a recommended grease and use a new lock washer.

The hub is drifted into position and the outer face of the bearing spacer must protrude beyond the outer face of the hub by .001 to .004 inch (.025 to .102 mm) when the bearing is fully home.

8:8 Fault diagnosis

(a) Noisy axle

1 Incorrect or insufficient lubricant
2 Worn bearings
3 Worn gears
4 Damaged or broken gear teeth
5 Incorrect adjustments on reassembly
6 General wear

(b) Excessive backlash

1 Worn gears, bearings
2 Worn drive shaft splines
3 Worn universal joints
4 Loose wheel attachments

(c) Oil leakage

1 Defective oil seal in hub
2 Defective oil seal in pinion
3 Defective gasket
4 Blocked breather
5 Overfilled rear axle

(d) Vibration

1 Propeller shaft out of balance
2 Worn universal joints
3 Defective centre bearing
4 Propeller shaft assembled out of phase

(e) Rattles

1 Worn damper rubber bushes
2 Dampers loose
3 U-bolts loose
4 Loose spring clips
5 Worn bushes in spring eyes or shackles
6 Broken spring leaves

(f) Settling

1 Weak or broken spring leaves
2 Badly worn shackles and bushes

(g) Axle knock

1 Badly worn splines on drive shafts
2 Worn universal joints

CHAPTER 9

FRONT SUSPENSION AND HUBS

9:1 Description

The components of the righthand front suspension and hub are shown in **FIG 9:1**. Included in the figure are the alternative brake systems, the drum brakes being standard and the disc brakes available either as an optional extra or standard on some versions. The lefthand side suspension is similar but note that many of the parts are handed and cannot be interchanged between sides.

The road wheel is attached to the hub 54, which also has the brake drum 75 or brake disc 79 attached to it by the screws 77 or bolts 80. The hub rotates about the stub axle of the swivel pin 1 on two opposed taper bearings 56 and 57 and is secured to the stub axle by the nut 59. The swivel pin also carries the dust shield 81 for the disc brake or the drum brake backplate 53 together with the drum brake components or caliper as applicable.

The hydraulic damper 23 is mounted on the frame of the car and the outer end of its arm carries the ball joint for the top attachment of the swivel pin, so that the damper arm acts as an upper wishbone. The lower end of the swivel pin screws into the lower link 28 which is in turn mounted between the outer ends of the lower arms 35 and 36. The link is mounted on a pivot pin 29 so that the suspension is free to move vertically.

Horizontal movement of the suspension is limited by the tie rod assembly 47. The inboard ends of the lower arms are free to pivot about the eyebolt 37 and the rear arm 35 is splined to the torsion bar 42. The rear end of the torsion bar is attached to the frame and the weight of the car and vertical road wheel movements are taken by the restoring force when the bar is twisted. Suspension oscillations are controlled by the damper 23.

Later cars (after 1975) are fitted also with a stabiliser or anti-roll bar, this is described separately in **Section 9:10**.

9:2 Maintenance

1 At intervals of 6000 miles (10,000 kilometres) grease through all four grease nipples on the front suspension (two per side). Greasing is best carried out with the car jacked up so that the weight is taken off the suspension and the grease can pass through easily. Turn the steering to full lock to make access to the grease nipples easier. Wipe the nipple clean and use a grease gun to pump in fresh grease. The grease nipples on one suspension are shown in **FIG 9:2** and those on the other suspension are similarly situated. Wipe away surplus grease and make sure that none has gone onto the tyres or flexible brake hoses.

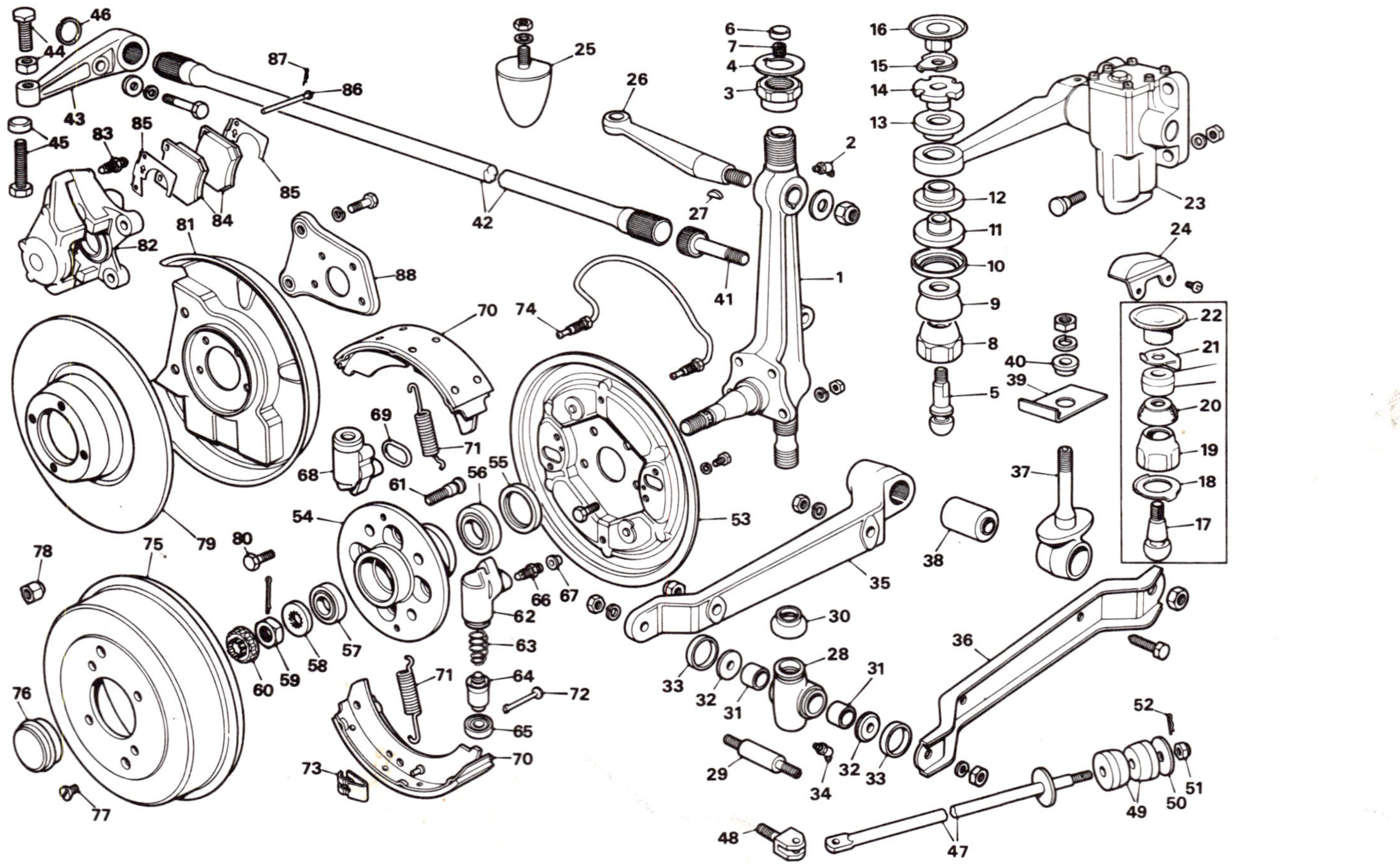

FIG 9:1   The components of a righthand front suspension assembly, showing disc and drum brake installations and Marina 2 (Series K) modifications (inset)

Key to Fig 9:1   1 Swivel pin and stub axle, righthand   2 Grease nipple   3 Locknut for ballpin   4 Tabwasher for ballpin   5 Ballpin*   6 Seat for ballpin   7 Spring for ballpin   8 Retaining nut for ballpin*   9 Dust cover for retaining nut*   10 Clip for dust cover*   11 Lower bush*   12 Housing for lower bush*   13 Upper bush*   14 Housing for upper bush*   15 Tabwasher*   16 Reaction pad*   17 Ballpin**   18 Tabwasher for ballpin**   19 Retaining nut for ballpin**   20 Dust cover for retaining nut**   21 Tabwasher for reaction pad**   22 Reaction pad**   23 Front shock absorber, righthand   24 Bump rubber for shock absorber   25 Rebound rubber   26 Steering lever, righthand   27 Key for lever   28 Lower link for swivel pin, righthand   29 Fulcrum pin for link   30 Rubber seal for link   31 Bush for link   32 Thrust washer for link   33 Sealing ring   34 Grease nipple for lower link   35 Lower arm, rear   36 Lower arm, front   37 Eyebolt   38 Bush for eyebolt   39 Reinforcement plate   40 Bush for plate   41 Serrated bolt   42 Torsion bar   43 Lever for torsion bar   44 Adjusting screw and locknut   45 Thrust pad and adjusting screw   46 Circlip for torsion bar   47 Tie rod   48 Fork for tie rod   49 Pad for tie rod   50 Plain washer   51 Nut   52 Retaining clip for tie rod   53 Brake backplate   54 Wheel hub   55 Oil seal for hub   56 Inner bearing   57 Outer bearing   58 Splined washer   59 Nut for stub axle   60 Retainer for nut   61 Wheel stud   62 Brake cylinder, righthand   63 Spring   64 Piston assembly   65 Cover for cylinder   66 Bleed screw for cylinder   67 Cap for bleed screw   68 Brake cylinder, lefthand   69 Sealing ring for cylinder   70 Brake shoe assembly   71 Spring for brake shoe   72 Steady pin for brake shoe   73 Spring for steady pin   74 Bridge pipe   75 Brake drum   76 Grease retaining cap   77 Screw for brake drum   78 Wheel nut   79 Front brake disc, righthand   80 Bolt for brake disc to hub   81 Mud shield for disc   82 Brake caliper, righthand   83 Bleed screw for caliper   84 Brake pads   85 Anti-squeal shims   86 Retaining pin for pads   87 Clip for retaining pin   88 Adaptor for brake caliper

* Model Series 9   ** Model Series 'K'

102

2 At intervals of 12,000 miles (20,000 kilometres), the front hub assemblies should be removed, cleaned, checked and refitted after packing with fresh grease. **Removing the grease cap and packing extra grease around the outside bearing is not sufficient as dirt can be forced into the bearing and the inner bearing may be running dry.**

9:3 Front hubs

A sectioned view of a hub assembly is shown in **FIG 9:3**. The upper part of the sectioned view shows the hub fitted with drum brakes while the lower part shows the hub fitted with disc brakes. The grease cap type B is fitted to TC models.

Removal:

1 Jack up the front of the car and place it securely onto stands, after slackening the road wheel nuts slightly. Remove the road wheel.
2 On models fitted with drum brakes, take out the two countersunk securing screws 3 and withdraw the brake drum, slackening off the brake adjusters if necessary to free the drum.
3 On models fitted with disc brakes, disconnect the caliper pipe first from the flexible hose and then from the caliper, using a container to catch the fluid as it drains and plugging the flexible hose to prevent further leakage of fluid. Take out the two bolts that secure the caliper to the suspension and slide the caliper off the brake disc.
4 Carefully prise off the grease cap 4. Remove the splitpin that secures the nut retainer. Unscrew and remove both the nut retainer and the nut and then slide off the serrated washer. The parts are shown as 5 in **FIG 9:3** and 52, 53 and 54 in **FIG 9:1**.
5 Pull the hub 6 off the stub axle, collecting the inner race of the outer bearing 7 as it comes free. Remove the oil seal 8 so that the inner race of the inner bearing can be withdrawn. The outer races of the bearings 9 can be drifted out of the hub if required, but if the bearings are satisfactory then they should be left in place.

Cleaning and examination:

Wipe out most of the old grease from the hub and bearings using newspaper or rags. The remainder of the grease can be washed out using petrol or paraffin. Wash the bearing races separately in clean fuel so that they do not pick up any dirt.

Check the circumference of the stub axle, onto which the oil seal acts, for scoring or damage.

Examine the outer races of the bearings, while still fitted to the hub, for any signs of wear, pitting or cracking. Similarly check the inner races. If any defects are found, both bearings must be renewed. **Note that bearings must be renewed completely as the inner and outer races are matched on manufacture.** Lubricate the inner races with light oil and check them in the outer races. Apply firm hand pressure and oscillate the race in its outer race to check for any roughness. If roughness is felt, try cleaning the bearings again and if it is still present after a thorough clean the bearing is defective and must be renewed.

FIG 9:2 The lubrication points on a front suspension

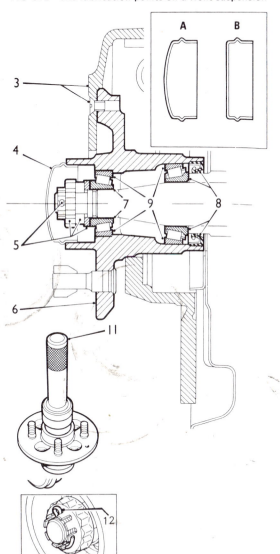

FIG 9:3 Sectioned view of the hub assembly. The upper portion shows the version fitted with drum brakes and the lower portion the version with disc brakes. Note also the splitpin legs turned circumferentially around the nut retainer

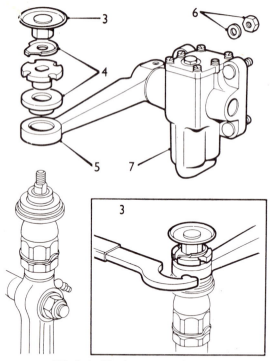

FIG 9:4   The damper attachments

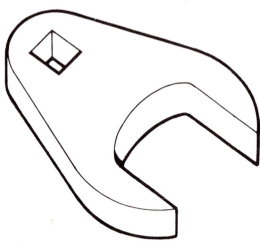

FIG 9:5   The swivel pin ball socket special spanner

Reassembly:

1 If the outer races 9 have been removed, drift the new ones back into place, preferably using the special tools 18G.134 and 18G.134.DM as shown in inset 12. If the special tools are not available, the races can be driven back using any suitable drift but take care to drive them in evenly and squarely.

2 Pack the inner race of the inner bearing liberally with high-melting point grease and fit it back into the hub.

Soak the new oil seal in engine oil and refit it back to the hub, lips facing into the hub, so that it keeps the inner bearing in place.

3 Slide the hub back into place on the stub axle. Pack inner race of the outer bearing with grease and slide it back into position on the stub axle. Refit the serrated washer and the stub axle nut followed by the nut retainer. Set the correct end float of .001 to .005 inch (.025 to .127 mm) and lock the nut retainer using a new splitpin. **The splitpin must be locked around the retainer circumferentially,** as shown in inset 12. Refit the grease cap 4, without filling it with grease.

Adjustment:

The most accurate method is to use a DTI (Dial Test Indicator) mounted on the hub, with its stylus resting vertically on the end of the stub axle, and check the end float by pulling and pushing firmly on the hub. The average owner may not have a DTI and the following method will set the end float within limits (.001 to .005 inch).

With the hub fitted in place and secured with the washer 52 and nut 53, spin the hub and gradually tighten the nut to a torque load of 5 lb ft (.69 kg m) or until slight drag is felt on the hub as it rotates. This ensures that the bearings are pressed fully back into position and all clearances taken up. Stop spinning the hub and slacken back the nut until it is just free. Tighten the nut finger tight.

Locate the nut retainer 54 so that the lefthand half of the splitpin hole in the stub axle is covered by one of the arms of the retainer. Slacken back the nut and retainer together until a new splitpin can be fitted to lock the retainer, and the adjustment is then correct.

It should be noted that if the top of the tyre is rocked in and out when the bearing is at its maximum end float a considerable amount of movement will be felt on the wheel. **Do not reduce the hub end float below .001 inch (.025 mm) to ensure that the bearings are not preloaded.**

Once the adjustment has been correctly set, refit the brake parts in the reverse order of removal. On drum brakes it will most likely be necessary to readjust the brake. On disc brakes, the hydraulic system must be filled and bled, and the brake pedal pumped several times to allow the self-adjusting of the brake to take place. Full instructions for dealing with the brakes are given in **Chapter 11.**

9:4 The dampers

The damper attachments are shown in **FIG 9:4.**

Before renewing a damper because it is suspect, check the fluid level in it. The filler plug is fitted to the top cover-plate and should only be removed after the area has been thoroughly cleaned, taking care that dirt is not knocked down from the wheel arch into the damper when the plug is out. Access to the plug is easiest with the road wheel removed. If the level is low, top up using the recommended Armstrong damper fluid to the bottom of the filler plug hole. **Do not overfill as a small air space is essential for correct operation.**

The damper can be checked by bouncing the suspension and seeing that the oscillations are rapidly damped out. When the arm has been disconnected from the upper ball joint, pump the arm up and down to check the resistance. If the movement is erratic, check the fluid level again as air may be trapped in the fluid and only come to the top after filling and operation. If the movement is still erratic, or resistance excessive, the damper is internally defective and must be renewed. **The damper cannot be dismantled or serviced, nor must the arm be removed from the damper.**

Removal:

1 Slacken the road wheel nuts, jack up the car then place it onto stands. Remove the road wheel and support the suspension from underneath on a small jack.
2 Free the tabwasher and unscrew the reaction pad nut 3 while holding the upper bush housing with the spanner 18G.1202, as shown in the inset.
3 Remove the lockwasher, upper bush housing and upper bush 4. Support the swivel pin to prevent the hub assembly from falling down, and lift the arm of the damper of the upper ball joint. If the parts are to be left, tie the swivel pin up with a piece of cord to prevent it from leaning over and straining the brake flexible hose.
4 Take off the nuts and washers 6 that secure the damper 7 and remove the damper from the car.

The parts are refitted in the reverse order of removal. Check the upper and lower bushes and renew them if they are damaged. Use a new reaction pad lockwasher. Tighten the reaction pad nut 3 to a torque of 35 to 40 lb ft (4.8 to 5.5 kg m), and the attachment nuts 6 to 26 to 28 lb ft (3.5 to 3.8 kg m).

9:5 The upper ball joint

The components which make up the upper ball joint assembly are shown in **FIG 9:1** as items 3 to 11.

Dismantling:

1 Disconnect the damper arm from the ball joint as described in the previous section. Lift off the lower bush 11 and its housing 12. Remove the dust cover 9 and its retaining clip 10.
2 Unlock the tabwasher 4 and unscrew the retaining nut 8 while holding the locknut 3. A special open ended spanner 18G 1192, shown in **FIG 9:5**, is designed for holding the locknut while unscrewing the retaining nut.
3 Remove the ballpin 5, seat 6 and spring 7. Unscrew the locknut 8 from the top of the swivel pin.

Reassembly:

Wash the parts and examine them, paying particular attention to the ballpin and its seat. Renew any worn or damaged parts, but note that new tabwashers 4 and 15 should always be obtained. Renew the dust cover 9 if it shows signs of cracking or perishing.

1 Screw the locknut on to the swivel pin and refit the tabwasher 4, spring 7, seat 6 and ballpin 5, screwing the retaining nut 8 down onto the swivel pin after applying some Duckham's Q5648 or similar grease to the ballpin. Ease back the locknut fully.
2 Tighten the retaining nut until the torque required to produce articulation of the ballpin is 32 to 52 lb inch (.38 to .56 kg m). Hold the retaining nut and tighten the locknut to 70 to 80 lb ft (9.6 to 11 kg m) using tool 18G 1192. Recheck the ballpin articulation torque.

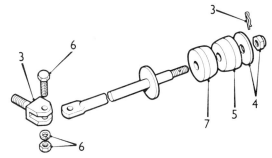

FIG 9:6   The tie rod attachments

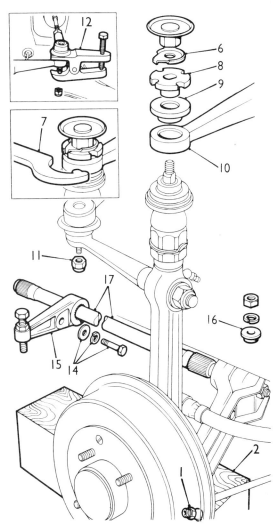

FIG 9:7   Removing the torsion bar

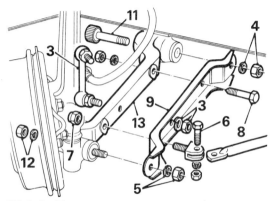

FIG 9:8 Dismantling the lower suspension arm assembly. Note that the anti-roll bar link 3 is not fitted to early model cars

3 Lock the retainer and the locknut with the tabwasher and complete the operation in the reverse order of dismantling.

9:6 The tie rod

The attachments are shown in **FIG 9:6**. Remove the spring clip 3, after jacking up the car and removing the road wheel, and undo the nut 4 so that it and its washer can be removed as well as the outer pad 5. Remove the nut, bolt and washer 6 to disconnect the tie rod from the suspension and remove the tie rod assembly. If necessary, remove the nut from behind the rear lower arm and take off the fork 8 from the suspension arms.

Check the inner and outer pads 7 and 5, renewing them if they are defective or damaged. Refit the tie rod in the reverse order of removal.

9:7 The torsion bars

The method of removing the torsion bar is shown in **FIG 9:7**.

Removal:

1 Remove the grease nipple 1 and place a block of wood 2 which is 8 inch (200mm) in height under the suspension as shown. Jack up the car and remove the road wheel then lower the car until the suspension is resting on the block of wood. On Series 2 models unscrew the two retaining nuts and remove the anti-roll bar link.

2 Disconnect the damper arm 10 from the upper ball joint, by removing the parts 6, 8 and 9 as described in **Section 9:4**. Support the suspension assembly to prevent it from tilting over. On Series 2 models pull the damper arm from the swivel pin ball joint

3 Remove the nut 11 from the steering ball joint. Use the tool 18G.1063 to disconnect the ballpin from the steering lever 12 on the suspension.

4 Raise the front of the car slightly on jacks to relieve the load on the torsion bar, but make sure that the suspension is still resting on the block of wood. Remove the bolt and washers 14 that secure the reaction lever 15. Slide the reaction lever 15 forwards along the torsion bar to free it from the chassis bracket.

5 Slacken the nut 16 that secures the eye bolt for the pivot of the lower suspension arms sufficiently to allow the suspension to drop by $\frac{1}{2}$ inch (12mm). Move the torsion bar 17 forwards sufficiently for its end to clear the lip on the chassis. Lower the rear end of the torsion bar and withdraw it rearwards from the suspension. Remove the circlip at the rear end of the torsion bar and slide off the reaction lever 15.

New torsion bars can be fitted to either side as there is no difference between them. **Once a torsion bar has been used it will acquire a slight set and must therefore always be refitted to the side from which it was removed.**

Refit the torsion bar in the reverse order of removal. Slacken the locknut and set the adjusting bolt on the reaction lever to its midway position. Make sure that all fittings are correctly torque loaded. Once the parts have been refitted, check the trim height and adjust it as required.

Checking trim height:

Stand the car on level ground, with two gallons of fuel in the tank. The cooling system must be full and the oil to the correct level in the engine and gearbox.

Measure vertically from the underside of the wheel arch to the centre of the hub, making sure that the measuring device is aligned vertically with the hub centre. The normal trim height is $15 \pm \frac{1}{4}$ inch (381 ± 6.35 mm) on early cars or $14.63 \pm \frac{1}{4}$ inch (371.6 ± 6.35 mm) on Series K. If it is outside these limits proceed as follows:

Fine trim adjustment:

Remove the adjusting lever lockbolt (on early models only) together with the spacer and spring washer 14.

Slacken the locknut (when fitted) and turn the adjusting bolt on the lever as necessary, clockwise to increase the trim height or anticlockwise to decrease it. Note that turning the adjusting bolt fully clockwise from the midway position gives approximately $\frac{3}{4}$ inch (19 mm) increase in the trim height, but fully anticlockwise movement from halfway gives $1\frac{1}{4}$ inch (32 mm) decrease in trim height. When correct, tighten the locknut or refit the lockbolt.

Coarse trim adjustment:

If the fine adjustment just described is not sufficient, the position of the lever on the splines of the torsion bar must be altered.

Securely chock the rear wheels and raise the front of the car on supports placed under the front chassis member. Remove the road wheel.

On late models remove the two nuts and remove the anti-roll bar link.

Unlock the reaction pad nut and remove the nut.

On early models hold the upper bush housing as shown at 7 in **FIG 9:7**. Remove the lockwasher 6, upper bush housing 8 and bush 9. On late models, remove the damper arm from the swivel pin ball joint using tool 18G 1063 if available.

On early models raise the damper arm and remove the lower bush and housing.

Unscrew the nut 11 and disconnect the ballpin from the steering lever. Lift up the damper arm and support the suspension on a wooden block, being careful not to strain the flexible brake hose.

Make alignment marks on the torsion bar lever, not the torsion bar itself, and the car body, then unscrew the lockbolt, spring and spacing washer and move the lever forward from the bar splines and reposition it one spline up or down as required. Make sure that the adjusting screw is correctly fitted to the lever.

Complete the operation in the reverse order of dismantling and then check the trim height and carry out any fine adjustment as necessary.

9:8 The lower suspension arm assembly

The components are shown in **FIG 9:8** and this figure is the one that should be referred to in this section. The parts are also shown in **FIG 9:1** and reference need only be made to it if specifically stated.

Removal:

1 Jack-up the car under the suspension unit and support it on stands. Remove the road wheel.
2 If applicable, remove the two securing bolts and nuts 3 and remove the anti-roll bar link 3.
3 Remove the nut and spring washer 4 from the eyebolt pin 11, noting that the pin is splined into position and its head concealed by the torsion bar.
4 Remove the front nut and spring washer 5 from the swivel lower link pin. Remove the nut and bolt 6 securing the tie rod to the fork. Remove the nut 7 and remove the tie rod fork.
5 Remove the nut and bolt 8 which clamps the front and rear lower arms, then remove the front lower arm 9.
6 Remove the torsion bar and the eyebolt pin 11.
7 Remove the rear nut and washer 12 from the swivel lower link pin and remove the rear lower suspension arm.

The parts are refitted in the reverse order of removal, noting that the tightening torque for the fork nut and the tie rod to fork nut are 48 to 55 lb ft (6.6 to 7.6 kg m) and 22 lb ft (3 kg m) respectively.

Take care not to strain the brake flexible hose by pulling the swivel pin too far outwards. Check and adjust the trim height of the suspension (see previous section).

Eye bolt assembly:

The parts are shown in **FIG 9:1**. If the bush 38 is worn, press it out of the eye bolt 37. Press a new bush back into place, lubricating it with water, soft soap or soap solution.

The reinforcement plate 39 need not be fitted with the later type of eye bolt, which has a 2.5 inch (63 mm) elliptical diameter.

9:9 Lower swivel pin link

The removal of the parts on cars fitted with drum brakes is shown in **FIG 9:9**. On cars fitted with disc brakes, the method is very similar, except that the caliper 82 and dust shield 81 must be removed in place of the drum brake parts (as shown in **FIG 9:1**) and the brake disc 79 is removed with the hub.

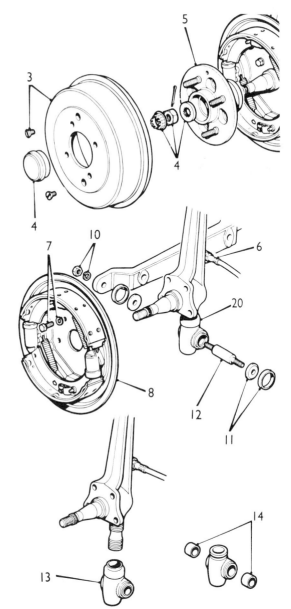

FIG 9:9   The lower swivel pin link

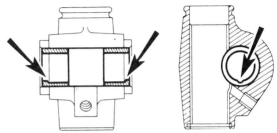

FIG 9:10   The correct positioning of the bushes in the lower link

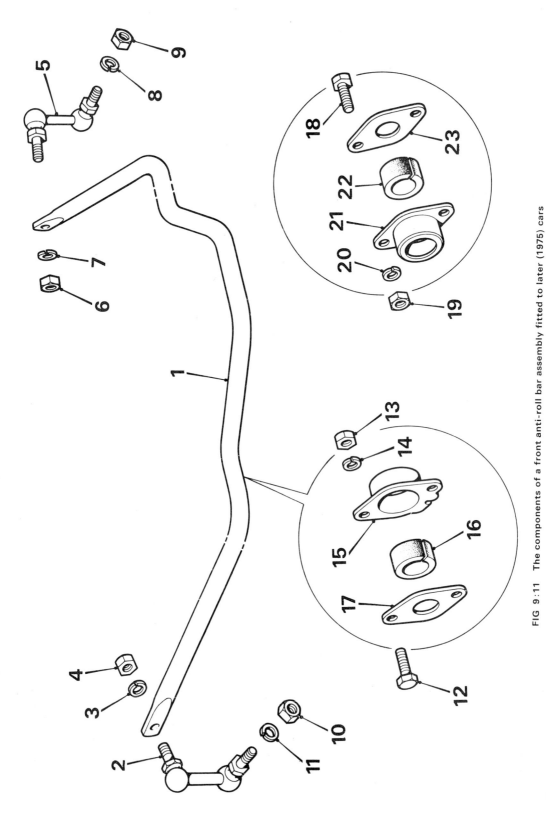

FIG 9:11 The components of a front anti-roll bar assembly fitted to later (1975) cars

Key to Fig 9:11   1 Anti-roll bar   2 Link, righthand   3 Spring washer   4 Nut   5 Link, lefthand   6 Nut   7 Spring washer   8 Spring washer   9 Nut   10 Nut
11 Spring washer   12 Bolt   13 Nut   14 Spring washer   15 Bearing carrier   16 Bearing   17 Bearing retainer   18 Bolt   19 Nut   20 Spring washer   21 Bearing carrier
22 Bearing   23 Bearing retainer

108

Dismantling:

1 Jack up the car and place it onto secure stands. Remove the road wheel. Take out the two screws 3 and withdraw the brake drum. On models fitted with disc brakes, remove the brake caliper. Extract the splitpin, remove the retainer nut and washer 4 so that the hub assembly 5 can be withdrawn (see **Section 9:3**).

2 Disconnect the flexible brake hose at 6, **holding the hose with a spanner while undoing the union nut and locknut that secures the hose to the bracket.** Take out the four bolts 7 and remove the brake backplate assembly (dust shield on disc brake models) and remove the backplate assembly 8.

3 Remove the front lower suspension arm as described in operations 2 and 3 of the previous section. Remove the remaining nut and washer 10 so that the swivel pin can be swung clear of the rear lower suspension arm.

4 Remove the seals and thrust washers 11 and withdraw the lower link pin 12. Unscrew the lower link 13 from the swivel arm, and remove the dust cover 20. If the bushes 14 are worn, they should be drifted out.

Examination:

Discard all the old seals and dust covers, fitting new ones on reassembly. Thoroughly clean the threads on the swivel pin and lower link so that they can be checked for wear. If the threads are worn then both the lower link and swivel pin must be renewed (disconnect the damper arm from the upper ball joint to remove the swivel pin assembly).

Examine the thrust washers and renew them if they are worn.

If the bushes 14 are worn, drift them out and press in new bushes, making sure that the grooves are aligned as shown in **FIG 9:10**. Once the new bushes have been fitted they must be line-reamed to .688 ± .0005 inch (17.48 ± .013 mm).

Check the pin 12 for wear or scoring and renew it if it is defective.

Reassembly:

The parts are reassembled in the reverse order of dismantling, after packing the area between the lower link bushes and the swivel pin threads with 2.5 cc of Q 5648 grease. Screw the lower link 13 fully back into place on the swivel pin then unscrew it one complete turn and fit the parts to it in this position.

Bleed and adjust the brakes after refitting the hub and setting it to its correct end float.

9:10 The anti-roll bar

This component, designed to reduce the amount of body roll when cornering, was introduced with the Marina 2 Series K, models. The anti-roll bar and its mountings are shown in **FIG 9:11**.

Removal:

1 Remove the two nuts 4 and 6, washers 3 and 7 and release the anti-roll bar from the links 2 and 5.

2 Note the fitted position of the two mounting assemblies (shown inset) and remove the four securing bolts and nuts.

3 Lift away the anti-roll bar, noting the L mark at the lefthand end. If necessary, the bushes can be slid off the bar and the links removed from the lower suspension arm.

Refitting is carried out in the reverse order, using a little rubber grease when threading on the rubber bushes.

9:11 Fault diagnosis

(a) Wheel wobble

1 Worn hub bearings
2 Weak front torsion bars
3 Uneven tyre wear
4 Worn suspension linkage
5 Loose wheel attachments

(b) Bottoming of suspension

1 Check 2 in (a)
2 Rebound rubbers worn or missing
3 Dampers defective

(c) Heavy steering

1 Neglected swivel pin lubrication
2 Incorrect suspension geometry

(d) Excessive tyre wear

1 Check 4 in (a); 3 in (b) and 2 in (c)

(e) Rattles

1 Neglected lubrication
2 Damper mountings loose
3 Worn bushes

NOTES

CHAPTER 10

THE STEERING SYSTEM

10:1 Description

There have been some slight modifications in the steering system since the introduction of the Marina in 1971 as may be seen from the composite exploded diagram in **FIG 10:1**.

The essential details of the system are not affected. A simple rack and pinion gear is employed, giving the most direct linkage between steering wheel and road wheels and the minimum of moving parts.

The steering wheel 1 is splined to the upper inner column 12 and the column 12 is in turn connected to the lower column 30 by a flexible coupling 29. A flexible joint connects the lower column to the pinion of the steering unit. Rotation of the steering wheel will then act to rotate the pinion by the same amount. The teeth of the pinion mesh with those of the rack so that rotation of the pinion drives the rack from side to side in the housing. Tie rods and ball joints connect the ends of the rack directly to the steering arms on the suspension swivel pins.

Shims are fitted so that wear in the parts can be taken up by adjustment of the pack.

10:2 Maintenance

There are no lubrication points in the system as the parts are lubricated on manufacture. The tie rod ends are sealed after manufacture and require no greasing.

When carrying out the 6000 mile service, the system should be checked through for excessive play or worn gaiters and security of parts. Any gaiters that are damaged must be renewed before they actually split and allow dirt to enter. If dirt has entered a tie rod end there is no method of flushing out the dirt and the only cure is to fit a new tie rod end. If the gaiter is renewed before it has actually split, pack a little extra grease into the tie rod end before fitting a new gaiter.

10:3 The steering wheel and steering column lock

The steering wheel and its attachments are shown in **FIG 10:1**. The lock is also shown in **FIG 10:1** but a better view of the parts is shown in **FIG 10:2**.

Steering wheel:

Before this can be removed from later cars, it is necessary first to remove the two halves of the cowl which, in turn, requires the disconnection of the carburetter mixture control. This is detached from the carburetter lever and pulled through the body grommet. The cowl halves are secured by cross-head screws.

Remove the safety pad by carefully prising it out from the wheel and then unscrew, but do not yet remove the centre nut 4. Use a suitable puller, according to type, to pull the steering wheel from the steering column after

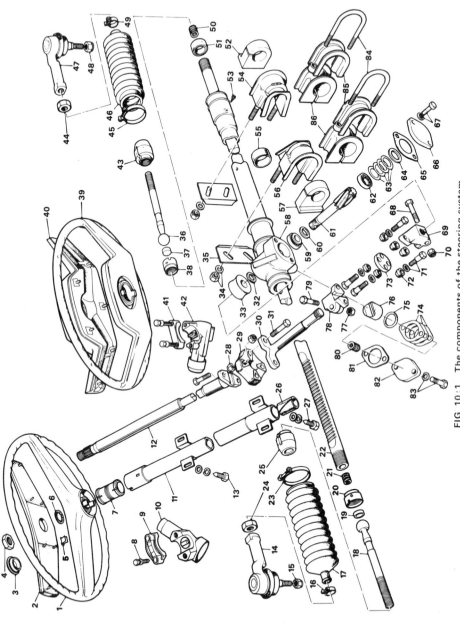

FIG 10:1   The components of the steering system

Key to Fig 10:1   1 Steering wheel*   2 Safety pad*   3 Motif*   4 Nut   5 Clip, safety pad to wheel   6 Shakeproof washer   7 Bush, upper   8 Shear bolt, steering lock   9 Clamp plate*   10 Steering lock*   11 Column outer, upper   12 Column inner, upper   13 Screw, spring and plain washer   14 Tie rod end   15 Nut, self-locking   16 Clip, small   17 Rack seal   18 Tie rod   19 Ball seat   20 Locknut, tie rod end   21 Thrust spring   22 Rack   23 Clip, large   24 Locknut   25 Ballhousing   26 Lower bush   27 Bolt, plain and spring washer   28 Nut   29 Flexible coupling   30 Column, lower   31 Bolt   32 Pinion oil seal   33 Sealing washer   34 Nut and plain washer   35 Locating plate   36 Tie rod   37 Ball seat   38 Locknut   39 Steering wheel**   40 Safety pad**   41 Clamp plate**   42 Steering lock**   43 Ballhousing   44 Locknut, tie rod end   45 Clip, large   46 Rack seal   47 Tie rod end   48 Nut, self-locking   49 Clip, small   50 Thrust spring   51 Rack bearing   52 Rack mounting rubber*   53 Screw rack bearing   54 Rack clamp*   55 Sealing rubber   56 Rack clamp*   57 Rack mounting rubber, model*   58 Pinion housing   59 Pinion bearing   60 Washer   61 Pinion   62 Pinion bearing   63 Shim   64 Shim, 0.60 inch (1.524 mm)   65 Shim gasket, 0.010 inch (0.254 mm)   66 End cover   67 Bolt and spring washer   68 Bolt   69 Flexible joint, half   70 Nut   71 Shouldered bolt   72 Rubber bush   73 Joint plate   74 Shim   75 'O' ring   76 Support yoke   77 Nut   78 Flexible joint, half   79 Bolt   80 Thrust spring   81 Joint gasket   82 Rubber bush   83 Bolt and spring washer   84 Rack U-bolts**   85 Rack clamps**   86 Rack mounting rubbers**   * Model series 9   ** Model series K

112

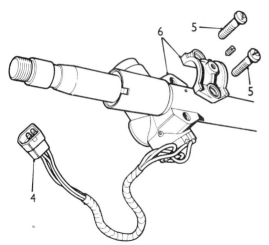

FIG 10:2 The steering lock attachments

first marking it to ensure correct replacement. Do not try to remove the steering wheel by hitting it with a hammer. On Series K cars the correct tool is 18G 2 and 2H; if this is used, the flat side of the adaptor should be towards the steering wheel.

Refit the steering wheel in the reverse order of removal. Ensure first that the nylon switch centre is correctly positioned before refitting the steering wheel. Make sure that the previously made marks align or, if a new steering wheel is being fitted, set the front wheels in the straight-ahead position and refit the steering wheel so that the spokes are level. Tighten the steering wheel nut 4 to a torque of 32 to 37 lb ft (4.4 to 5.1 kg m). When refitting the safety pad 2, locate it by the outer pins first as this will ensure that the pad has an even gap on both sides.

Steering column lock:

The lock is secured to the column by shear bolts on all models but there are two different procedures for gaining access to the lock after removing the steering wheel as described above.

On early model cars, remove the column cowl, the lower facia and the instrument panel.

On all models disconnect the electrical harness connectors for the ignition and multi-purpose switches.

On late cars, remove the four screws securing the outer steering column to the bulkhead and withdraw the outer column through the facia panel. Remove the felt bush from the inner column.

Drill out, or use an extractor to remove, the shear-head bolts and remove the clamping plate and lock/switch assembly.

The switch is refitted in the reverse order of removal, using new shear-head screws 5. Refit the switch, tightening the shear-head screws 5 just sufficiently to hold the switch in place, and locating it using the grub screw of the clamp plate seating into the recess in the column. Check the full operation of the switch. When satisfied that the switch is operating satisfactorily, tighten the shear screws 5 until their heads break off at the waisted portion.

Refit the lower facia, instrument panel and steering wheel in the reverse order of removal.

10:4 Upper steering column

The attachments of the upper steering column are shown in FIG 10:3.

Removal:

1 Remove the steering wheel (see previous section) as well as the lower facia panel and instrument panel on Saloon and Estate cars (Model Series 9). Slacken the screw that retains the combined switches, see insert 4, disconnect their leads from the harness at the connector and remove the switches. Disconnect the harness for the steering column lock switch at its connector.

2 Remove the two sets of nuts and washers 6 that secure the inner upper column to the flexible coupling.

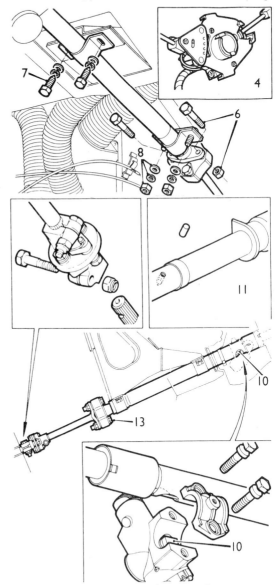

FIG 10:3 The upper column attachments

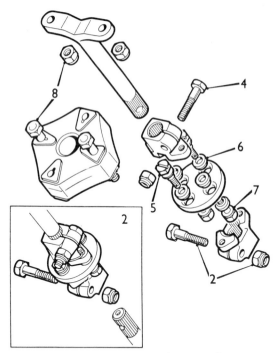

FIG 10:4 The steering column couplings

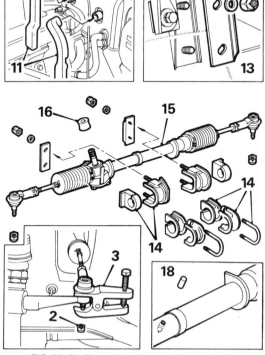

FIG 10:5 Removing the steering rack unit

Remove the two sets of bolts and washers 7 that secure the upper clamp of the outer column. Support the column and take off the two sets of nuts (bolts on later cars) and washers 8 that secure the lower clamp. The upper steering column assembly can then be removed from the car.

Refitting:

The parts are refitted in the reverse order of removal. Engage the steering column lock 10 to lock the column. Centralize the steering rack as shown in inset 11 and reconnect the parts. Tighten the coupling bolts 6 to a torque load of 20 to 22 lb ft (2.77 to 3.04 kg m). The nuts 8 and bolts 7 are tightened to 14 to 18 lb ft (1.94 to 2.49 kg m).

If the lower bush (item 26 in **FIG 10:1**) is worn or damaged, it can be renewed when the upper column assembly has been removed from the car.

Upper bush:

This can be renewed without having to remove the upper column assembly. Disconnect the battery, remove the steering wheel (see previous section), slacken the screw which secures the combined switch assembly and slide the switch assembly off, over the top of the inner column.

A special extractor 18G.1191 is made for extracting the old bush (item 7 in **FIG 10:1**) and the same tool with an adaptor is made for refitting the new bush.

If care is taken the old bush can be hooked out and the new one pressed back into place with a suitable piece of pipe as a sleeve. If hand pressure is not sufficient, use a large washer and nut to draw the bush back in. When refitting the new bush, make sure that the chamfered end enters first and that the slots in the bush align with the depression in the outer column.

10:5 Steering column couplings

The parts are shown in **FIG 10:4**.

Remove the upper steering column assembly, as described in the previous section. Remove the pinch bolt and nut 2 that secure the lower coupling to the pinion shaft on the steering rack unit. The lower steering column assembly complete can now be removed from the car.

Remove the pinch bolt and nut 4, and pull the flexible joint assembly complete free from the lower column splines. The flexible coupling can be freed from the column by taking out the bolts 8.

Unlock and remove the four shouldered bolts 5 from the flexible joint. Remove the rubber washers 6, noting how their conical faces mate with the countersunk face of the joint plate. Collect the plain washers 7 from the bolts.

The parts are reassembled and refitted in the reverse order of removal, after cleaning and renewing worn parts. If a new flexible coupling (item 29 in **FIG 10:1**) is fitted, leave the band on the coupling until the coupling has been bolted back into place. Once the coupling is in place, break the compressing band and discard it.

When aligning the parts, lock the steering column with its lock and centralize the rack unit, as described in the previous section. Leave the steering rack unit centralized when refitting the steering wheel, so that the spokes are horizontal in the straight-ahead position. **Remove the centralizing pin before attempting to drive the car or check the action of the steering column lock.**

10:6 Removing the steering rack unit

For the various stages in this operation refer to **FIG 10:5**.

First raise the front end of the car and support it firmly on stands placed under the front chassis members. Remove the securing nuts and disconnect the tie rod ballpin ends from the steering levers using an extractor such as 18G 1063. Do not use a hammer on the threaded pin even with a slave nut (see items 2 and 3).

On early model cars, remove the lower facia, instrument panel and parcel tray and disconnect the electrical leads to the column mounted switches at the connectors.

Remove the pinch-bolt securing the flexible joint to the rack pinion.

On early model cars, remove the four screws securing the steering column to the support brackets and lift out the steering column assembly. Remove the two drain tubes 11 from the heater.

On Marina 2, slacken the intermediate shaft pinch-bolt and slide the joint upwards.

Remove the two nuts 13 retaining each rack clamp bracket to the bulkhead, on early cars noting the position of the packing strip relative to the body panel.

Remove the steering rack U-bolts brackets and rubbers according to model as shown at 14. The steering rack 15 can now be withdrawn through the wheel-arch opening. Remove the pinion seal 16.

Refitting:

Engage the steering lock and centralise the rack by moving the sealing rubber and inserting a $\frac{1}{4}$ inch (6.35 mm) diameter rod 18 in the hole in the rack and casing.

Continue by reversing the order of removal, noting the following torque values:

Rack clamp nuts   20 to 22 lb ft (2.77 to 3.04 kg m)
Tie rod ballpin nuts   20 to 24 lb ft (2.77 to 3.3 kg m)
Flexible joint pinch-bolt 17 to 20 lb ft (2.35 to 2.77 kg m)

Do not forget to remove the $\frac{1}{4}$ inch rod from the rack casing and check and adjust the front wheel alignment as described in **Section 10:8**.

10:7 Servicing the steering rack unit

The components of the unit are shown in **FIG 10:1**. Remove the unit as described in the previous section.

Dismantling:

1 Slacken the locknuts 24 and 44. Unscrew the tie rod ends 14 and 47 from the tie rods 18 and 36 and then screw off the two locknuts 24 and 44. Free the clips 16, 23, 45 and 49 then slide the bellows 17 and 46 off from the rack housing and tie rods.

2 The locknuts 20 and 38 are staked down into the slots of the housings 25 and 43. Prise out the locking from the slot, noting that it will be necessary to fit new locknuts 20 and 38 on reassembly. Hold the locknut and unscrew the housing. Special spanners 18G.706 and 18G.707, shown in **FIG 10:6**, are made for holding the locknut and undoing the housing. Remove

the tie rods 18 and 36, collecting their ball seats 19 and 37 as well as the springs 21 and 50. Prise out the locking indents that secure the locknuts 20 and 38 to the rack 22 and unscrew the locknuts from the rack.

3 Take out the pan-headed screw 53 and remove the rack bearing 51 from the housing. Remove the two sets of bolts and washers 83 so that the cover 82, joint washer 81 and shim pack 74 can be removed from the housing. Withdraw the rack support yoke 76 and remove the spring 80 and O-ring 75 from it.

4 Remove the two sets of bolts 67 securing the pinion cover 66. Remove the pinion cover followed by the shim gasket 65, shim 64 and shim pack 63. Push out the pinion shaft 61 so that the pinion bearing 62 is removed with it. Take out the oil seal 32 and extract the pinion bearing 59 with its washer 60. Slide the rack 22 out of the housing.

Examination:

Thoroughly clean all the components by washing them in fuel. Examine the rack and pinion for cracks, wear or damage, paying particular attention to the teeth. Check the bellows for signs of splitting or cracking. Renew any components that are damaged or badly worn.

Reassembly:

1 Refit the bearing 51 to the housing and secure it with the screw 53. Coat the screw with sealing compound before refitting it and **make sure that it does not protrude through into the bore of the bearing.** If a new bearing is being fitted, position it so that its flats are offset to the retaining screw hole. Use a .119 inch (3.0 mm) drill through the retaining hole in the housing to drill through the new bearing, for the attachment screw. **Remove all swarf and burrs from the inside of the bearing.**

2 Refit the rack 22 into the housing. Fit the bearing 59 and washer 60 to the pinion 61 and slide the assembly back into the housing. The rack should be centralized by inserting a peg through the housing and rack (through the hole in the housing normally covered by the sealing rubber 55). Insert the pinion assembly so that when the teeth are meshed the locating groove **A** in the pinion is parallel to and on the same side as the rack teeth, as shown in **FIG 10:7**. Remove the peg from the locating hole.

3 Refit the bearing 62. Fit sufficient shims 63 and 64 to ensure that the shim pack stands proud of the end of the housing. Refit the coverplate 66, omitting the shim gasket 65, and tighten the bolts 67 by hand only. Use feeler gauges to measure the gap **B** between the cover and housing, shown in **FIG 10:7**. Remove the cover and bolts and adjust the shim pack thickness, by selective fitting of shims, until the gap **B** (still without the shim gasket 65 fitted) is correct at .011 to .013 inch (.279 to .330 m). When the shim pack has been correctly adjusted, remove the cover and refit it with the shim gasket 65 in place, making sure that the shim 64 is nearest to the end cover end. Dip the threads of the bolts 67 into sealing compound and use them, with their spring washers fitted, to secure the cover 66. Tighten the bolts 67 to a torque of 12 to 15 lb ft (1.6 to 2.0 kg m). Fit a new pinion seal 32 back into place. Remove the centralizing peg.

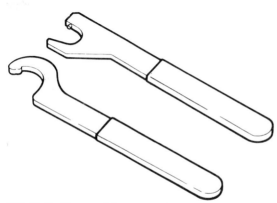

FIG 10:6 The special spanners for servicing the rack unit ball joints

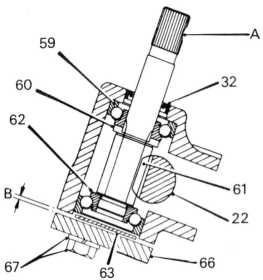

FIG 10:7 Section through the pinion of the rack unit

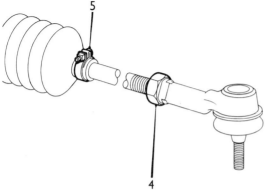

FIG 10:8 Adjusting the tie rods

4 Refit the rack support yoke 76, joint 81 and cover 82. Secure the parts in place with the bolts 83. Tighten the bolts 83 while turning the pinion backwards and forwards through an angle of 180 degrees until it is just possible to rotate the pinion using a force of 15 lb in (.17 kg m). The bearing preload gauge 18G.207 and the adaptor 18G.207A will make the checking of the torque accurate and fairly easy. Use feeler gauges to measure the clearance between the housing and the cover. Remove the cover and its attachment bolts. Refit the spring 80 and O-ring 75 to the yoke 76. Make up a shim pack 74 which is .002 to .005 inch (.05 to .13 mm) greater in thickness than the gap measured with feeler gauges. Refit the cover and secure it by tightening the bolts 83 to a torque of 12 to 15 lb ft (1.6 to 2.0 kg m), not forgetting to refit the lockwashers. Check the force required to start the pinion rotating. **The force required must not exceed 15 lb in (.17 kg m).**

5 Screw new locknuts 20 and 38 back onto the ends of the rack, right to the ends of the threads. Refit the springs 21 and 50. Slide the tie rods 18 and 36 back through the housings 25 and 43 and fit the seats 19 and 37 back into place. Screw the housings 25 and 43 back onto the rack 22 until the tie rod is pinched. Screw the locknuts 20 and 38 outwards until they contact the housings 25 and 43, **making sure that the tie rods are still pinched.** Hold the locknuts and slacken the housings outwards by $\frac{1}{8}$ turn each to allow the tie rod to articulate. Hold the housing firmly, so that it does not turn about the rack, and tighten the locknut up to it to a torque of 33 to 37 lb ft (4.6 to 5.6 kg m). The tie rod should now articulate smoothly and require a force of 32 to 52 lb in (.37 to .6 kg m) to make it move. Punch the edges of the locknuts into the slots in the rack and housings to lock the parts.

6 Refit the two bellows, but do not yet fit the small clip to the pinion end rack bellows. Inject $\frac{1}{3}$ pint (190 cc) of a recommended oil (Hypoid SAE 90) into the bellows and then fit the clip.

7 Fit the tie rod locknuts 24 and 44 and screw on each tie rod end 14 and 47 equally until the distance between ballpin centres is 43.7 inch (111.0 cm). Secure the tie rod ends with the locknuts.

10:8 Front wheel alignment

This should always be checked after the steering rack unit has been removed and refitted as well as when major work has been carried out on the front suspension. Incorrect front wheel alignment will show by excessive tyre wear, which leaves the edge of the tread worn to a characteristic feathered edge.

It is most advisable to take the car to an agent, who will check the alignment accurately using optical equipment or special gauges.

The front wheel alignment will be near the correct limits if both tie rod ends are set so that the length between ball centres on each tie rod is 43.7 inch

The adjustment point for each tie rod is shown in **FIG 10:8. Both tie rods must be adjusted by an equal amount,** to ensure that the steering wheel spokes are horizontal when the wheels are straight-ahead.

If the owner wishes to check the alignment then a level piece of ground must be found. Some form of trammel will also make the task easier. The trammel rests on the ground and has two pointers mounted on it, at wheel centre height, which are just slightly less far apart than the inner wheel rims on the front wheels. Instead of measuring the total dimension only the gap between one pointer and the wheel rim need be measured, while making sure that the other pointer is in contact with the other wheel rim.

Drive the car onto level ground and set the front wheels to the straight-ahead position. The rack can be locked using a suitable peg. Push the car forwards to settle the bearings. Measure, as accurately as possible, the distance between the inner wheel rims at the front of the wheel and at wheel centre height. Mark the positions with chalk and push the car forwards so that the wheels turn exactly half a revolution and the chalk marks are again at wheel centre height, but at the rear of the wheels. **Never push the car backwards while checking the track.** Again measure the distance between the wheel rims at the chalk marks. The difference between the two measurements represents the front wheel alignment.

The correct setting is $\frac{1}{16}$ inch (1.6mm) toe-in. If the setting is incorrect, slacken the locknuts 4 and the bellows clips 5. Screw the tie rods in or out of the tie rod ends so as to alter their effective length and the front wheel alignment. **Both tie rods have a righthand thread and they must both be of the same effective length between ball centres when the adjustments are complete.**

When the adjustment is correct, tighten the locknuts 4 to a torque of 35 to 40 lb ft (4.8 to 5.5 kg m) and tighten the clips for the bellows. Finally, make a recheck on the wheel alignment.

10:9 Fault diagnosis

(a) Wheel wobble

1 Unbalanced wheels and tyres
2 Slack steering connections
3 Incorrect steering geometry
4 Excessive play in the steering rack unit
5 Weak torsion bars on suspension
6 Worn or loose front hub bearings
7 Loose wheel attachments

(b) Wander

1 Check 2, 3 and 4 in (a)
2 Uneven tyre pressures
3 Uneven tyre wear
4 Weak dampers or rear springs
5 Body distorted so that front suspension not in line with rear axle

(c) Heavy steering

1 Check 3 in (a)
2 Very low tyre pressures
3 Neglected lubrication
4 Wheels out of alignment
5 Steering rack unit incorrectly adjusted
6 Steering column bent or misaligned
7 Steering column bushes tight
8 Steering flexible coupling or joint defective
9 Defective ball joints or tie rod ends

(d) Lost motion

1 Check 8 and 9 in (c)
2 Loose steering wheel or worn splines
3 Worn rack and pinion teeth
4 Worn suspension system or swivel pin swivels

NOTES

CHAPTER 11

THE BRAKING SYSTEM

11:1 Description

Drum brakes are fitted to the rear wheels of all versions. Either drum or disc brakes can be fitted to the front wheels, depending on version. All four wheel brakes are operated by hydraulic pressure from the master cylinder when the brake pedal is pressed. The hydraulic pressure generated in the master cylinder is led to the brakes by a system of metal and flexible pipes. It should be noted that the pressure to the rear brakes is fed to the axle by a single flexible hose on the righthand suspension. A short metal pipe connects this flexible hose to the bottom port of the righthand rear brake wheel cylinder. The upper port on the righthand wheel cylinder is connected to the bottom port of the lefthand side wheel cylinder by a metal pipe running along the rear axle casing and the top port of the lefthand side wheel cylinder is fitted with a bleed screw. **It is vital that the inlet pipe to a wheel cylinder is always connected to the bottom port otherwise it will be impossible to bleed out all the air from the system when air has entered.**

The handbrake lever operates the rear brakes only on all versions, using a system of cables to operate the brakes mechanically.

The disc brakes, if fitted, are of the standard fixed caliper type. Each half of the caliper contains a piston and under hydraulic pressure these two pistons move towards each other. As the pistons come together they clamp the' rotating disc, attached to the wheel hub, between friction pads to exert the retarding force on the disc and consequently on the wheel and tyre. Seals are fitted between the piston and bore and these seals deform slightly when the piston moves to apply the brake. As soon as the hydraulic pressure is released, the seals return to their original shape and draw back the pistons to give a running clearance between the pads and disc. If the pads wear, the piston can slide through the seal, allowing wear to be taken up.

The drum brakes are of the internally expanding type, in which the shoes and linings are pressed outwards to contact the rotating brake drum. On all the rear brakes only a single wheel cylinder is fitted. On the models fitted with front drum brakes, each brake has two wheel cylinders so that both shoes are 'leading' when the car is moving forwards. On a leading shoe, the leading edge of the shoe is pressed into contact with the drum by the action of the wheel cylinder and the self-wrapping action

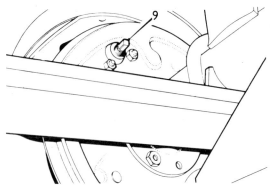

FIG 11:1 The adjustment point on the rear brake of a 1.3 model. 1.8 models are fitted with self-adjusting rear brakes.

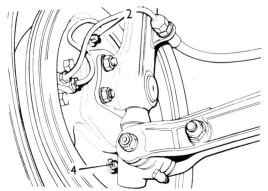

FIG 11:2 The adjustment points on a front drum brake

tends to pull the brake on further, thus giving assistance. Note that a leading shoe will trail when the car is driven in reverse and the servo action will not be present.

On the 1.3 Saloon and Coupé and the 1.8 Estate models the rear brakes are fitted with mechanical adjusters which have to be reset at regular intervals as the linings wear. On the 1.8 Saloon and Coupé models for the Swedish market self-adjusting brakes are fitted, which automatically adjust when the handbrake is operated.

A vacuum-assisted brake servo may be fitted. The unit fits between the brake pedal and master cylinder to add to the pressure on the master cylinder pushrod exerted by the brake pedal. For a given retardation the unit will reduce the pressure required at the brake pedal.

Metric brake fittings are used on these cars and it is essential that only metric replacements are fitted. Most fittings can be identified by being marked with the letter M or coloured BLACK.

11:2 Maintenance

Fluid level:

At regular intervals check the level of the fluid in the master cylinder reservoir. **Wipe the top clean before removing the filler cap. Ensure that the level never falls to the danger mark on the outside of the reservoir.** When disc brakes are fitted, the level in the reservoir will slowly drop as the pads wear. Any sudden drop or increase in the rate of dropping indicates a leak

in the system. **Check the system thoroughly and rectify any leaks found with the utmost urgency.**

On models fitted with disc brakes, use UNIPART 550 or a fluid that meets specification SAE.J.1703a. On models fitted with all drum brakes, use UNIPART 410 or a fluid that meets specification SAE.J.1703. **The use of the incorrect fluid in the system can be extremely dangerous as some fluids will attack the material of the seals in the system, causing them to fail.**

1.3 vehicles exported to France, Belgium or Luxembourg have an extension fitted to the reservoir. The fluid level must be maintained to the mark indicated on the extension.

On vehicles exported to some Scandinavian and European countries a dual circuit braking system is incorporated and the level of the fluid in the tandem master cylinder must be to the top of the division baffle.

Disc brakes:

These are self-adjusting. At intervals of 6000 miles (10,000 kilometres) they should be checked for pad wear and other defects. New pads must be fitted when the friction material on them has worn down to $\frac{1}{16}$ inch (1.6 mm).

Manually adjusted rear brakes:

A single adjuster, shown in **FIG 11:1**, is fitted to each brake. The brakes should be adjusted when the pedal travel becomes excessive. Chock the front wheels and jack up the rear of the car. Make sure that the handbrake is fully released and that its cables are not pulling on the levers of the brake assembly. If the adjuster is covered with dirt, brush away the dirt using a wire brush and if necessary apply a drop or two of penetrating oil to the threads. Turn the adjuster in a clockwise direction, viewed from the centre of the car, until the brake shoes are felt to be in firm contact with the drum and the wheel cannot be rotated. Slacken back the adjuster until the wheel just rotates freely without the brake rubbing. Adjust the other rear brake in a similar manner.

At intervals of 6000 miles, remove the brake drum so that dust and dirt can be brushed and blown out. Check the lining thickness and fit new shoes if the linings are worn down nearly to the rivet heads. Check the brake internally for damage or oil and grease leaks.

Automatically adjusted rear brakes:

These are automatically adjusted by application of the handbrake. On these models it is important that the brake drums are removed at intervals of 5000 miles so that the action of the automatic adjusters and lining wear can be checked. Clean out dust and dirt, check for leaks and renew the shoes if the linings are worn nearly down to the rivets. If the brakes are not checked regularly the linings can easily wear right down, as no routine adjustments are required which would normally serve as a reminder.

Front drum brakes:

Two adjusters are fitted to each brake as shown in **FIG 11:2**. Apply the handbrake firmly and jack up the front of the car. Brush away road dirt and lubricate with a drop of penetrating oil if required. Turn the adjuster 2 in a clockwise direction, viewed from the centre of the car, until the brake shoe is in firm contact with the drum and the wheel cannot be rotated. Slacken back the adjuster until the wheel just rotates freely without binding. Repeat the adjustment on the lower adjuster 4 of the brake. The other front brake is then adjusted in a similar manner.

The front brakes should have their drums removed and checked at the same servicing interval as the rear brakes, and the same conditions apply.

The handbrake:

This must only be adjusted after the rear brakes have been correctly adjusted. If handbrake retardation is poor, check through the system for defects before adjusting the cable. Make sure that the rear linings are not excessively worn, the cables and levers moving freely and that clevis pins on attachments are not excessively worn or sticking.

The adjustment point is shown in **FIG 11:3.** Its position on the linkage is shown in **FIG 11:20.** Fully release the handbrake lever and then pull it up four notches. If the effect is not satisfactory, slacken the locknut 3. Hold the cable with a spanner and turn the adjusting nut 4 clockwise until the rear wheels are firmly held from rotating. When the adjustment is correct, tighten the locknut 3. Release the handbrake fully and check that the rear wheels rotate freely without binding.

The handbrake cable is fitted with one of the six grease nipples on the later cars. Apply a grease gun to the nipple on the cable, after wiping it clean, and inject three or four strokes of grease. This should be done at intervals of 6000 miles (10,000 kilometres).

Brake servo:

If a brake servo is fitted, the filter on the unit should be renewed at intervals of 36,000 miles (60,000 kilometres) or 3 years. The method of renewing the filter is shown in **FIG 11:4.** From below the parcel shelf, pull back the dust cover 13. Pull off the filter retainer 14 and withdraw the old filter 15. Diagonally cut the new filter 15, as shown in the inset, fit it over the pushrod and press it into place. Refit the retainer 14 and dust cover 13.

Preventative maintenance:

Never use any fluid in the system except the type recommended. Fluid that has been drained or bled from the system is best discarded.

Absolute cleanliness is essential when working on any part of the hydraulic system.

When carrying out the 6000 mile service, check the brake pipes and flexible hoses for damage, leaks or corrosion. Have an assistant apply heavy pressure to the brake pedal, with all the parts assembled, and check through the system for leaks or weak spots. Corroded metal pipes or defective flexible hoses should be renewed as they will be a weak point that may fail under the stress of heavy braking. The brake pedal must not be pressed when the brake drums are off, or a disc brake caliper removed, otherwise the pressure will force out the pistons.

It is recommended that the fluid is drained out of the system at intervals of 18 months, and the system refilled and bled using fresh fluid. Brake fluid absorbs moisture from the air which lowers its boiling point, and it is for

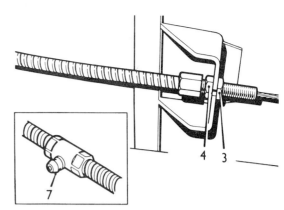

FIG 11:3   The adjustment and lubrication point on the handbrake cable

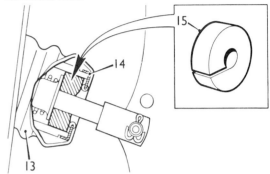

FIG 11:4   Renewing the air filter on a brake servo unit

this reason that the fluid should be renewed, otherwise it may boil in the brakes under the stress of heavy braking and cause brake fade.

It is also recommended that the system is flushed through with methylated spirits at intervals of 3 years and all the components dismantled and checked for wear, followed by reassembly using all new seals. Any components found to be worn or defective should be renewed.

11:3 Flexible hoses

When removing or refitting a flexible hose, the flexible portion must never be twisted or strained.

The attachment of a typical flexible hose is shown in **FIG 11:5.** The hose shown is a front suspension one but the attachments are similar on the rear hose. To disconnect the hose, hold it at its hexagons 3 with a spanner and undo the union nut 1 with another spanner, taking care not to twist the metal pipe.

Still holding the hose with a spanner, undo the locknut 2 and remove it complete with its lockwasher. The hose can then be withdrawn from its bracket. Refit the hose in the reverse order of removal, noting that the system must be filled and bled.

If a hose is blocked and cannot be cleared by blowing through it, it is defective. **Do not attempt to clear blocked hoses by poking wire through them.**

The average safe life of a flexible hose is 5 years. For this reason it is advisable to renew the flexible hoses after $4\frac{1}{2}$ years (when changing the hydraulic fluid).

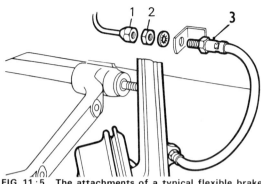

FIG 11:5 The attachments of a typical flexible brake hose

11:4 Renewing the friction pads

The method of renewing the friction pads on the disc brakes is shown in **FIG 11:6**.

1 Jack up the front of the car and remove the road wheel.
2 Remove the spring clips 3 and withdraw the pad retaining pins 4. The pads and anti-squeal shims 5 can then be withdrawn from the caliper. If the pads are difficult to withdraw, pass a length of wire or cord through the holes in the pad and use a wooden handle through the wire to give good purchase so that the pads can be pulled out. The pads must be renewed if the friction material has worn down to $\frac{1}{16}$ inch (1.6 mm). The pads are interchangeable from side to side of the caliper and if wear is uneven between the pads they may be interchanged, provided that there is sufficient lining material left to last until the next check.
3 Brush out all dust and grit from inside the caliper. If washing is required, only methylated spirits (denatured alcohol) or hydraulic fluid may be used. Any other solvent will attack the material of the seals.

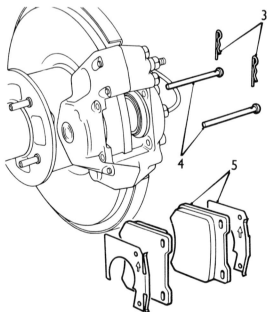

FIG 11:6 Renewing the disc brake friction pads

4 Press the pistons back into the cylinders, preferably using the special tool 18G.590. **The level of the fluid in the master cylinder will rise during this operation so syphon off any surplus to prevent it from overflowing. Hydraulic fluid will quickly remove paint, so avoid any spillage.** It may help to open the bleed screw on the caliper when pressing back the pistons, as surplus and old fluid will then be ejected, but it may then be necessary to bleed the brakes after the new pads have been fitted.
5 Refit the new pads and old anti-squeal shims in the reverse order of removal, making sure that the arrows on the anti-squeal shims are pointing upwards. Secure them with the retaining pins 4 and clips 5. Refit the road wheel and lower the car back to the ground.
6 Renew the pads on the other front brake in a similar manner. **Before driving the car, pump the brake pedal hard several times to take up the adjustment in the disc brakes.** Make sure that the same grade of pad is fitted on both sides to each brake. For models fitted with a servo use F2430 pads and for models without a servo use DON.227 pads.

11:5 Renewing drum brake linings

On all types of drum brake new or exchange shoes must be fitted if the linings are worn down nearly to the rivet heads or if the linings are contaminated with oil or grease.

If the linings are contaminated, do not waste time trying to wash or bake out the oil or grease. Some oil will always remain, unless the treatment is so drastic as to ruin the lining, and will creep out under the stress of heavy braking.

The owner should not attempt to reline the brake shoes himself as the result is never as satisfactory as a professional job at best, and at worst the brakes will be extremely dangerous and liable to fail. Exchange shoes, with new linings riveted and ground to shape, are obtainable and usually a deposit is asked for and returned when the old shoes are taken in.

Never renew just one shoe in a brake and it is always advisable to renew the shoes in complete axle sets. Do not intermix different grades of lining. The recommended lining material for all drum brakes, with or without servo, is F2626.

When renewing brake shoes, jack up the car and place the appropriate end of the axle on chassis stands. Remove the road wheel. Take out the two countersunk screws that secure the brake drum to the hub and withdraw the hub. On models fitted with mechanical adjusters, slacken back the adjusters to completely free the shoes from the drum. A little judicious even tapping with a copper or hide-faced mallet may be required to free drums that stick in place. Try to remove the drum squarely otherwise it will jam on the shoes.

Checking brake drums:

Blow out loose dust and dirt. Wash off any oil or grease with fuel or methylated spirits. Check the operating surface for scores or cracks. Light scores can be turned out in a lathe but if they are deep or the drum is cracked a new drum must be fitted. The drum can be checked for cracks by hanging it on a wooden handle through the centre and tapping it with a light metal tool. If the drum rings it is satisfactory but a flat note indicates a crack.

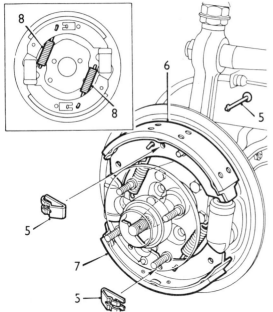

FIG 11:7   Removing the shoes from a front drum brake

Removing shoes from front brake:

The attachments are shown in **FIG 11:7**.

1 Grip the shoe restraining pins 5 with a pair of pliers and turn them through 90 deg., so that the T-head moves into the slot of the restraint spring and the spring can be removed. Withdraw the restraining pins from the back of the backplate.

2 Use a large screwdriver or similar tool to lever the upper shoe carefully out of its abutments in the wheel cylinders, levering out and then moving the shoe away from the backplate so that it comes free. Take care not to damage the dust seal on the wheel cylinder.

3 Remove the lower shoe 7 from its cylinder abutments in a similar manner. Once the shoes have been freed, the return springs 8 can be unhooked from the backplate and the shoes and springs removed.

Removing shoes from manually adjusted rear brake:

The attachments are shown in **FIG 11:8**.

1 Hold the shoe restraining pin 5 at the back of the backplate to prevent it from turning. Grip the washer of the restraint with a pair of pliers, press it in against the spring and turn it through 90 deg. so that the T-head of the pin can pass through the slot in the washer. Remove the washers, springs and pins 5.

2 Lever the trailing shoe 6 out of its slot in the adjuster, moving the shoe away from the backplate when it is out of its slot. Lever the other end of the shoe out of the slot in the wheel cylinder.

3 Once the trailing shoe is free, the tension on the return springs will be released sufficiently for the leading shoe 7 to be eased out of its slots by hand. Disconnect a return spring from a shoe and remove the parts from the brake. Remove the retaining spring and support plate 9 from the leading shoe.

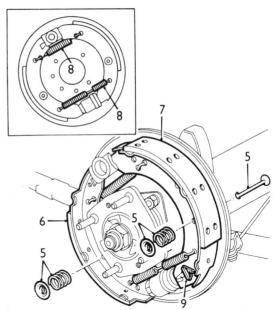

FIG 11:8   Removing the shoes from a 1.3 model rear brake

Removing shoes from automatically adjusted rear brake:

The attachments are shown in **FIG 11:9**. The method of removal of the shoes is similar to the method used on the manually adjusted models. Once the shoes have been removed, and the support plate 7 removed from the leading shoe 6, take out the automatic adjuster 8 from the wheel cylinder and slacken off any adjustment by rotating the ratchet wheel.

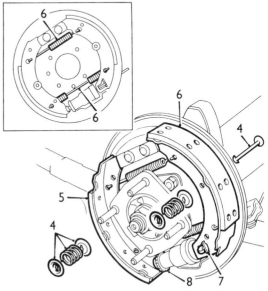

FIG 11:9   Removing the shoes from a 1.8 model rear brake

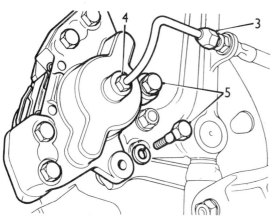

FIG 11:10 The brake caliper attachments

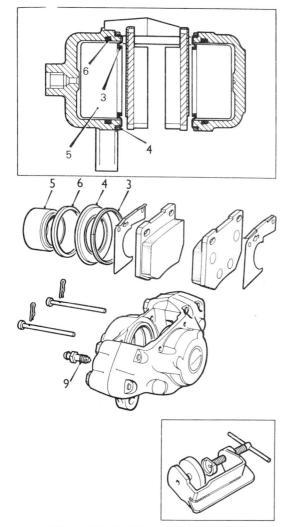

FIG 11:11 Servicing a disc brake caliper

Reassembly:

Clean the inside of the backplate with Girling Cleaning fluid or methylated spirits. Check for leaks from the wheel cylinders or other defects, such as grease leaking past worn oil seals. On the rear brakes of both models, make sure that the wheel cylinders slide freely in their slots in the backplate.

Very lightly lubricate all pivot points and adjuster cams with Girling Brake Grease, **making sure that no grease contacts the rubber seals or lining material.** On the manually adjusted rear brakes, make sure that the adjuster screws in and out of the backplate freely and that the two adjuster links are positioned correctly in the housing, with the angle of the links against the angle of the adjuster wedge. Note that the links can be withdrawn and the adjuster screwed out from the backplate for cleaning and lubrication.

Refit the shoes in the reverse order of removal, making sure that the hands are clean and no grease comes into contact with the lining material. It is advisable to renew the shoe return springs when fitting new brake shoes. Make sure that the return springs are correctly fitted, as shown in the appropriate figure.

Secure the shoes with the restraint pins and springs. Gently tap the shoes central with the handle of a hammer so that the brake drum can be refitted. Secure the drum with its two countersunk screws. Adjust the brake, as described in **Section 10:2,** noting that the brakes are adjusted on 1.8 models by operating the handbrake several times.

Refit the road wheel(s) and lower the car back to the ground.

11:6 Servicing disc brakes

The renewal of the friction pads is dealt with in **Section 11:4.**

Caliper removal:

The attachments of the caliper are shown in **FIG 11:10.** Disconnect the metal pipe from the flexible hose by undoing the union nut 3. Plug the flexible hose to prevent excess hydraulic fluid draining out. Free the metal pipe from the caliper by undoing the union nut 4. Take out the two bolts 5 and slide the caliper off.

Refit the caliper in the reverse order of removal. Tighten the bolts 5 to a torque of 50 lb ft (6.9 kg m). When the caliper is in place and the pipe reconnected, fill and bleed the hydraulic system.

Brake disc:

The brake disc can only be removed after the front hub assembly has been withdrawn from the stub axle on the front suspension (see **Chapter 9, Section 9:3**). Mark the relative positions of the hub and disc before taking out the four bolts that secure the disc to the hub. Gently tap the disc free from the hub.

Refit the brake disc in the reverse order of removal, tightening the four bolts that secure it to the hub to a torque of 38 to 45 lb ft (5.25 to 6.22 kg m).

When the hub has been refitted, mount a DTI (Dial Test Indicator) onto the suspension so that its stylus is resting vertically on the outer operating face of the disc at a radius of 4.75 inch (120.7 mm) and check that the runout of the disc does not exceed .006 inch (.152 mm) through one revolution of the hub assembly.

If the runout is excessive, remove the disc and make absolutely sure that the mating faces of the disc and hub are scrupulously clean, as specks of dirt will alter the runout. If dirt is not the cause, try rotating the disc relative to the hub to see if the runout is minimized in the new position. If excessive runout cannot be cured, a new disc must be fitted.

In normal use slight concentric scoring will build up on the discs. If the scoring is deep or radial, braking efficiency will be affected and a new disc must be fitted.

Deposits on the disc can be cleaned off by soaking with trichlorethylene and gently scrubbing with worn emery-cloth. **Carry out this operation in a well-ventilated space (or out of doors) as the fumes from tri-chlorethylene are harmful.**

Mudshield and brake caliper bracket:

These can be removed from the suspension, after the hub assembly has been removed, by taking out the bolts that secure them to the swivel pin.

Caliper servicing:

Remove the caliper from the car and take out the brake pads with their anti-squeal shims. **Under no circumstances separate the two halves of the caliper.** The components are shown in **FIG 11:11**.

Carefully prise out the dust cover retaining rings 3 and remove the dust covers 4. Fit a piece of cloth into the caliper and use compressed air through the inlet port to blow the pistons out of their bores. If a piston sticks, clamp the other piston back into place and reconnect the caliper to the hydraulic system. Bleed the brake through the bleed screw 7. Wrap the caliper in cloth, to catch fluid which will spurt when the piston comes free, and apply steadily increasing pressure to the brake pedal until the piston frees. **Do not press the brake pedal if the other caliper is free or the drums removed from the rear brakes.**

Remove the pistons 5 and then take out the seals 6 from their recesses in the bore, using a small tool but **taking great care not to damage or score the bore.**

Wash all the parts, except the brake pads, in methylated spirits or Girling Cleaning Fluid. **Do not use any other solvent.** Discard the old seals 6 and dust covers 4. Check the pistons 5 for scoring or wear and renew them if they are defective. If the cylinder bore shows signs of corrosion, scuffing, scoring or wear a complete new caliper assembly must be fitted.

Wet the new seals 6 in hydraulic fluid and insert them back into the bores, using only the fingers and making sure that the seal is fully seated and not twisted. Wet the pistons with hydraulic fluid and press each one in turn back into the bore, using the fingers first and then pressing them in with the special tool 18G.590, shown in the inset, until each piston protrudes by .31 inch (.8 mm). **When first entering the piston into the bore, take great care not to cock it and jam it in the bore.**

Refit the dust cover 4 onto the piston and secure it to the caliper with the clip 3.

The caliper is then ready for refitting.

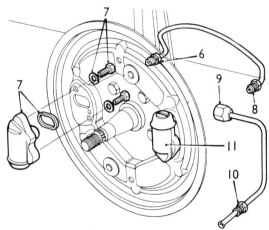

FIG 11:12 The attachments of the wheel cylinders on a front drum brake

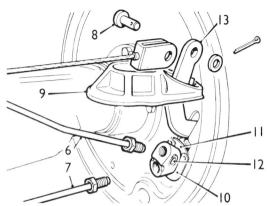

FIG 11:13 The attachments of a rear brake wheel cylinder, righthand

11:7 Drum brake wheel cylinders

These can be removed from the brake backplate after the brake drums and shoes have been removed (see **Section 11:5**). If the brake backplate itself needs to be taken out, the hub must be removed first. See **Chapter 8, Section 8:2** for rear hubs and **Chapter 9, Section 9:2** for front hubs.

Removing front brake wheel cylinders:

The attachments of a wheel cylinder are shown in **FIG 11:12**. With the wheel, drum, and shoes removed disconnect the bridge pipe at 6 from the forward cylinder, noting that hydraulic fluid will flow out if the system has not been drained. Take out the two bolts and remove the wheel cylinder 7 with its sealing gasket. Disconnect the bridge pipe at 8 from the rear cylinder. Disconnect the supply pipe from the flexible hose at 9, and from the wheel cylinder at 10. The rear wheel cylinder 11 can then be removed by taking out its attachment bolts.

The parts are refitted in the reverse order of removal. The supply pipe 10 is connected to the bottom port of the rear wheel cylinder and the bridge pipe 8 to the top port.

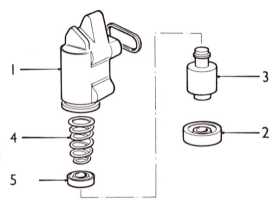

FIG 11:14 The components of a front drum brake wheel cylinder

Key to Fig 11:14 1 Body 2 Dust cover 3 Piston 4 Spring 5 Seal

The bridge pipe 6 is connected to the bottom port of the front cylinder and the bleed screw fitted to the top port. Tighten the cylinder attachment bolts to a torque of 4 to 5 lb ft (.55 to .7 kg m). Refit the shoes and brake drum. Fill and bleed the system then adjust the brake resistor.

Removing rear brake wheel cylinder:

The attachments of the righthand wheel cylinder are shown in **FIG 11:13**. Remove wheel, brake drum and shoes. Disconnect the main feed pipe 6 from the bottom port of the wheel cylinder on righthand side brakes. The bridge pipe 7 runs along the axle casing to connect the two wheel cylinders and it is attached to the top port on the righthand side but to the bottom port on the lefthand side. Disconnect the bridge pipe 7. Remove the splitpin and washer so that the clevis pin 8, connecting the handbrake cable to the brake lever, can be removed. Remove the ruber boot 9. Remove the retaining plate 10, by tapping it off with a screwdriver. Remove the spring plate 11. The wheel cylinder assembly 12 can then be withdrawn from the backplate, into the brake, and the handbrake lever 13 removed from it.

The parts are refitted in the reverse order of removal. Smear the slot in the backplate lightly with Girling Brake Grease before refitting the wheel cylinder. The retaining

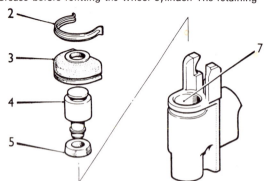

FIG 11:15 The components of a rear brake wheel cylinder

Key to Fig 11:15 2 Clip 3 Dust cover 4 Piston 5 Seal 7 Body

plate 10 must be slid or driven back into place so that its holes align over the pips of the spring plate 11. Check that the wheel cylinder slides freely in its slot. Reconnect the pipes 6 and 7, making sure that they are connected to the correct ports. Refit the shoes and drum. Fill and bleed the braking system. On the 1.3 models, set the brake adjustment using the mechanical adjusters. On the 1.8 models, operate the handbrake several times to adjust the rear brakes.

Servicing a wheel cylinder:

The components of a front wheel cylinder are shown in **FIG 11:14** and those of a rear wheel cylinder in **FIG 11:15**.

Remove the dust cover, after freeing the clip if fitted. Withdraw the piston assembly from the bore, collecting the spring if fitted. Remove the cup seal from the piston.

Discard the old dust seal and cup seal, fitting new parts on reassembly. Wash the parts in any suitable solvent but give them a swill in methylated spirits or Girling Cleaning fluid before reassembly. This ensures that there are no traces of other solvents left to attack the material of the seals.

The unit is reassembled in the reverse order of dismantling. Dip the cup seal into hydraulic fluid and refit it while it is wet to the piston. The lips of the seal must face into the bore of the cylinder. Use only the fingers to refit the seal, making sure that it is fully and squarely seated in its recess. When refitting the piston into the bore, take great care not to bend back or damage the lips of the seal.

11:8 The master cylinder

Removal:

The master cylinder attachments to models fitted without a servo are shown in **FIG 11:16**. On the models fitted with a servo, the unit is bolted directly to the servo and the reference to withdrawing the clevis pin 4 can be ignored, otherwise the removal is the same.

Remove the filler cap and syphon out the hydraulic fluid from the reservoir. Disconnect the metal pipe 2 from the master cylinder, **using rags to catch any spillage.** Remove the nuts and washers 3 securing the master cylinder. From inside the car, remove the clevis pin 4 that secures the pushrod to the brake pedal and from inside the engine compartment withdraw the master cylinder.

Refit the master cylinder in the reverse order of removal, noting that on models without a servo the clevis pin must be passed through the upper hole in the brake pedal. Fill and bleed the hydraulic system.

Dismantling:

The components of the unit are shown in **FIG 11:17** and a sectional view in **FIG 11:18**.

1 Pull back the dust cap 2. Lightly press the pushrod down the bore and remove the circlip 3. The pushrod with its integral stop washer 4 can then be removed from the unit. Apply air pressure at the port, or shake out the internal parts 5 by tapping the open end of the cylinder onto the palm of the hand.

2 Use a small screwdriver through the coils of the return spring to lift up the lip on the spring retainer so that the retainer can be slid off the piston 6. Remove the

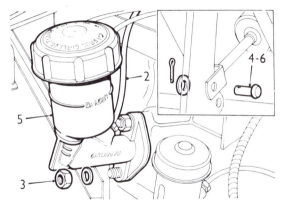

FIG 11:16 The attachments of the master cylinder

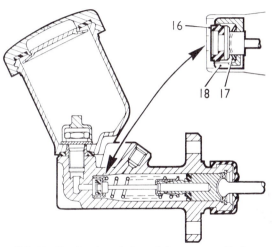

FIG 11:18 Sectioned view of the master cylinder

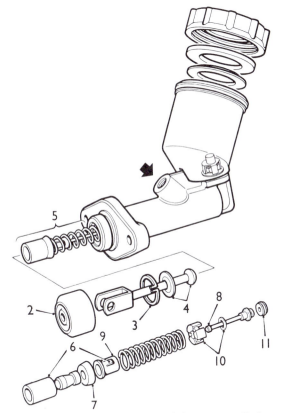

FIG 11:17 The components of the master cylinder

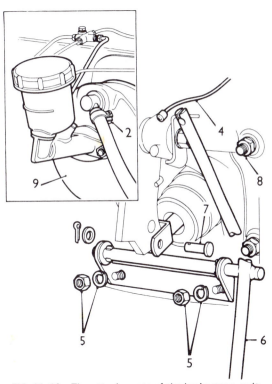

FIG 11:19 The attachments of the brake servo unit

cup seal 7 from the piston. Lightly compress the return spring and slide the head of the valve stem 8 sideways in the retainer so that it can pass out through the larger parts of the keyhole in the end of the retainer 9.

3 Slide off the valve spacer 10 and washer from the valve stem. Remove the valve seal 11 from the end of the stem.

Examination:

Discard the old seals and fit new ones on reassembly (available in service kits). Wash the parts in methylated spirits and allow them to dry. Check the bore of the cylinder and renew the complete unit if the bore is at all scored, ridged or worn.

Check that the ports are clear, cleaning them out with a blunt-ended piece of wire if they are blocked or dirty.

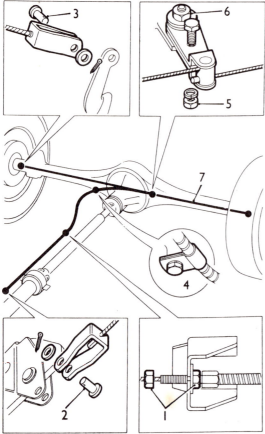

FIG 11 : 20 The handbrake cables and their attachments

Reassembly:

The internal parts should be dipped into clean hydraulic fluid and reassembled and refitted while wet.

Refer to **FIG 11 : 18.** Refit the valve seal 16 (see item 11) to the valve stem so that its smallest diameter is seated on the valve head. Slide on the curved washer 17 (see item 10) with its curved side towards the shoulder as shown. Refit the spacer 17 (see item 10) with its legs towards the curved washer.

Refer to **FIG 11 : 17.** Refit the return spring followed by the retainer 9. Centralize the stem of the valve in the retainer to locate it. Use the fingers only to refit the new seal 7 to the piston, so that its lip will face into the bore of the cylinder, and make sure that it is fully and squarely seated in its recess. Press the retainer 9 back onto the piston, making sure that the tongue on the retainer is pressed fully and squarely down behind the lip of the piston.

Again wet the internal parts with hydraulic fluid. Press them back down the bore of the master cylinder, **taking great care not to bend back or damage the lips of the seal as they enter the bore.** Insert the pushrod and use it to press the internal parts down the bore while refitting the circlip 3. Check that the internal parts return

freely under the action of the return spring before refitting the dust cover 2. The end of the pushrod and inside of the dust cover should be smeared with Girling Brake Grease (supplied in the kit).

11 : 9 The brake servo

The attachments of the unit are shown in **FIG 11 : 19.** Note that when a servo is fitted, the servo pushrod is always attached to the lower of the two mounting holes on the brake pedal.

The renewal of the servo filter is dealt with in **Section 11 : 2.**

Removal:

Remove the brake master cylinder as described in the previous section. Disconnect the vacuum hose from the non-return valve 2 on the unit. The non-return valve can be removed from the case and renewed if it is defective.

From inside the car, remove the parcel shelf. Disconnect the throttle cable 4 from the throttle pedal. Remove the nuts 5 and take off the throttle pedal assembly 6. Disconnect the servo pushrod from the brake pedal by taking out the clevis pin 7. Remove the nuts 8 which secure the unit and then withdraw the unit from the engine compartment.

Servicing:

The filter should be renewed if it is choked. The non-return valve can be renewed, lubricating its sealing washer lightly with Girling Grease 64949009. A seal and end plate assembly is fitted around the pushrod that connects to the master cylinder. The seal and plate can be carefully prised out and new parts pressed back into position, after lubricating them with Girling grease.

If the unit shows any other defects it must be renewed.

Reassembly:

The unit is refitted in the reverse order of removal, making sure that the pushrod attaches to the lower hole. Refit the master cylinder then fill and bleed the braking system.

11 : 10 Bleeding the hydraulic system

This is not routine maintenance but it must always be carried out when air has entered the hydraulic system, either through allowing the fluid level in the reservoir to fall so low that air is drawn into the system, leaks in the system, or after dismantling and reassembly.

Before starting the operation, remove the filler cap from the reservoir and fill it as far as it will go without spilling. During the operation, keep a constant check on the level, topping up as required to keep the level above the danger mark. Use UNIPART 550 on models fitted with disc brakes and UNIPART 410 on models fitted with all drum brakes.

Fluid that has been bled from the system should be discarded. Only if the fluid is perfectly clean may it be used again, after storage in a clean sealed container for 24 hours to allow all air to disperse. **Never return fluid directly from bleeding to the master cylinder reservoir.**

Start bleeding at the front brake furthest from the master cylinder, followed by the other front brake and finally the lefthand side rear brake (noting that only one bleed screw is fitted to the rear brakes).

Attach a short length of small-bore plastic or rubber tube to the bleed screw of the brake to be bled and dip the free end of the tube into a little clean hydraulic fluid in a glass container. An assistant will now be required. Open the bleed screw by $\frac{1}{2}$ turn. The assistant presses the brake pedal fully down to the floor and then gives three short rapid strokes before allowing the pedal to fly back on its own. Carry on this sequence until the fluid coming out of the bleed tube is perfectly clear and free from air bubbles. Tighten the bleed screw as the pedal is being pressed down on the first slow long stroke of the sequence.

Bleed the remaining brakes using the same method. Check that the bleed screws are sufficiently tight to prevent leaks. If the system has been fully dismantled and the pedal still feels spongy after bleeding, use the car for a day or so and then rebleed the system. The tiny air bubbles will have had time to coalesce and will be easier to bleed out.

After brake bleeding is completed, top up the reservoir to the correct level and refit the filler cap.

11 : 11 The handbrake

The attachments of the cables are shown in **FIG 11 : 20** and the attachment of the handbrake lever is shown in **FIG 11 : 21.**

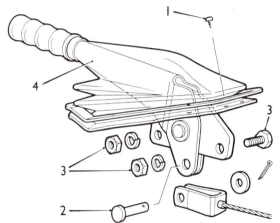

FIG 11 : 21 The attachments of the handbrake lever assembly

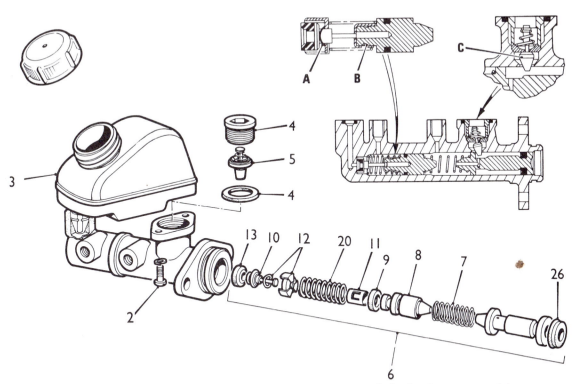

FIG 11 : 22 Section and exploded views of the tandem master cylinder fitted to export models

Key to Fig 11 : 22   2 Reservoir retaining screws   3 Reservoir   4, 5 Tipping valve   6 Piston assemblies   7 Intermediate spring   8 Secondary piston   9 Seal   10 Valve   11 Thimble   12 Spacer and curved washer   13 Valve seal   20 Spring   26 Primary seal

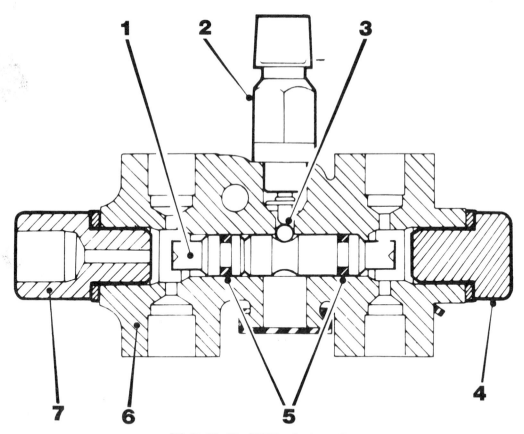

FIG 11 : 23   The PDWA valve in section

Key to Fig 11 : 23   1 Two-part piston assembly   2 Switch   3 Switch operating ball   4 Small end plug   5 Piston seals
6 Body   7 Large end plug

Removing cables :

1 Slacken the adjuster nut and locknut 1 so that the cable is released from its bracket. Remove the splitpin, washer and clevis pin 2 that secure the front end of the cable to the handbrake lever.

2 Disconnect the cables from the levers on the rear brakes by removing the splitpins, washers and clevis pins 3. Free the clip that secures the handbrake cable clip to the axle case by taking out the bolt 4.

3 Remove the nut, washer and bolt 5 that hold the compensating levers together and secure the trunnion off the cables. Slacken the nut 6 so that the trunnion can be removed from the compensating levers. Remove the cable from the car.

The parts are refitted in the reverse order of removal. Renew all clevis pins that are worn and use new splitpins to secure the clevis pins.

Adjust the cable, at the point 1, as described in **Section 11 : 2.**

The lever assembly :

Ease back the floor covering and take out the four screws 1 that secure the gaiter 4 in place. Remove the clevis pin 2 which secures the cable to the lever. Slide

the gaiter up and off the lever. Remove the nuts and bolts 3 that secure the assembly and lift out the handbrake lever parts from the car.

Refit the handbrake lever in the reverse order of removal and check the handbrake adjustment.

11 : 12 The tandem brake system

Cars destined for certain territories may be fitted with a dual line system which provide separate hydraulic circuits for the rear and the front pairs of brakes. By this means a failure in one circuit will still permit balanced braking on the other pair of wheels which should enable the driver to bring the car safely to a halt or even proceed slowly to wherever the fault is to be rectified.

The first essential component in this system is the tandem master cylinder which, by having two pistons operating in the lengthened bore, pressurises the two circuits equally or, in the event of a failure, the one good circuit remaining at full pressure although with longer pedal travel. The tandem master cylinder is shown in section and exploded on **FIG 11 : 22** and its removal and dismantling can be carried out in a similar manner to that described in **Section 11 : 8.**

The two hydraulic lines from the master cylinder pass through a device known as the Pressure Differential Warning Actuator (PDWA) valve, which includes a passage linking the two circuits and housing a cylindrical shuttle valve or piston. In the event of a break in one of the circuits, pressure in that circuit will be reduced and the shuttle in the PDWA will move in its bore to that side of the unit and in so doing will actuate an electrical plunger type switch which, in turn, actuates a warning lamp on the instrument panel. The device is shown in section in **FIG 11:23** and requires no maintenance in normal service.

Bleeding the brakes:

The method to be employed differs from that described in **Section 11:10** as follows:

Attach bleeder tubes to the bleed screw on the lefthand front and lefthand rear brakes, noting that this latter controls the bleeding for both rear brakes.

Commence bleeding as before but using light partial strokes of the pedal until all the air has been expelled from these two bleeding points and then move to the righthand front brake and pump all the air out of this circuit.

If the PDWA should be actuated in the course of the operation and cause the warning light to glow, complete the operation and then attach a bleed tube to a brake at the opposite end of the car and carefully press down the brake pedal until the light goes out. Release the pedal immediately and tighten the bleed screw. Remove the tubes and check that both sections of the fluid reservoir are full.

11:13 Fault diagnosis

(a) Spongy pedal

1 Leak in the fluid system
2 Air in the fluid system
3 Worn master cylinder
4 Leaking wheel cylinders
5 Gaps between shoes and linings on drum brakes
6 Excessive hub end float (disc brakes only)

(b) Excessive pedal movement

1 Check 1 and 2 in (a)
2 Excessive lining or pad wear
3 Very low fluid level in reservoir

(c) Brakes grab or pull to one side

1 Seized piston in wheel cylinder or caliper
2 Seized handbrake cable or compensator
3 Wet or oily friction linings
4 Broken shoe return springs
5 Mixed linings of different grades
6 Unbalanced shoe adjustment
7 Scored, cracked or distorted brake drums or discs
8 Uneven tyre pressures or uneven tyre wear
9 Defective suspension or steering

MARINA

NOTES

CHAPTER 12

THE ELECTRICAL SYSTEM

12:1 Description

All the versions covered by this manual are fitted with a 12-volt electrical system in which the negative terminal of the battery is earthed. **Care must be taken to ensure that the correct polarity is observed when connecting up circuits, as some components will be irreparably damaged if they are connected with the wrong polarity.**

Standard models are fitted with a DC generator, driven by a belt from the engine, to supply the needs of the electrical system as well as charging the battery. A separate control unit regulates the output of the generator to the demands of the battery and system.

An AC alternator can be fitted as an optional extra in place of the conventional generator. The alternator has its own in-built rectifier pack, to change the AC current to DC which is acceptable to the battery, as well as its own regulator. The alternator will charge at a slower speed and provide a higher current as compared with a generator, so it is most useful where much stop-start driving and short journeys are carried out. The alternator also has greater reliability by virtue of its design and construction.

A lead/acid battery is used to store electrical power for operating the accessories when the engine is stopped, as well as supplying the heavy current required by the starter motor for starting the engine. The battery also acts as a voltage stabilizer for the system.

Wiring diagrams are shown in **Technical Data** at the end of this manual, to enable those with electrical experience to trace and rectify wiring faults. A test lamp or any 0 to 20 voltmeter will do for testing the continuity of circuits, by connecting the tester between the suspect terminal and a good earth on the car. **Cheap and unreliable instruments must not be used when checking performance or adjusting components, as they cannot measure to the accuracy required.** For accurate checks, high grade instruments must be used, preferably instruments of the moving-coil type.

Instructions are given in this chapter for servicing the components of the system but it must be realized that it is a waste of time and money to attempt to repair items which are seriously defective, either electrically or mechanically. In such cases, advantage should be taken of the B90 exchange scheme run by Lucas to fit new or reconditioned units in their place.

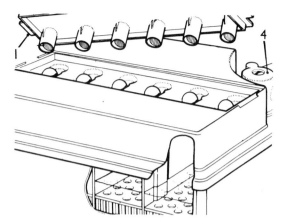

FIG 12:1 Topping up an Exide battery

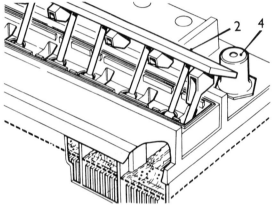

FIG 12:2 Topping up a Lucas battery

12:2 The battery

The battery is the heart of the electrical system and if it is in poor condition the operation of the whole electrical system will suffer. The battery is also the component that will suffer first from neglected maintenance.

Maintenance:

Always keep the top of the battery clean and dry. Wipe away any dampness, spillage or dirt from the top of the battery. If acid has spilt, or dirt allowed current to leak, the metal surrounds around the battery can become corroded. Take out the battery and wash the area with dilute ammonia or baking powder dissolved in warm water. When the acid has been neutralized, flush the area with plenty of clean water and allow to dry. Use anti-sulphuric paint to prevent further corrosion.

Keep the battery connectors clean and tight. Poor contact here is one of the commonest causes of the starter motor failing to operate satisfactorily. Wash away corrosion with dilute ammonia followed by clean water. Oxides can be gently scraped away with a sharp knife, though it should be noted that special tools are made for cleaning the posts and connectors. Smear the posts and connectors with petroleum jelly to prevent further corrosion.

At regular intervals check the electrolyte level in the battery, topping up with pure distilled water only. Do not add acid, electrolyte or additives. The Exide type battery is shown in **FIG 12:1**. Remove the vent cover and check that the level is up to the bottom of the filler tubes. Do not top up if the level is above the bottom of the filler tubes. The Lucas-type battery is shown in **FIG 12:2** and the level can be checked through the translucent case or after freeing the vent cover. On Lucas batteries the level should be just above the top of the separators.

If the level is low, pour distilled water into the trough until all the cell fillers are full and the bottom of the trough just covered, then refit the vent cover and the cells will automatically take the right amount of distilled water. **Do not use naked lights to examine the battery. Do not top up if the battery has been recharged from a separate charger within half-an-hour otherwise the gases vented may cause flooding.**

Electrolyte, of the correct specific gravity, should only be added to replace spillage or leakage.

Charging:

The best rate of charging is 10 per cent of the battery's rated capacity, though a trickle charger will be quite sufficient for boosting the battery or even recharging it from flat.

Heavy-duty boost chargers should be avoided if at all possible as they will ruin a battery that is in poor condition. **When charging the battery, leave the vent cover fitted otherwise the gases will force electrolyte out.**

A battery can be checked using a hydrometer but it will be fully charged when it is gassing freely on the charging current. Note that these gases given off are explosive, so avoid making sparks when refitting a freshly charged battery.

When using a heavy-duty boost charger on models fitted with an alternator, disconnect the charging circuit or the heavy duty cable from the positive terminal (+ve) on the battery.

A poor battery can sometimes be partially reclaimed by giving it three or four cycles of discharge and charge. Connect the battery across a lamp bank that takes approximately 5 amps (Watts=Volts X Amps) and discharge it until the bulbs are noticeably dim. Recharge the battery, then discharge it again. After the fourth cycle, charge the battery ready for use. This treatment is also said to prolong the life of a good battery if carried out twice a year.

Electrolyte:

Concentrated sulphuric acid is a very dangerous chemical so buy electrolyte ready-mixed. Electrolyte of the correct specific gravity should only be added to the battery to replace spillage or leakage.

If electrolyte is spilled, it should be immediately neutralized with baking powder or dilute ammonia and then flushed away with plenty of clean water.

Testing:

Single-cell heavy-duty testers cannot be used on either make of battery.

Provided that the battery has not been just topped up, the charge of the cells can be checked with a hydrometer.

If the battery has just been topped up the car should be used for a short while to mix the electrolyte (this should also be done after topping up in very cold weather). Draw sufficient electrolyte from each cell in turn into the instrument to ensure that the float is clear of the sides and bottom. Take the reading at eye level and at the same time note the condition of the electrolyte. Dirt, specks or a cloudy appearance indicate a defective cell and this will be confirmed if the reading of that cell differs radically from the other five cells.

The readings give the following indications:

For climates above 27°C (80°F):

1.270 to 1.290	..	..	Cell fully charged
1.1190 to 1.210	..	..	Cell half charged
1.110 to 1.130	..	..	Cell discharged

Replace spillage with electrolyte of 1.270 specific gravity.

For climates below 27°C (80°F):

1.120 to 1.230	..	..	Cell fully charged
1.130 to 1.150	..	..	Cell half charged
1.050 to 1.070	..	..	Cell discharged

Replace spillage with electrolyte of 1.120 specific gravity.

The figures are given assuming a standard electrolyte temperature of 16°C (60°F). If the actual temperature is different from the standard, then convert by adding .002 to the reading for every 3°C (5°F) rise in temperature and subtract for every 3°C (5°F) drop in temperature.

Storage:

Short-term storage provides no problems provided that the battery has been well maintained. If the battery is to be stored for long periods, make sure that it is fully charged, the top dry and the posts well covered with petroleum jelly. Keep the battery stored in a cold dry place, well away from extremes of temperature.

At monthly intervals give the battery a freshening-up charge and at three-month intervals discharge it, using a lamp bank, and fully recharge it. If this is not done the battery will slowly self-discharge and the plates sulphate up, to the ruination of the battery.

12:3 Servicing electrical motors

All the motors fitted to the car operate on the same principles and are basically very similar in constructional detail. It should be noted that a generator can be considered as a specialized form of motor in which mechanical energy is fed in and electrical energy taken out.

The removal and dismantling of the various motors will be dealt with in the relevant sections, but to save constant repetition, general instructions for dealing with all motors are collected into this section.

Brush gear:

Dismantle the motor sufficiently to expose the brush gear. **Great care must be taken not to damage the brushes on the edge of the commutator as they are withdrawn or refitted,** and on some motors it will be necessary to partially withdraw the brush from its holder and secure it in this position with the spring resting on the side instead of on the top of the brush. The assembly can then be slid off the commutator, or refitted, without damaging the brushes. Once the assembly is back in place use a rod or hook to lift the spring onto the top of the brush.

Renew the brushes if they are excessively worn. On motors where the connectors are soldered into place, grip the connector with a pair of pliers to prevent solder from creeping up them and making them stiff. On the starter motor, cut the old connector so that approximately $\frac{1}{4}$ inch of old connector is left and pass this tag through the loop of the new connector before soldering the new connector into place. The old tag can be bent over but make sure that there is no danger of the tag or new connector earthing against the yoke of the motor.

Check that the brushes move freely in their brush holders. If the brushes stick, remove them and polish their sides on a smooth file. Clean the brush holders with a piece of cloth moistened with fuel or methylated spirits before refitting the brush. If the original brushes are being refitted, make sure that they are refitted into their original positions and facing the same way as before removal. This ensures that the bedding-in is not lost.

Use a suitably-modified spring balance to check the pressure of the brush springs. Fit new springs if the old ones are weak or broken.

Brushes are usually supplied ground to shape on the end. If further bedding-in is required, make up a wooden rod the same diameter as the commutator (or use the commutator itself) and wrap it with a fine grade of glass-paper. Fit the brush holder complete with brushes over the mandrel and rotate the mandrel inside the brushes for a few turns. Bedding-in in use will then finally fit the brushes accurately.

Before reassembling the motor, brush and blow out all dust and dirt. Wipe the commutator over with a piece of cloth moistened in methylated spirits or fuel.

Commutator and armature:

If the commutator is worn or scored the armature assembly must be removed from the motor. Light score or burn marks can be polished off using a fine grade of glasspaper. Never use emerycloth as this will leave abrasive particles embedded in the copper.

If the damage is deep it can be skimmed off in a lathe, provided that the minimum diameter of the commutator is not reached. Use the highest speed possible and a very sharp tool. Starter motor commutators must never be undercut. On generators and motors where the insulation is undercut between the segments, grind a hacksaw blade so that it is the exact width of the insulation and use it to undercut the insulation to a depth of $\frac{1}{32}$ inch. Take a light final skim cut using a diamond or carbide-tipped tool. Failing such a tool, polish the commutator, as it rotates, using a fine grade of glasspaper. Remove all swarf and metal dust from the commutator before reassembly.

Very little can be done to the remainder of the armature, apart from checking it for physical damage. A special tester is required for checking shortcircuits in the coils, though they may be suspected if individual commutator segments are burnt. Check that there are no loose laminations, segments or wiring, as well as checking the laminations for scoring. Scoring all round the laminations indicates excessively worn bearings or loose polepieces, while scoring on one side only indicates a bent armature shaft. **A defective armature shaft cannot be repaired and it must not be machined or an attempt made to straighten it.** The only cure is to fit a new armature.

Field coils:

On some of the smaller motors, permanent magnets are fitted in place of field coils. Care must be taken when dismantling such motors as the magnet, attached inside the cover, will draw the armature out with it, to the possible damage of the brushes.

The field coils can be checked by connecting a test lamp and 12-volt battery across the terminals and between a terminal and the yoke. In the first case the lamp should light, showing continuity, and in the second case it should not light, showing that the insulation is satisfactory. A more accurate test is to connect an ammeter in place of the test lamp and measure the current flow. The resistance can then be calculated using Ohms law (Voltage divided by Current equals Resistance). Obviously a resistance meter will give a direct reading of resistance and should therefore be used in preference.

The field coils on starter motors and generators are held in place by the polepieces, which are in turn secured by large screws to the yoke. The screws must be tightened to a high torque using a wheel-screwdriver and then locked by staking or punch dots. An ordinary screwdriver cannot exert the torque required to slacken or tighten these screws so renewal of field coils should be left to an agent.

Bearings:

Either ballbearings or bushes may be used. Ballbearings are usually held in place by a riveted retainer plate. To remove rivets use a drill larger in diameter than the stem but smaller than the head. File a flat on the rivet head and then centre punch it as a guide. Drill carefully until the head is so weakened that it can be tapped off with a small cold chisel, then use a suitable punch to drive out the rivet stem. Before refitting ballbearings, make sure that they are packed with grease.

Porous bronze bushes are used on some larger motors. Sometimes they can be extracted by driving them out using a suitable punch. If the bushes are fitted in blind holes, screw a tap of the correct size into the bush and use the tap to draw the bush out. Soak the new bush in oil for 24 hours before fitting it. The period can be reduced by heating the oil over a bath of boiling water for two hours, leaving the oil to cool before taking the bush out of it. Press the new bush back into place, using a stepped mandrel whose spigot is just longer than the bush and has a highly finished surface of the same diameter as the armature shaft. **Do not machine or bore the bush.**

Smaller motors are fitted with spherical self-aligning bushes, usually held to the end cover by a riveted spring clip plate. Spares may not be readily obtainable and if the bush is worn the complete end cover must usually be renewed. Check that such bushes move freely in their clips and that their bores are not worn. Lubricate them with a few drops of oil before reassembly.

Insulation:

Clean away all metal and carbon dust from the inside of the motor. Use an air-line or tyre pump as well as a small brush. Oil or grease can be washed away using methylated spirits or clean fuel. The field coils and armature must not be wetted with solvent but only wiped over with a moistened cloth.

The best method of testing resistance is to use a resistance meter, though not the type known as a 'megger' which generates a high voltage. A test lamp and 12-volt battery can also be used but if this method is to be employed it is better to have a neon test bulb and 110 AC volt supply.

12:4 The starter motor

The different types of starter motor that can be fitted and their performance figures are given in Technical Data.

For cold climates, special pre-engage starter motors are fitted. A sectioned view of a typical pre-engage motor is shown in **FIG 12:3**. On these models, the first action of the starter solenoid is to move the drive pinion into engagement with the flywheel teeth and further movement of the solenoid closes the heavy duty contacts to energize the motor itself. Generally servicing of this type of motor follows the instructions for servicing standard motors.

Starter motor fails to operate:

1 Check the condition of the battery terminals, making sure that they are clean and firmly held down by the screws. At the same time check that the battery is charged. If, when operated, the horn sounds weak or the lights are dim then it is likely that the battery is low in charge.

2 Switch on some lights which can be seen from the driving seat and again operate the starter switch. If the lights go dim then the starter motor is taking current. One cause of the motor failing to rotate at all is that it is jammed in mesh. Select a gear and rock the car backwards and forwards. If this fails to free the starter motor, use a spanner on the squared end of the armature shaft, exposed at the end of the motor, to try to rotate the motor backwards and so free it. If all methods of freeing the motor fail, or the motor is free but does not rotate, then it must be removed for further examination. Broken or worn pinion teeth are a cause of jamming and the teeth on the flywheel should also be checked, by examining them through the starter motor aperture while slowly turning the engine over. Dirt on the drive pinion will also cause it to jam (either keeping it in engagement or preventing it from engaging).

3 If the lights do not go dim when the starter is operated then the motor is taking no current. Disconnect the single control wire from the solenoid and check that current is reaching the terminal of the wire when the switch is operated, using a test lamp or voltmeter. If current is not reaching the terminal, trace back through the system until the fault is found and can be rectified. If current is reaching the control terminal for the solenoid, listen for the click as the solenoid operates. If there is no click the coils are defective and

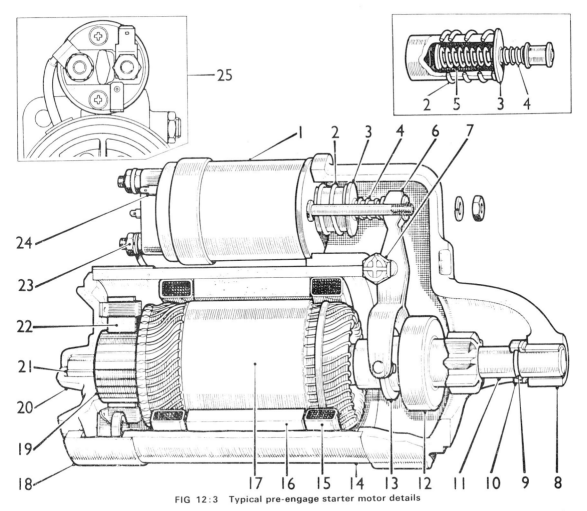

FIG 12:3   Typical pre-engage starter motor details

Key to Fig 12:3   1 Solenoid   2 Plunger return spring   3 Plunger   4 Lost motion spring   5 Drive engagement spring
6 Engaging lever   7 Pivot pin   8 Fixing bracket   9 Retaining ring   10 Thrust collar   11 Armature shaft extension   12 Clutch
13 Drive operating plate   14 Yoke   15 Field coil   16 Pole shoes   17 Armature   18 Cover band   19 Commutator   20 End bracket
21 Bush bearing   22 Brushes   23 Solenoid STA terminal   24 Solenoid operating terminal   25 Alternative layout of terminals

a new solenoid must be fitted. On the separate solenoids, the starter can still be operated by pressing in the rubber covered end of the solenoid plunger. Burning of the contacts in the solenoid can be another cause of starter motor failure. If the solenoid clicks and the motor does not operate (similarly when the solenoid is operated manually), try shorting across the heavy-duty terminals with a thick piece of metal. The starter motor now operating shows that the contacts are burnt and again the only cure is to fit a new solenoid.

Removal:

Disconnect the battery. Disconnect the leads from the starter motor. Remove the nuts and bolts which secure the starter motor and withdraw it from the engine.

The motor is refitted in the reverse order of removal.

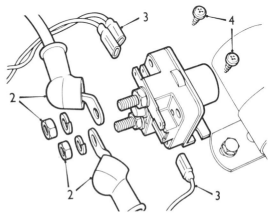

FIG 12:4   The starter solenoid attachments

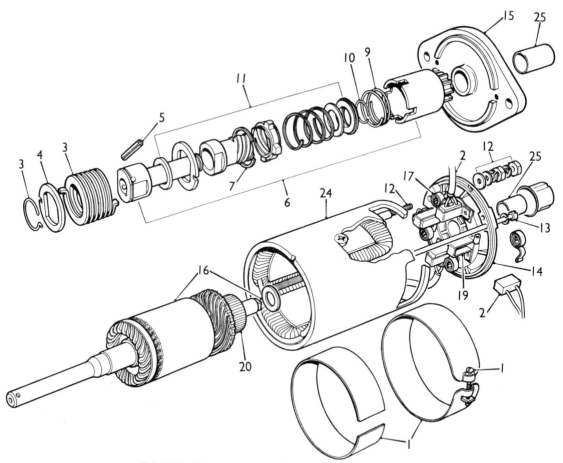

FIG 12:5 The components of the M418G starter motor

Solenoid:

Solenoid faults can be found using the checks out-lined for starter motor failure. The attachments of the solenoid are shown in **FIG 12 : 4.** The solenoid is removed in the numerical order of the attachments.

Dismantling M418G starter motor:

The components of the unit are shown in **FIG 12 : 5.** The brushes are accessible after the coverband 1 has been removed.

The armature assembly, drive end plate and pinion components can be removed separately from the yoke 25. Remove the coverband 1, lift up the springs 17 and with-draw the brushes 2 from their holders 19. Remove the ter-minal nuts and washers 12. Take out the two through-bolts 13 so that the commutator end plate 14 can be taken off and the armature assembly withdrawn from the yoke 24. This dismantling is usually sufficient for most servicing and cleaning operations. For full dismantling proceed as follows:

1 Remove the coverband 1, and withdraw the brushes 2 from their holders. Compress the main drive spring 3 and remove the snap ring 3. Drive out the roll-pin 5 and remove the assembly parts 6. Remove the spring ring

7 so that the centre sleeve and screwed sleeve can be removed from the barrel. Remove the spring 9 and spring retaining grip 10 from the barrel. Detach the locating collar and remove the parts 11.

2 Remove the nuts and washers of the terminal assembly 12. Take out the two through-bolts 13 and remove the commutator end cover 14. Free the drive end bracket 15 and withdraw the armature and its thrust washer 11 from the yoke 24.

3 The bushes 25 can be pressed or driven out if they are worn, pressing new oil-soaked bushes back into place.

The starter motor is reassembled in the reverse order of dismantling. Check the components as described in **Section 12 : 3.** Check the parts of the drive pinion assembly and renew any that are worn or damaged.

Dismantling M35J starter motor:

The components are shown in **FIG 12 : 6.** This type of starter motor has a commutator where the brushes act on the vertical face instead of on the circumference as is more usual.

1 Remove the two screws 1 so that the drive end bracket complete with armature 2 and pinion assembly

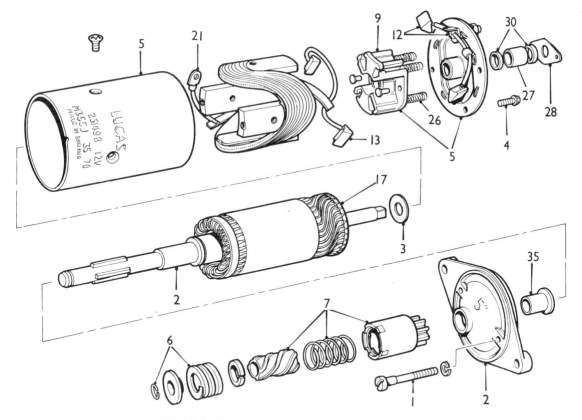

FIG 12:6   The components of the M35J starter motor

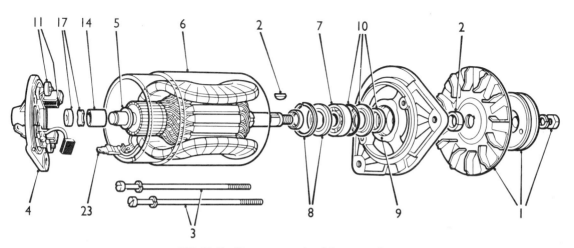

FIG 12:7   The components of the generator

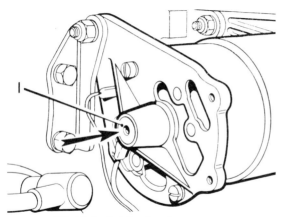

FIG 12:8 Lubricating the generator

can be withdrawn from the yoke. Collect the thrust washer 3 from the end of the shaft 2.

2 Take out the two screws 4 and remove the commutator end bracket 5 complete with brushgear assembly 9.

3 Compress the mainspring and remove the snap ring 6. The pinion parts 7 can then be removed from the armature shaft 2.

The components are checked following the instructions in **Section 12:3**. The spring tension of the brushes is checked, using new brushes and a push-type spring gauge with the brushes pressed in until they protrude by approximately $\frac{1}{16}$ inch (1.6 mm). If the spring pressure is weak, the complete end bracket assembly 5 must be renewed. When checking the insulation of the field coils, unrivet the terminal 21 and keep it well clear of the yoke, checking between each field coil brush and yoke in turn. The plate 28 must be unrivetted before the bush 27 and felt seals can be renewed, using a $\frac{1}{2}$ inch tap to withdraw the bush. The bush 35 can be pressed straight out and a new bush pressed straight in.

The motor is reassembled in the reverse order of dismantling.

Testing:

For full tests, a torque rig and accurate meters capable of measuring a large current are required. The performance figures for the various starter motors are given in Technical Data.

The motor can be roughly checked by mounting it in the padded jaws of a vice. If the motor is hand-held the starting torque will make it kick heavily. Use heavy duty leads and connect the positive terminal of the battery to the terminal on the motor. Firmly hold a heavy duty lead, connected to the negative terminal of the battery, against the yoke of the motor. If the motor is satisfactory, it will rotate at high speed in its normal direction of rotation. Note that the current even under free-running can reach 65 amps on some motors.

12:5 The generator

The components of the generator are shown in **FIG 12:7. Section 12:3** should be referred to for instructions on servicing and checking the parts of the generator.

Routine maintenance:

1 At intervals of 6000 miles (10,000 kilometres) check the tension of the drive belt. The method of checking and adjustment is given in **Chapter 4, Section 4:4**.

2 While checking the fan belt tension, inject a few drops of oil through the hole in the end of the boss of the bracket, shown in **FIG 12:8**. Do not overlubricate otherwise oil will seep through onto the commutator.

3 It is advisable to remove the generator from the engine and check the brushgear for wear at 24,000 mile intervals.

Checking generator output:

1 If the output is low, check the drive belt to make sure that it is at the correct tension and not slipping because of defects in the belt. If the car is only used for stop-start motoring with short journeys, it is possible that the generator has not had a chance to recharge the battery, particularly in winter when accessories are used more and the engine is stiffer to turn. A regular boost charge on a trickle charger will help to overcome this difficulty, but consideration should be given to fitting an alternator in place of the generator.

2 Disconnect the two leads from the D and F terminals on the generator, making sure that their ends cannot accidentally earth. Bridge the terminals on the generator with a jump lead and connect them to earth through a voltmeter. Start the engine and gradually increase its speed. The voltage reading should rise steadily and rapidly with the increase in engine speed. **Do not race the engine in an attempt to obtain a reading and do not allow the engine to speed up beyond the point at which the voltmeter reads 20 volts.** A very low maximum reading indicates defective brushgear while a maximum of 4 to 5 volts indicates defective armature or field coils.

3 It is advisable to reconnect each lead between the control box and generator in turn to the generator, disconnect it from the control box and repeat the test at the end of the lead. This ensures that the leads are satisfactory. The test can also be repeated using the earth point of the control box as the earth point for the voltmeter, as a check on the control earthing.

4 If a voltmeter is not available a rough test can still be carried out. Disconnect the leads from the generator

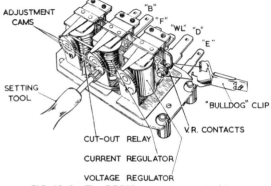

FIG 12:9 The RB340 generator control box

and bridge the terminals on the generator. Remove the drive belt and connect a lead direct from the battery positive terminal to the bridged leads on the generator. If the generator is satisfactory it will operate as a motor and spin freely in its normal direction of rotation. It is advisable to carry out this test when fitting a new generator, as not only does it check the generator but it also sets the generator to the correct polarity of the system.

5 Remove the jumper lead from the terminals of the generator and correctly reconnect the leads of the circuit.

Generator removal:

Disconnect the battery. Disconnect the leads from the D and F terminals on the generator. Slacken the three bolts and nuts that secure the generator, and if necessary slacken the bolt that secures the generator stay to the water pump. Press down the generator to slacken the fan belt tension and remove the belt from the generator pulley. Take out the three sets of attachment bolts so that the generator can be lifted out of the car.

Dismantling:

For complete dismantling the parts are removed in the numerical order shown in **FIG 12:7**. Hold the pulley in a vice with an old fan belt or piece of rope wrapped around it when undoing the pulley nut. The bearing 7 can be

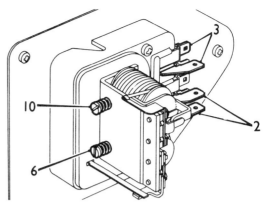

FIG 12:10 Adjusting the RB106 generator control box

removed after the armature shaft has been pressed out through it and the circlip 8 removed. The bush 14 can be extracted using a $\frac{5}{8}$ inch tap screwed into it.

For servicing, the generator need not be fully dismantled. Remove the two through-bolts 3 and the end bracket 4. The armature, drive end bracket and pulley assembly can then be withdrawn from the yoke. When reassembling the parts, lift the brushes partially out of their holders and the springs are then lifted back into place, after reassembly, using a piece of rod through the cooling slots in the end bracket 4.

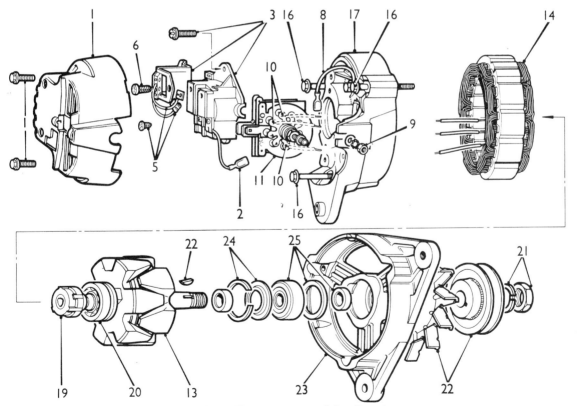

FIG 12:11 The components of the alternator

12:6 The generator control box

Two types of control box are fitted. Models with left-hand steering use a Lucas RB340 control box while models fitted with righthand steering use a Lucas RB106 control box.

The details of the RB340 unit are shown in **FIG 12:9**. Before making any adjustments to the control box of either type, check the following:

1 Check the drive belt tension to the generator and check that the generator is supplying current (see previous Section).

2 Check all the leads and connections between the control box and generator, making sure that there are no loose connections, broken leads or faulty insulation. Check the leads of the generator and earth point of the control unit as described in the previous section.

3 Check the connections on the battery and the earth strap at the frame. Make sure that the battery is capable of holding a charge.

4 After long service the contacts in the unit become dirty and can cause erratic readings. Regulator contacts may be cleaned with a strip of fine silicone carbide paper or carborundum stone. **Cut-out contacts must only be cleaned with a strip of glasspaper as any other material will damage them.** When the points have been cleaned, blow away loose dirt and wipe them over with a piece of cloth moistened with methylated spirits.

Whenever adjustments or checks are carried out on the control box it is essential that only accurate high-grade instruments are used. Unless otherwise stated, the reading, and adjustment, must be completed within 30 seconds of starting the engine, otherwise the coils will heat up and give a false reading for setting. If settings take longer than 30 seconds, stop the engine and allow the coils to cool.

RB340 voltage regulator adjustment:

This can be checked without removing the cover, though the cover must be removed to make adjustments.

1 Disconnect the leads from the B terminal and check that battery voltage is reaching the supply cable. Join the two cables together to allow the engine to be started. Disconnect the lead from the WL terminal and connect a voltmeter between the WL terminal and a good earth.

2 Start the engine and run it to a dynamo speed of 3000 rev/min, noting the reading on the voltmeter. If the adjustment is correct the readings will be between open-circuit voltage settings given in the following table:

3 If the reading varies by more than ± .03 volts, try cleaning the points. If the reading is steady but outside the correct limits, adjust to the settings given in the previous table. Stop the engine and remove the cover from the unit. Use the special tool shown to turn the voltage regulator cam clockwise slightly to raise the setting and anticlockwise to lower it. Note that only small adjustment will be necessary and that the engine should be stopped after every check and before another fine adjustment is made.

4 When the correct adjustment is reached, refit the cover and restore the circuit to normal.

RB340 current regulator adjustment:

If the system is still not charging correctly after the voltage regulator has been adjusted, set the current regulator as follows:

1 Remove the cover. Disconnect the leads from the B terminal and bridge them together as before. Isolate the voltage regulator by clipping its points together with a clip as shown.

2 Connect an ammeter between the bridged cables and the B terminal on the regulator. Start the engine and run it to give a steady generator speed of 4500 rev/min. If the adjustment is correct the ammeter will be reading 22 ± 1 amp, with a maximum fluctuation of 1 amp.

3 If the reading is outside the limits, turn the centre adjuster clockwise to raise the setting and anticlockwise to lower it. Stop the engine when making adjustments and restart it to check the setting. When the adjustment is correct, stop the engine, remove the clip, refit the cover and restore the circuit to normal.

RB340 cut-in voltage:

1 Disconnect the cable from the WL terminal on the unit and connect a voltmeter between the WL terminal and a good earth on the car. Start the engine and switch on the headlamps.

2 Gradually increase the speed of the engine while watching the voltmeter. The reading will steadily rise, reach a peak, and then drop slightly. Note the peak reading, which should be 12.7 to 13.3 volts. Note that the test can be done without the headlamps on but the peak may then be more difficult to determine.

3 If the adjustment is incorrect, stop the engine and remove the cover. Restart the engine and adjust the cut-out cam clockwise to increase the setting and anticlockwise to lower the reading. Increase the engine speed and check the setting, allowing the engine to slow down far enough for the points to open before making further adjustments. Refit the cover and restore the circuit.

Voltage regulator setting limits:

Ambient temperature	Open-circuit voltage setting	When checking in service	
		In between	Reset to
0° to 25°C (32° to 77°F)	14.5 to 15.5 V	14.0 to 14.5 V	14.5 V
		15.5 to 16.0 V	15.5 V
26° to 40°C (79° to 104°F)	14.25 to 15.25 V	13.75 to 14.25 V	14.25 V
		15.25 to 15.75 V	15.25 V

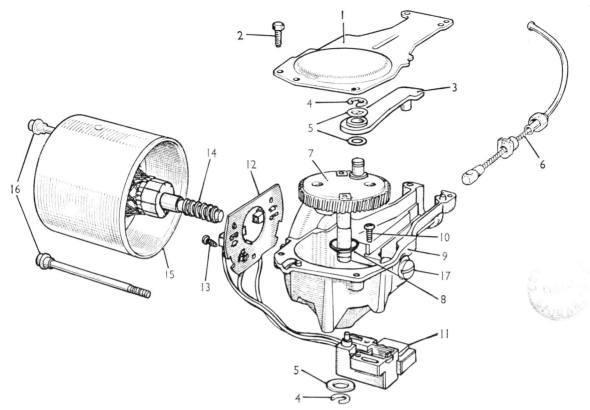

FIG 12:12   The windscreen wiper motor components

Key to Fig 12:12   1 Gearbox cover   2 Screws   3 Connecting rod   4 Circlip   5 Washers   6 Cable rack assembly
7 Shaft and gear   8 Dished washer   9 Gearbox   10 Screw   11 Limit switch assembly   12 Brush gear   13 Screw   14 Armature
15 Cover assembly   16 Through bolts   17 Armature adjusting screw

RB340 Drop-off voltage:

1 Disconnect the leads from the B terminal, bridge them together and connect a voltmeter between the leads and B terminal. Start the engine and run it up until the speed is above the cut-in speed. Slowly allow the speed to drop while watching the voltmeter. The reading will fall steadily and suddenly drop to zero, indicating that the contacts have opened. Note the voltmeter reading just before the points open and if the adjustment is satisfactory the reading will be 9.5 to 11.0 volts.

2 If the reading is outside the limits, remove the cover. Bend the fixed contact support to alter the drop-off voltage. Closing the gap will raise the voltage and opening will lower the voltage.

3 Refit the cover and restore the circuit to normal.

RB106 open circuit voltage:

1 Remove the cover and disconnect the leads from the A and A1 terminals, shown as 2 in **FIG 12:10,** and connect the cables together to allow the engine to run, after checking that battery voltage is reaching the supply cable. Connect a voltmeter between the D and E terminals, shown as 3.

2 Start the engine and run it at a steady generator speed of 3000 rev/min. The reading on the voltmeter should lie between 16.0 and 16.6 volts at an ambient temperature of 20°C (68°F). For every 10°C (18°F) rise in ambient temperature subtract .1-volt from the setting and add .1-volt for every equivalent drop in temperature. If the adjustment is incorrect, turn the screw 6 clockwise to raise and anticlockwise to lower the setting.

3 Stop the engine. Restart it and slowly run it up to a generator speed of 4500 rev/min. Check that the voltage reading is a maximum of 17.1 volts (after making allowance for ambient temperature difference from standard). Refit the cover and restore the circuit to normal.

RB106 cut-in voltage:

1 Remove the cover and connect a voltmeter between the terminals 3. Start the engine and increase the speed until there is a momentary drop in the voltmeter reading, indicating that the contact points have closed. If the adjustment is correct, this drop should occur at 12.7 to 13.3 volts, allowing for ambient temperature.

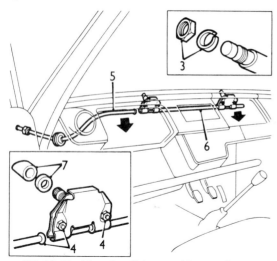

FIG 12:13   The wiper linkage and its attachments

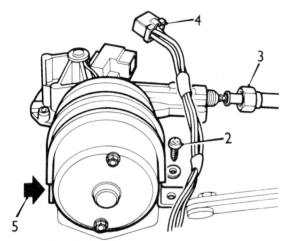

FIG 12:14   The wiper motor attachments

2 If the adjustment is incorrect, turn the adjusting screw 10 clockwise to increase the voltmeter reading and anticlockwise to reduce it. Carry out this adjustment as rapidly as possible to prevent heating of the coils from altering the reading. Refit the cover and restore the circuit to normal.

12:7 The alternator

The components of the alternator are shown in **FIG 12:11**. The unit is dismantled in the numerical order of the parts shown in the figure, noting the following points:
1 When unsoldering the stator leads from the rectifier pack at 10, note their positions so that they can be resoldered back to their original terminals. **When unsoldering any wires connected to the diodes in the rectifier pack, use a hot iron so that the solder melts rapidly and grip the diode pin with a pair of long-nosed pliers to act as a heat-sink and prevent heat from reaching the diode.** This also applies when resoldering the leads.

2 Before removing the stator 14, mark its position in relation to the end brackets.
3 If the rotor bearing 25 has to be removed the slip rings 19 must first be taken off, after unsoldering their connections to the stator.

The alternator is reassembled in the reverse order of dismantling, after checking and cleaning the parts.

Precautions:

The following precautions must be carried out when an alternator is fitted:
1 Never make or break the charging circuit while the engine is running.
2 Always ensure that the system is at the correct polarity, as reverse voltages can damage the alternator.
3 When carrying out arc-welding repairs to the bodywork or charging the battery on a heavy duty boost charger, always disconnect the charging circuit to prevent the alternator from picking up stray induced voltages.

Servicing:

Generally servicing can be carried out following the instructions given in **Section 12:3**. The field coil resistance is measured between the rotor slip rings. The stator windings have a very low resistance and need not be checked for resistance, but they should be checked for continuity and insulation. Check between any pair of stator leads then repeat the test using one of the original leads and the third lead.

The slip rings must not be machined and usually wiping with a cloth moistened with methylated spirits is sufficient though they may be lightly polished with fine glasspaper if required.

Diodes:

These are tested with a 12-volt battery and 1.5 watt test lamp. Connect the lamp and battery in series across the diode pin and its heat sink, then repeat the test with the polarity reversed. If the diode is satisfactory the bulb will light when the current flows in one direction but it will prevent current flowing in the reverse direction and the lamp will not light. If the lamp lights in both directions, or fails to light at all then the diode is defective and the rectifier assembly 11 must be renewed.

12:8 The windscreen wipers

A Lucas 14W two-speed wiper motor is fitted as standard, and the components of the motor are shown in **FIG 12:12**.

Poor or no operation:

Check the fuse and if it has blown trace through the circuit for faults such as defective insulation.

If the wipers operate sluggishly, first check through the wiring for points of high resistance. Use a voltmeter to check that all points in the circuit give battery voltage. A test bulb can be used, in which case it should glow as brightly when connected between terminals (with the

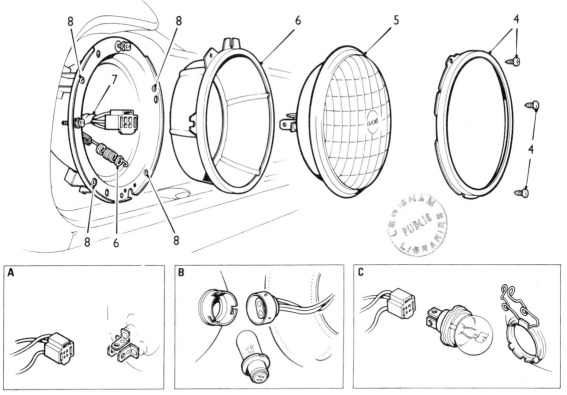

FIG 12:15   The headlamp attachments

motor disconnected) and earth as it does across the battery. Clean up and tighten any loose or poor contacts.

Remove the gearbox cover 1 from the motor and disconnect the connecting rod 3 from the cable rack by removing the circlip 4. Connect an accurate ammeter into the circuit and measure the operating current after the motor has been running for a minute. At normal speed the motor should take 1.5 amps and at high-speed it should take 2 amps. The normal speed is 46 to 52 cycles/minute while the high-speed is 60 to 70 cycles/minute.

If the motor does not operate satisfactorily on its own then the fault lies in the motor. Abnormal current demands by the motor can be caused by faulty brush gear or defective armature, while high currents will be caused by internal shortcircuits or excessive internal resistance. No field coils are fitted as the exciter field is produced by a permanent magnet in the cover 15.

If the motor operates satisfactorily on its own, check the linkage, shown in **FIG 12:13**. Remove the wiper arms from the spindles of the wheel boxes and use a spring balance to check that the pull required to move the cable operating rack (after disconnection from the motor) does not exceed 6 lb (2.72 kg). If this force is exceeded then the tubes are damaged or misaligned or the wheelboxes are damaged. The parts of the linkage can be removed following the numerical order given in **FIG 12:13,** after the instrument panel and glove box have been taken out (see **Chapter 13**) and the wiper arms and cable rack removed.

Removing the motor:

The attachments of the motor are shown in **FIG 12:14.** Take out the screw 2 which secures the motor strap. Undo the cable union nut 3 and disconnect the connector 4. Remove the wiper arms from the wheelbox spindles. Press the motor clamp strap into its release slot 5 and lift out the motor. Withdraw the cable rack with the motor.

Refit the motor in the reverse order of removal, guiding the cable rack through the tubing of the linkage. When the motor is in place, operate it and switch it off so that it is in the park position. Refit the wiper arms so that they are also correctly in their parked positions.

Dismantling the motor:

1 Disconnect the cable rack by removing the circlip 4 and lifting out the connecting rod, carefully collecting the washers 5. Check that the end of the gearshaft is free from burrs and damage, polishing it with emery-cloth if necessary. Withdraw the shaft and gear 7, noting the position of the dished washer 8. Do not remove the crankpin mounting plate from the gear unless it is essential, and if it must be removed carefully mark the relation of the pin to the gear.

2 Indelibly mark across the cover 15 and gearbox flange 9, noting that if the cover is assembled 180 deg. out the motor will run in reverse. Take out the two through-bolts 16 and withdraw the cover by **no more** than

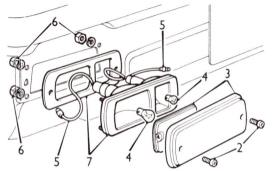

FIG 12:16 The front sidelight assembly

$\frac{3}{16}$ inch. Ease the brushes off the commutator and then completely withdraw the parts, **taking care to prevent grease from getting onto the brushes.**

3 Remove the screws 10 and 13 to free the limit switch 11 and brush gear assembly 12.

Servicing and reassembly:

The parts are serviced following the instructions given in **Section 12:3.** Wipe out any old grease and lubricate the bearings and shafts with Shell Turbo 41 grease on reassembly. The gearbox and cable rack should be packed with Ragosine Listate grease.

Reassembly is the reverse of the dismantling operation, but take care when refitting the cover not to damage the brushes or contaminate them with grease. The screw 17 controls the armature end float, and it should be adjusted to give a float of .004 to .008 inch (.1 to .21 mm). Packing washers can be fitted under the head to increase the end float but the underside of the head must be turned down in a lathe if the end float is excessive. On some models a locknut and screw will be found and these can be used to set the adjustment without any trouble.

12:9 The headlamps

The attachments of a headlamp are shown in **FIG 12:15,** and the insets to the figure show the different methods of fitting the bulb. In the inset A sealed beam units are used, where the whole light unit 5 is a bulb with the filaments sealed into it. Do not handle bulbs with the bare hands but use a piece of tissue or clean cloth.

Removal:

Disconnect the battery. Remove the four screws securing the front grille at the top of the body. Lift out the grille. Remove the three rim securing screws 4 and lift out the light unit 5 and disconnect it as shown in the appropriate inset.

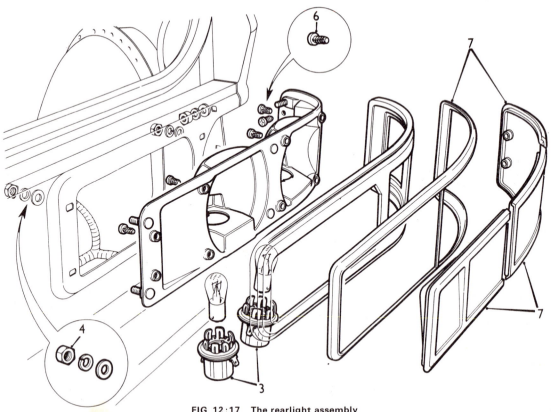

FIG 12:17 The rearlight assembly

If more parts require removal, disconnect the spring 6 and lift out the shell, freeing it from the two adjusting screws. Free the snap connectors at the wing valance for the leads 7. Drill out the rivets 8 and detach the lamp shell complete with wiring from the body.

The parts are refitted in the reverse order of removal.

Beam setting:

Remove the grille in order to gain access to the two adjusting screws on each headlamp. The beams can be set by standing the car a little distance from, and squarely to, a plain vertical wall. The upper adjusting screw controls the vertical alignment and the screw on the side the horizontal alignment.

It is more accurate to take the car to an agent who will set the beams precisely, and within the legal limits, using special beamsetter equipment.

12:10 Direction indicators

If the flash rate on one side alters or stops, check the bulbs on that side as a blown filament will badly affect the flashing rate. The attachments of the front lights are shown in **FIG 12:16** and the bulbs are accessible after the two screws 2 and lens parts 3 have been removed. The attachments of the rear lights are shown in **FIG 12:17**.

The Estate models and Vans are mounted vertically, flasher uppermost, and may be contoured around the rear quarter corners to give a wide radius of visibility.

The bulbs are accessible after the holders have been freed from inside the luggage compartment. **Check that the bulb holders or connections have not accidentally been displaced by luggage or items in the boot.**

If the flashers fail to operate, disconnect the leads 2 from the flasher unit, shown in **FIG 12:18,** and use a suitable tester to check that battery voltage is reaching the unit. Connect the two leads together and operate the direction indicator switch. The lamps should operate correctly, but without flashing. If lamps do not operate, trace through the wiring to find the fault and at the same time make sure that the earth points of the lamps are satisfactory. If the lamps do operate correctly, the flasher unit itself is at fault and must be renewed. Unclip the old unit from its holder and fit a new one back into place. Handle the unit with care and do not plug it back into a live circuit.

12:11 Temperature and fuel gauges

Both these instruments operate from a special voltage stabilizer, and the whole system uses the expansion and contraction of bi-metallic springs, as they heat and cool when current is passed through them. If either instrument is defective, trace through the wiring and check for faults. If both instruments fail then it is likely that the voltage stabilizer unit itself is defective. Ordinary instruments cannot be used for testing the systems. The voltage stabilizer opens and closes its contacts so that over a period of time the current flow through the system is exactly the same as if the systems were connected to a stable 10-volt supply. If a voltmeter is used to take the reading it will give alternating periods of full battery voltage and no voltage. Special test instruments are essential and for this reason the car should be taken to an agent who can then pinpoint the fault and change the

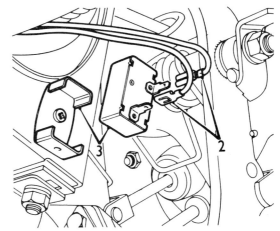

FIG 12:18 The flasher unit attachments

defective unit, without the process of trial and error that the owner would have to carry out. **Never connect parts of the system across full battery voltage.**

12:12 Fuses

Fuses are fitted to protect the circuits, and they will blow on an overload. On some models a line fuse is fitted and this must not be overlooked if the rear lights fail.

Do not fit fuses of a higher rating than is called for in an attempt to cure intermittently blowing fuses. A higher rating fuse may fail to blow and make the wiring burn out instead.

On early model cars the fuse box is mounted on the inner body panel on the righthand side behind the facia, on Series 2 cars it is located on the back of the parcel shelf.

According to model there may be two, four or five fuses in the box. Two spare fuses are also provided, one of each rating when this is applicable. Further details of the circuits protected may be found in the **Wiring Diagrams** in the **Appendix.**

12:13 Fault diagnosis

(a) Battery discharged

1 Terminals loose or dirty
2 Shortcircuit in part of system not protected by fuse
3 Alternator/generator not charging
4 Battery internally defective

(b) Battery will not hold charge

1 Low electrolyte level
2 Battery plates sulphated or distorted
3 Electrolyte leakage from cracked case
4 Plate separators ineffective

(c) Alternator output low or nil

1 Loose or broken drive belt
2 No battery supply to field coils (in rotor)
3 Defective wiring
4 Control unit failed (defective diodes)
5 Brushes excessively worn or slip rings dirty

(d) Generator output low or nil

1 Loose or defective drive belt
2 Defective wiring
3 Control box failed or incorrectly adjusted
4 Defective brush gear
5 Defective armature or field coils
6 Mechanical defects in generator

(e) Starter motor lacks power or will not operate

1 Battery discharged, loose or dirty connectors
2 Starter jammed in mesh
3 Starter switch defective
4 Starter solenoid defective
5 Brush gear defective
6 Armature or field coils defective
7 Engine abnormally stiff

(f) Starter motor runs but does not turn engine

1 Dirt jamming pinion open
2 Broken teeth on pinion or flywheel ring gear

(g) Starter motor rough or noisy

1 Loose mountings
2 Damaged pinion or flywheel teeth

3 Weak or broken pinion spring
4 Motor mechanically defective

(h) Lamps inoperative or erratic

1 Battery low
2 Bulb filaments blown
3 Defective wiring
4 Faulty earth points
5 Defective lighting switch
6 Blown fuse

(i) Fuel or temperature gauges do not register

1 No battery supply to voltage stabilizer
2 Defective voltage stabilizer
3 Broken cable
4 Defective gauge
5 Defective transmitter
6 Poor earth on transmitter unit

(j) Fuel or temperature gauges erratic

1 Defective wiring
2 Defective voltage stabilizer
3 Defective transmitting units
4 Defective gauges

CHAPTER 13

THE BODYWORK

13:1 Bodywork repairs

Large scale repairs to bodywork are best left to experts. Even small dents can be tricky as too much or injudicious hammering will stretch the metal and make the dent worse instead of better. Gentle tapping to reduce the dent will help but the best method available to the owner is filling and spraying, particularly when self-spraying cans of exactly matching paint are readily available. Minor dents and scratches should be touched in with a retouching kit before the metal underneath has a chance to corrode.

As the car gets older the surface finish will lose its lustre and fade slightly so there may be a slight difference between new paint and the old finish. Spraying a complete wing or panel will make any difference in colour far less obvious. Original lustre and colour can be partially restored using a mild cutting compound type cleaner, but this must not be used too often as it removes paint to expose a new layer underneath.

If an area is to be sprayed or filled, wash it thoroughly with white spirits to remove all traces of wax polish. Even more drastic treatment will be required to remove silicone-based polishes. If possible, take off any trim or handles in the area as a better result will be obtained with these removed. Lightly scuff the whole area to give a

good key for the new finish and rub down any corrosion to bare metal. Apply a coat of primer over bare metal areas. Build up the damaged area to just proud of the surface, using filler or paste stopper as required. When the surface is hard, rub it down using 400 grade 'Wet and Dry' paper and clean water. Wash off slurry and apply further coats of filler or stopper if required. Spend plenty of time and patience at this stage in removing all blemishes and obtaining a perfect surface, as any marks at this stage will stand out glaringly on the final polished surface. When the surface is smooth, wash it down with plenty of water and let it dry and then wash off the slurry that was missed in the first wash.

Mask off surrounding areas using newspaper and masking tape.

Spray a complete panel evenly all over, including the edges, but if only a patch is being sprayed the paint should be 'feathered' at the edges. Apply two or more thin coats, rubbing down between each coat, rather than one thick one which may run.

Remove the masking and leave the paint to dry for at least a night. Use a mild cutting-compound to lightly polish the surface and remove any spray dust. Leave the paint to fully harden for a period of weeks, not days, before applying wax polish.

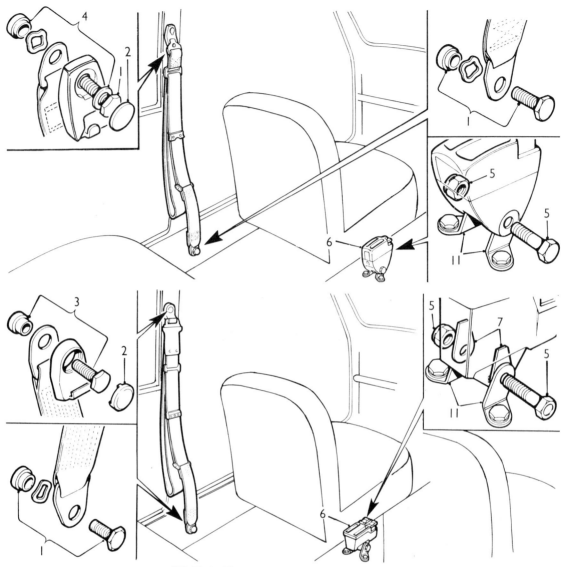

FIG 13:1   The attachments of static seat belts

13:2   Seat belts

Strong points for attaching seat belts are built into the car and usually cars are supplied with belts already fitted. A standard simple belt can be fitted, or an optional reel type belt. The attachments for the standard static seat belts are shown in **FIG 13:1**, and those for the optional reel type belts are shown in **FIG 13:2**. When fitting Kangol reel type belts, make sure that the arrow in the inset 20 is vertical. To adjust the arrow position, slacken the screw beside it and turn the arrow to the vertical, then retighten the screw.

Do not attempt to alter the attachments of the belts and periodically check that the attachments are tight and secure. If the belts become soiled, they may be washed by gently sponging with non-detergent soap and warm water and then allowed to air dry naturally. **Do not apply any cleaning chemicals, bleaches or dyes to the belts.**

Reel type belts can be checked by driving at 5 mile/hr and sharply applying the brakes. The reel should lock instantly.

If in any doubt about the condition, attachments or details of the seat belts, consult an agent.

13:3   Door interior trim

Typical trim pad details are shown in **FIG 13:3**. Take out the screw and spacer 1 from the window regulator handle 2 and remove the handle and circular washer. Remove the armrest 3 by taking out the two attachment

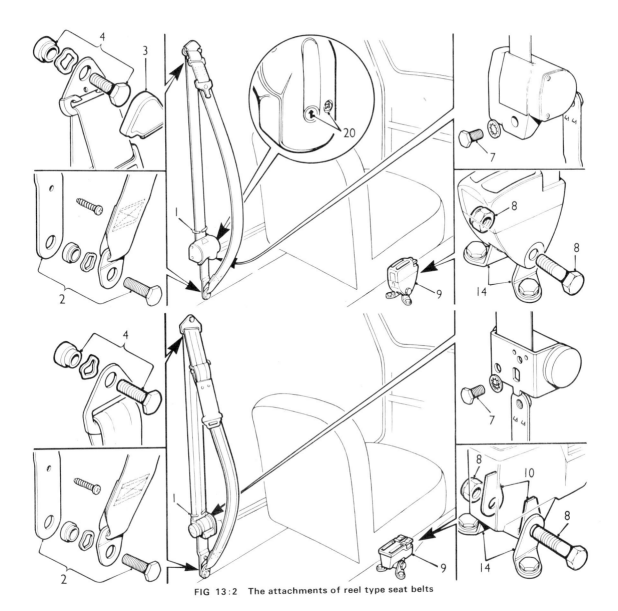

FIG 13:2 The attachments of reel type seat belts

screws or, if applicable, remove the pull handle which also is retained by two screws. On later cars these are covered by a snap-on protector.

The bezels for the remote control handles on early cars may be slid off, on later models they are retained by a single cross-head screw. On later cars also the door locking button must be unscrewed before the trim pad can be carefully levered off, pulling the retaining clips out of their holes in the door panel.

Refit the trim panel in the reverse order of removal.

Door trim capping:

Remove the arm rest interior handle, bezels and trim panel. Take out the screws that secure the capping and unclip it from the door.

Refit the capping in the reverse order of removal, making sure that the door glass seal and wiper are correctly positioned.

13:4 Door glass and regulator

The parts are shown in **FIG 13:4**.

Removal:

1 Remove the door interior trim pad as described in the previous section. Lower the glass until the glass regulator channel 14 is accessible through the aperture in the inner panel.

2 Remove the four screws and washers 3 that secure the regulator 4. The inset shows the regulator fitted to rear doors. When removing the regulator, free the

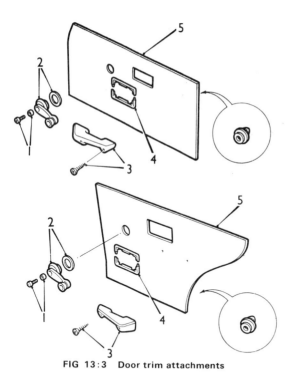

FIG 13:3 Door trim attachments

arm from the channel 14 and withdraw the unit through the aperture in the inner door panel. Hold the glass up by hand or support it with rubber wedges between it and the door.

3 On front doors lower the glass right down to the bottom, but on rear doors raise it to the top and support it. If a finisher strip is fitted, remove it. Spring off the six clips 6 securing the outer weatherstrip and remove the strip 6. Similarly remove the wiper strip 7 by freeing its six clips 7. Remove the window channel rubber 8.

4 Drill out the pop rivet 9, remove the screw and washer 10 securing the bottom of the centre window channel, and remove the channel 11 by turning it through 90 deg. and aligning the narrowest section with the glass aperture in the door. Remove the quarter light assembly 12.

5 The window glass can now be removed, if necessary taking off the regulator channel and its rubber 14 from the glass.

Refit the parts in the reverse order of removal, making sure that the regulator channel is fitted centrally on the glass. Grease regulator and pivot points.

13:5 Door locks

There are some slight differences in the locks fitted to early and late model cars and typical illustrations of the front and rear door arrangements are given in **FIGS 13:5** and **13:6** respectively.

Removal:

1 Remove the door trim panel as described in **Section 13:3**. Remove the three screws and shakeproof washers that secure the remote control assembly 3 and remove the lock screw. Disconnect the long

remote control rod 4 from the safety locking lever. On front doors, disconnect the remote release rod 19 from the clip 21 (rod 18 from clip 20 on rear doors). Remove the remote control unit.

2 On the front door only, remove the screw that secures the bottom of the centre window channel (see item 10 in **FIG 13:4**), and disconnect the outside handle transfer lever 13 from the lifting stud on the cross control lever.

3 On the rear doors only, disconnect the screwed rod 11 from the cross control lever.

4 Disconnect the remote release rod 19 from the operating lever on the front lock. On the rear lock disconnect the rod 18 from the freewheel assembly on the lock.

5 On the front door, disconnect the lock rod clip 15 from the lock rod 14. On both doors disconnect the short lock rod 8 from the lock assembly. Mark the position of the lock assembly relative to the door, take out the attachments screws and remove the assembly.

The parts are refitted in the reverse order of removal. Lightly lubricate pivot points before refitting the parts. The operation of the remote control unit can be adjusted by altering the lengths of the control rods.

Exterior handle and private lock:

The attachments of the parts are shown in **FIG 13:7**. Remove the door trim pad, as described in **Section 13:3**. Remove the screws or nuts 2 that secure the clamp plate 3 and take out the plate.

On the front door, disconnect the private lock control rod from the locking bar cross-shaft at the clip 4 and disconnect the screwed rod 5 from the exterior handle.

On the rear door, disconnect the screwed rod 6 from the cross lever. In both cases the exterior handle can now be removed.

The private lock is secured by the circlip shown in the figure and can be taken out after removing the circlip, spring washer and special washer.

The parts are refitted in the reverse order of removal. The screwed rod 5 or 6 should not be altered when dismantling or reassembling the parts. Check the adjustment before refitting the trim panel.

Close the door and partially operate the outside handle and check that there is free movement of the lever before transfer lever and screwed rod move. Fully operate the exterior handle and check that the lock is released before the handle is fully operated. If the settings are not correct, alter the effective length of the screwed rod 5 or 6 to correct.

Striker plate:

This is secured to the pillar by two countersunk screws. **Do not slam the door if the striker is out of adjustment.**

Tighten the striker screws sufficiently to hold the striker in place while allowing it to move under pressure. Gently shut the door and pull or push on the door until it is in line with the body. Carefully open the door so as not to move the striker. Make lines around the striker so that it can be aligned horizontally. Make vertical adjustments of the striker until the door can be closed easily, without rattling, dropping or having to be lifted. Tighten the striker adjustment screws fully in this position. When correctly adjusted, it should be possible to press the door in slightly against the compression of the door seal.

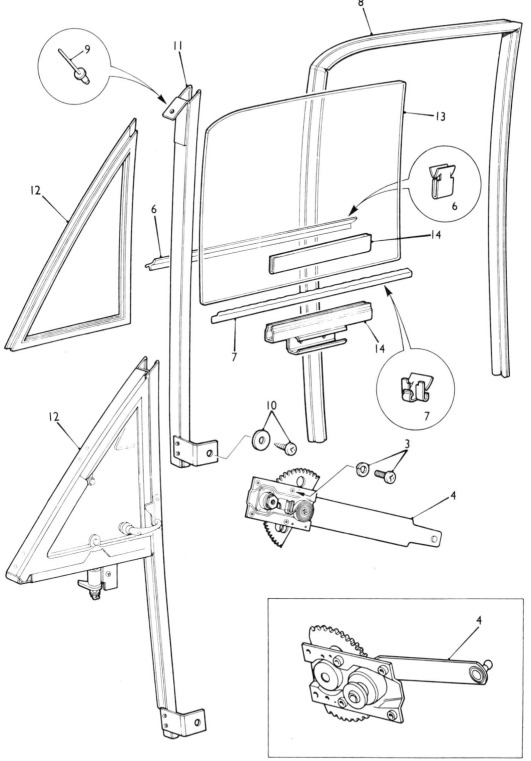

FIG 13:4   The door glass and regulator components

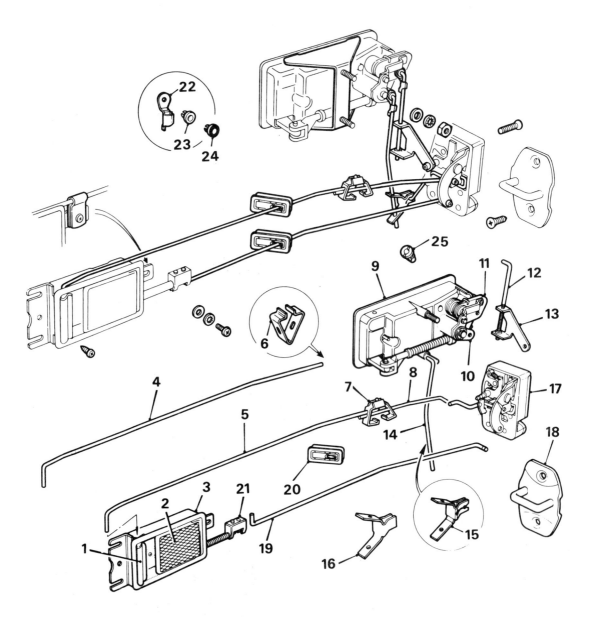

FIG 13:5 Typical front door lock components

Key to Fig 13:5   1 Safety locking lever   2 Remote release handle   3 Remote control assembly   4 Remote lockrod, long (early type)   5 Remote lockrod, long (later type)   6 Remote lockrod clip (early type)   7 Remote lockrod clip (later type) 8 Remote lockrod, short   9 Outside handle   10 Lock barrel freewheel lever   11 Outside handle release lever   12 Screwed rod   13 Transfer lever   14 Lockrod (outside handle)   15 Lockrod clip (early type)   16 Lockrod clip (later type)   17 Disc lock assembly   18 Lock striker   19 Remote release rod   20 Door rod guide   21 Retaining clip   22 Rod clip   23 Rod bush (early type)   24 Rod bush (later type, black finish)

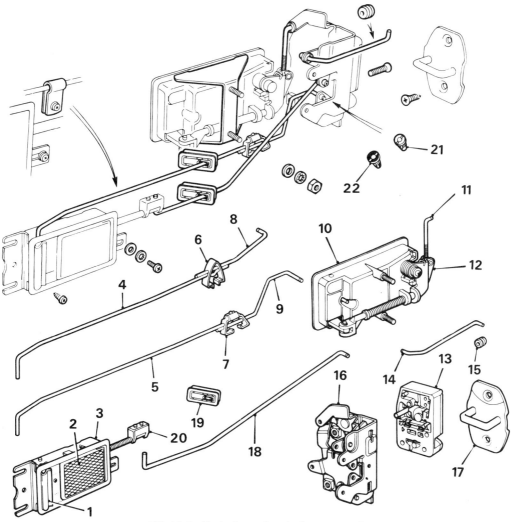

FIG 13:6 Typical rear door lock components

Key to Fig 13:6   1 Safety locking lever   2 Remote release lever   3 Remote control assembly   4 Remote lockrod, long
(early type)   5 Remote lockrod, long (later type)   6 Remote lockrod clip (early type)   7 Remote lockrod clip (later type)
8 Remote lockrod, short (early type)   9 Remote lockrod, short (later type)   10 Outside handle   11 Screwed rod   12 Outside
handle release lever   13 Disc lock assembly   14 Child safety lever rod   15 Door grommet   16 Freewheel assembly
17 Lock striker   18 Remote release rod   19 Door rod guide   20 Retaining clip   21 Rod bush (early type)   22 Rod bush
(later type, black finish)

13:6 Door attachments

The door attachments are shown in **FIG 13:8.**
Remove the door trim panel. Mark the position of the
stiffening plates inside the door at 2. Support the door
and remove the nuts 3, with their washers, and the
stiffening plates 4. The door 5 can then be lifted off.

Refit the door in the reverse order of removal.

The remainder of the figure shows the attachments of
the hinges to the body. Note that the front parcel tray
must be removed and the trim pulled back to remove the
front hinges, and the trim must be removed from the
B post to remove the rear hinges.

13:7 The bonnet

The bonnet hinge attachments are shown in **FIG 13:9.**
To remove the bonnet, open it and support it open on its
stay. Mark around the hinges and bonnet at 4 so as to
make refitting easier. Have an assistant support the bonnet
and remove the screws 5 that secure the hinge to the
bonnet. Lift off the bonnet, **taking great care to
prevent its corners from scratching the paintwork
on the body.**

Refit the bonnet in the reverse order of removal. If the
bonnet does not line up accurately, leave all screws just
tight enough to prevent the bonnet from moving under

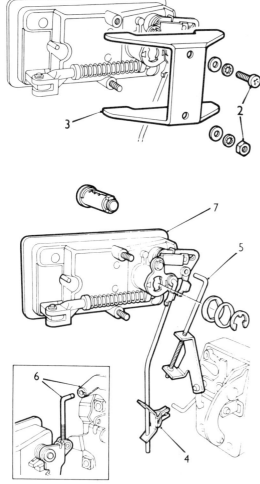

FIG 13:7 The exterior handle attachments

its own weight and pull or push it into alignment. Once the bonnet is in place, do not overtighten the attachment screws.

The bonnet lock components are shown in **FIG 13:10.** The bolts retaining the radiator support brackets, shown in inset 2, are only fitted to 1.8 models. If the parts require removal, they are freed in the numerical order shown in the figure.

When refitting the lock parts, the release cable should be located in the clip 4 and trunnion 3 so that a minimum movement of $\frac{1}{2}$ inch (13 mm) is required on the control before the bonnet is released, and the bonnet should release before the control has been pulled out by 2 inch (50 mm) of movement.

The lockpin on the bonnet should be set to the dimension A at 2 inch (50.8 mm). Some adjustment on the bolts 6 is possible to ensure that the pin enters the lock centrally. When the bonnet is closed check if it rattles, in which case shorten the dimension A. If the bonnet is difficult to close, slightly lengthen the dimension A.

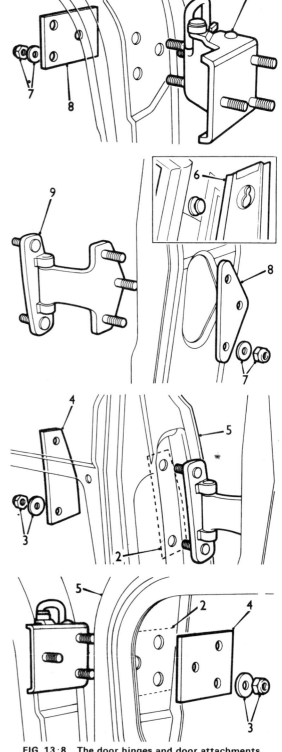

FIG 13:8 The door hinges and door attachments

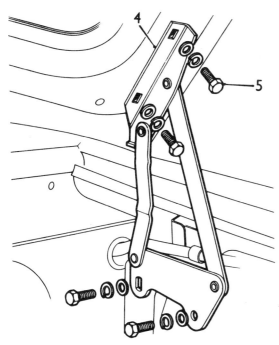

FIG 13:9   The bonnet hinge

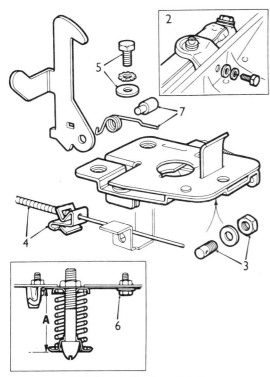

FIG 13:10   The bonnet lock

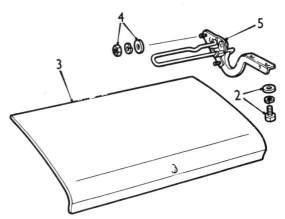

FIG 13:11   The luggage locker lid

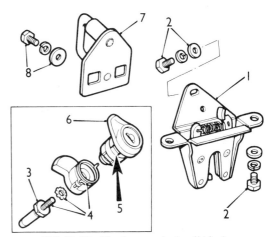

FIG 13:12   The luggage locker lid lock

13:8 The luggage compartment lid

The attachments of the lid are shown in **FIG 13:11**. The lid alone can be removed by taking out the bolts 2 that secure the hinge to the lid, after marking the position of the hinge relative to the lid. The hinges can then be removed from the car by taking off the nuts and washers 4.

The holes are slotted to allow the lid to be accurately aligned with the body when it is refitted. Do not over-tighten the attachment bolts when refitting the lid.

The lock components are shown in **FIG 13:12**. Mark the position of the catch plate 1 relative to the lid and remove the lock catch by taking out the three screws and washers 2. Slacken the locknut and unscrew the spindle 3 so that the spindle striker, shakeproof washer and spring 4 can be removed. Break off the ears 5 on the retaining clip and remove the seal and lock barrel 6. The striker 7 on the body can be removed, after marking its position, by removing the bolts 8.

Refit the parts in the reverse order of removal, using a new retaining clip on the barrel housing.

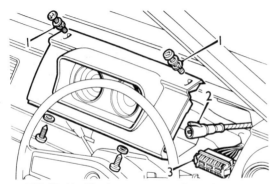

FIG 13:13   The instrument panel attachments

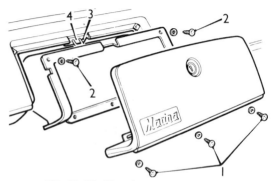

FIG 13:15   The glove box attachments

13:9 The windscreen

The method of attaching the backlight and quarter light is the same as for the windscreen, but references to the wiper arms and cleaning out the ventilation system can be ignored. If a heated backlight is fitted, the leads must be disconnected before removing the glass.

Deluxe models are fitted with a plastic insert which locks the rubber weatherseal into place. This type of insert should be refitted, once the glass and weatherseal is in place, with a glazier tool 18G.468.B which has a loop for opening the rubber to allow the insert to slide in, and a roller which then presses it firmly into place.

Super Deluxe models have a bright metal insert. In both cases the insert should be freed using a blunt screwdriver and on the Super Deluxe models the insert is also refitted using a blunt tool.

If the glass has broken and fallen away, take care to remove all particles from the car. **If a windscreen has broken it is particularly important to ensure that there are no particles left in the ventilation system, even if it means dismantling the system, as the action of the heater can blow the particles into the front seat occupants' faces.** If the glass has broken but not fallen out, it will be easier to remove if sheets of paper are stuck on both sides.

If the glass has to be removed in an unbroken state, remove the insert from around the weatherseal. Use a wooden wedge to free the lip of the weatherseal inside the car and remove the glass by pressing on it firmly with a padded hand or foot. Start at the top corner and have an assistant outside to take the glass as it comes free.

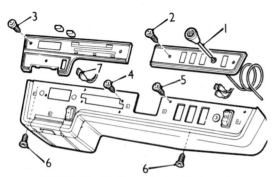

FIG 13:14   The lower facia attachments

Remove the wiper arms before working on the windscreen.

Once the glass has been removed, check the flange in the body aperture for damage or distortion. Dress out dents with a block of metal and hammer and file down any protrusions with a smooth file. If the flange is left distorted, it can set up stress points which will cause the new glass to break in service.

Lay the glass onto a padded bench and refit the weather seal to it. Apply sealer between the glass and rubber. Apply a bed of mastic sealer to the body flange. **It should be noted that as the glass is sealed into place, it is unlikely that the old weatherseal will be in good condition after removal and it is always advisable to fit a new one on reassembly.**

Lay a length of cord around the groove in the weatherseal into which the aperture flange will fit, making sure that the cord is long enough to overlap at the ends leaving enough hanging out to get a good grip on.

Pass the ends of the cord through the aperture and have an assistant accurately and firmly press the glass and weatherseal assembly against the aperture. Grip the ends of the cord and pull them out of the groove, parallel and towards the centre of the glass, so that the lip of the rubber is lifted over the flange and into place.

Refit the embellisher or insert. Wipe away surplus sealant with a cloth moistened with white spirits. **Avoid the excessive use of white spirits otherwise the solvent will creep between the glass and rubber and wash out sealant.**

13:10 The facia and instrument panel

Instrument panel:

The attachments are shown in **FIG 13:13**. It should be noted that the panel must be removed to change the instrument bulbs or the voltage stabilizer for the fuel and temperature gauges.

Disconnect the battery. Take out the four screws 1 which secure the panel in place. Partially withdraw the panel. Press the release lever and disconnect the speedometer drive cable from the back of the instrument. Disconnect the multi-connector 3 and if a tachometer is fitted, disconnect the lead at the back of the instrument. The panel can then be removed from the car.

Refit the panel in the reverse order of removal, noting that the longer screws are fitted above the instruments.

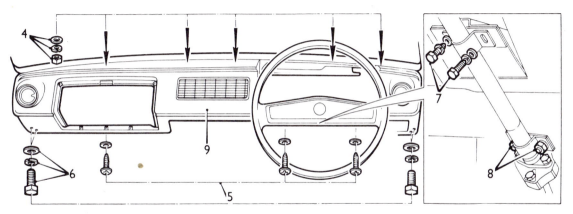

FIG 13:16   The facia attachments (Saloon and Estate cars)

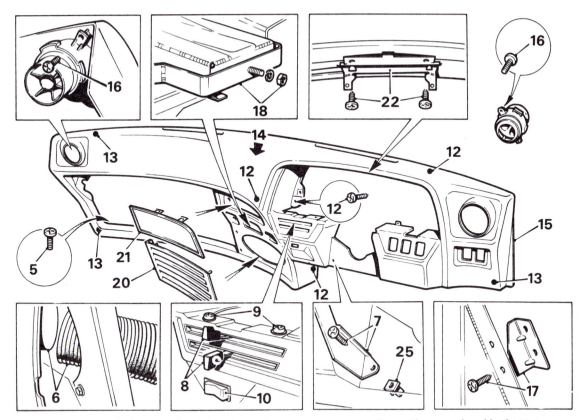

FIG 13:16A   The facia panel on Series 2 cars showing components and operations mentioned in the text

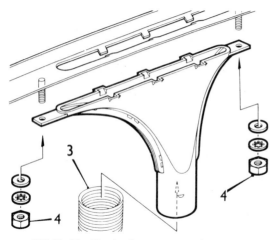

FIG 13:17   The demister vent attachments

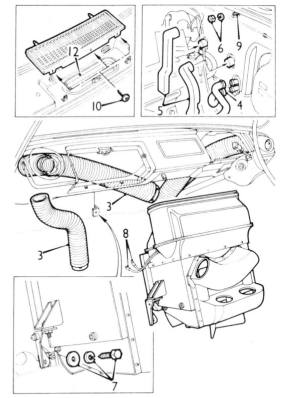

FIG 13:18   The heater attachments

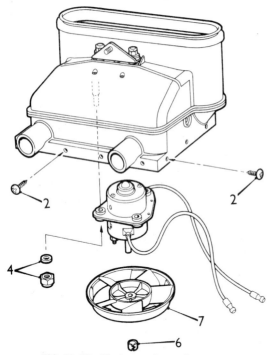

FIG 13:19   The heater fan and motor

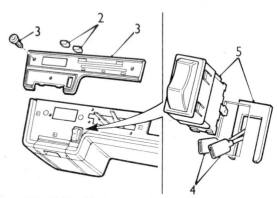

FIG 13:20   The heater switch and control panel

Lower facia panel:

The attachments are shown in **FIG 13:14**. Free the choke cable 1 from the carburetter and pull out the inner cable. Remove the screws 2 and 3 securing the switch panels and remove the panels. Note that the battery should be disconnected before removing switch panels. Remove the two screws 4 securing the heater controls. Remove the three screws 5 and the two screws 6. Move the panel slightly forward so that the heater switch and

lighting switch connections can be freed. Remove the panel, at the same time withdrawing the choke outer cable.

Refit the parts in the reverse order of removal.

Glove box:

The attachments are shown in **FIG 13:15** and the parts are removed in the numerical order shown in the figure. Refit the parts in the reverse order of removal.

The facia (Saloon and Estate cars):

The facia attachments are shown in **FIG 13:16**. Remove the instrument panel, lower facia and glove box. The parts are then removed in the numerical order shown in the figure. The bolts 7 securing the upper steering column upper clamp must be removed but the nuts for the lower clamp 8 need only be slackened.

The parts are refitted in the reverse order of removal.

The facia (Vans):

To remove the facia panel on Van models proceed as follows:

Remove the cowling around the central instrument group, this is secured by a single screw on either side, and then remove the speedometer. This is retained by four screws. Make sure that the electric leads which must be removed are clearly identified.

Remove the glove box (four screws) and the windscreen demister ducts.

Remove the ash tray clamp plate (one nut and washer) and pull out the ash tray assembly.

Take out the four screws and remove the two halves of the cowling over the steering column lock and switches. Unclip the cowl support bracket.

Slacken the cable trunnion screw holding the choke cable at the carburetter. Remove the cable and collect the screw assembly.

Remove the two knobs on the heater controls, pull off the trim panel and take out the two screws.

Remove the two nuts and bolts securing the facia to the outer support brackets. Remove the three screws securing the facia to the support stays and the six nuts from the studs in the windscreen lower panel.

Move the facia panel out sufficiently to remove the bezel for the windscreen washer pump and disconnect the electrical connections to the switches. Fully withdraw the panel, pulling the choke cable through its grommet on the scuttle.

The facia panel is refitted in the reverse order to the above.

Facia panel (Marina 2):

Several details of these assemblies are shown in **FIG 13:16A** for assistance in removing the panel. Proceed as follows:

Disconnect the battery and remove the steering wheel as described in **Section 10:3**.

Remove the instrument cluster. This is done by first removing the surrounding cowl (two screws on top) and then the screws securing the instrument cluster housing. Disconnect the clip for the speedometer cable and the wiring multi-connector. According to type disconnect the remaining electrical leads, main beam warning, clock etc.

Remove the glove box, this is secured by a number of screws easily reached when the lid is opened, but note the leads to the interior light and switch on some models.

Remove the two nuts, screws 5 and clip retaining the parcel shelf. Disconnect the tubes 6 from the air vents.

Remove the two screws 7 securing the steering column bridge piece. Pull the knobs 8 off the heater control levers and then remove the two screws 9 and move the control assembly to one side.

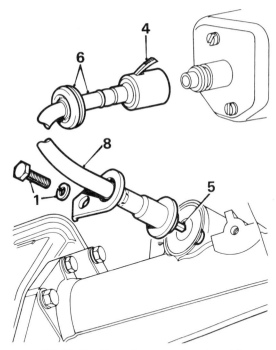

FIG 13:21   Removing a speedometer cable

Key to Fig 13:21   1 Securing screw and washer
4 Release lever   5 Inner cable   6 Outer casing and grommet
8 Cable assembly lower end

Release all the switches 10 from the panel and disconnect any Lucar type or multi-plug connectors, also the leads to the cigar lighter when fitted.

Remove the five facia securing screws 12 and three nuts 13. Press the centre of the panel downwards and release it from the centre retaining clip 14. The complete facia assembly can now be lifted out.

Any further dismantling can be carried out as required by referring to the small illustrations in the insets.

Refit the facia panel by reversing the removal procedure.

The printed circuit:

Access to the printed circuit wiring assembly is gained by first removing the instrument panel as described above.

Remove the voltage stabilizer and withdraw the warning and panel lamp holders from the speedometer and gauge units. Remove the tachometer panel lamp bulb holder.

Take out the three screws and the voltage stabilizer tag connectors. Remove the four sleeve screws and special washers securing the gauge units. Remove the screw securing the tachometer panel lamp lead.

Remove the five (six with tachometer) plastic retaining pegs.

Remove the screw and washer securing the printed circuit, lift up the circuit and take out the spacer. Remove the printed circuit.

Refitting the printed circuit is carried out in the reverse order to the above.

13:11 The heater

The heating and air distribution unit used on all model cars is illustrated in **FIG 13:19** but there are some slight differences in layout according to model type and year. The following details relating to a typical installation should enable the home operator to remove and refit the heater if this should become necessary.

The attachment of a demister vent is shown in **FIG 13:17**. The instrument panel and glove box must be removed to gain access to the nuts which secure the duct.

The heater attachments are shown in **FIG 13:18**. Before the heater can be removed, the facia lower panel and instrument panel must be removed. Disconnect the ducts 3 from the heater. Drain the cooling system (see **Chapter 4**) and disconnect the coolant hoses 4. Remove the two drain tubes 5. Remove the nut and washer 6 which secure the top of the heater to the bulkhead and remove the two sets of bolts and washers 7 which secure the sides of the heater to the bulkhead. Pull the top of the heater rearwards to free it from the stud and then pull the bottom of the heater rearwards until the unit can be canted over and removed from under the facia support rail on the passenger side of the car.

Before refitting the heater, remove the intake grille and hang the heater on the top stud. The seal can then be correctly positioned, working through the aperture for the heater intake grille.

Once the seal is in position, the heater can be refitted in the reverse order of removal.

Heater fan and motor:

The attachments of the motor to the heater are shown in **FIG 13:19** and they are accessible after the heater has been removed and the plenum chamber taken off.

Heater radiator:

Once the heater has been removed, the radiator can be taken out of the heater. Remove the rubber packing piece from the front of the heater, and take out the screws that secure the cover so that the cover and radiator can be withdrawn.

Refit the radiator to the heater in the reverse order of removal, sticking the rubber packing lightly to the cover.

Heater switch:

The attachments are shown in **FIG 13:20**. Disconnect the battery. Pull off the heater control lever knobs and take out the three screws 3 that secure the finishing panel. Disconnect the leads 4. The switch 5 can then be removed using the special tool(s) 18G.1201 to depress the spring legs on the switch so that it can be pulled out of the facia. **Note that this special tool is used for removing all switches in a similar manner.**

13:12 Renewing a speedometer cable

Refer to **FIG 13:21**. Remove the screw and spring washer 1 retaining the cable locking flange to the gearbox and pull the cable out of the drive pinion.

On Saloon and Estate models the instrument panel must be removed. On Vans the instrument cowl must be removed to gain access to the speedometer which is retained by four screws.

Press the release lever 4 on the cable connector and pull it away as shown.

Withdraw the inner cable 5. If the cable is broken the two sections can be removed from either end of the outer casing.

Pull the outer casing (if required) through the brake pedal housing allowing the connector end to remove the grommet 6. It may be necessary to move the heater drain tubes to one side to clear the cable.

Refit in the reverse order.

13:13 Tail doors, Vans and Estate cars

Van:

To remove a tail door on a Van, support the weight of the door and remove first the two nuts retaining the top hinge to the door and then the two nuts retaining the bottom hinge and the friction stay bracket.

Pull the stay bracket off the hinge studs and detach the door from the hinges.

When refitting the door, do not fully tighten the hinge retaining nuts until the door has been checked for correct alignment with surrounding body panels and, in the case of the righthand door, that the locking bars engage properly in their sockets.

Estate:

To remove the tailgate, first open it fully and mark the position of the hinges with a pencil.

Support the tailgate and remove the three screws from each hinge.

Refit in the reverse order.

Door lock—Van:

From inside the door remove the two hexagon screws retaining the lock mechanism to the door and lift the lock off the square shank of the outside handle.

Slide the locking bars out of their guides one at a time and detach the lock and bars assembly, noting their relative positions.

Door lock—Estate:

Remove the interior trim pad from the tailgate, this is retained by a number of spring clips which are levered out of their holes in the metal panel.

Unclip the retainer and pull the operating rod away from the outside handle assembly.

Remove the three screws and spring washers and lift the lock assembly away from the tailgate.

The striker plate is secured by three screws and its position is adjustable so as to ensure a tight fit for the door in its aperture.

APPENDIX

Inches	Decimals	Milli-metres	Inches to Millimetres		Millimetres to Inches	
			Inches	mm	mm	Inches
1/64	.015625	.3969	.001	.0254	.01	.00039
1/32	.03125	.7937	.002	.0508	.02	.00079
3/64	.046875	1.1906	.003	.0762	.03	.00118
1/16	.0625	1.5875	.004	.1016	.04	.00157
5/64	.078125	1.9844	.005	.1270	.05	.00197
3/32	.09375	2.3812	.006	.1524	.06	.00236
7/64	.109375	2.7781	.007	.1778	.07	.00276
1/8	.125	3.1750	.008	.2032	.08	.00315
9/64	.140625	3.5719	.009	.2286	.09	.00354
5/32	.15625	3.9687	.01	.254	.1	.00394
11/64	.171875	4.3656	.02	.508	.2	.00787
3/16	.1875	4.7625	.03	.762	.3	.01181
13/64	.203125	5·1594	.04	1.016	.4	.01575
7/32	.21875	5.5562	.05	1.270	.5	.01969
15/64	.234375	5.9531	.06	1.524	.6	.02362
1/4	.25	6.3500	.07	1.778	.7	.02756
17/64	.265625	6.7469	.08	2.032	.8	.03150
9/32	.28125	7.1437	.09	2.286	.9	.03543
19/64	.296875	7.5406	.1	2.54	1	.03937
5/16	.3125	7.9375	.2	5.08	2	.07874
21/64	.328125	8.3344	.3	7.62	3	.11811
11/32	.34375	8.7312	.4	10.16	4	.15748
23/64	.359375	9.1281	.5	12.70	5	.19685
3/8	.375	9.5250	.6	15.24	6	.23622
25/64	.390625	9.9219	.7	17.78	7	.27559
13/32	.40625	10.3187	.8	20.32	8	.31496
27/64	.421875	10.7156	.9	22.86	9	.35433
7/16	.4375	11.1125	1	25.4	10	.39370
29/64	.453125	11.5094	2	50.8	11	.43307
15/32	.46875	11.9062	3	76.2	12	.47244
31/64	.484375	12.3031	4	101.6	13	.51181
1/2	.5	12.7000	5	127.0	14	.55118
33/64	.515625	13.0969	6	152.4	15	.59055
17/32	.53125	13.4937	7	177.8	16	.62992
35/64	.546875	13.8906	8	203.2	17	.66929
9/16	.5625	14.2875	9	228.6	18	.70866
37/64	.578125	14.6844	10	254.0	19	.74803
19/32	.59375	15.0812	11	279.4	20	.78740
39/64	.609375	15.4781	12	304.8	21	.82677
5/8	.625	15.8750	13	330.2	22	.86614
41/64	.640625	16.2719	14	355.6	23	.90551
21/32	.65625	16.6687	15	381.0	24	.94488
43/64	.671875	17.0656	16	406.4	25	.98425
11/16	.6875	17.4625	17	431.8	26	1.02362
45/64	.703125	17.8594	18	457.2	27	1.06299
23/32	.71875	18.2562	19	482.6	28	1.10236
47/64	.734375	18.6531	20	508.0	29	1.14173
3/4	.75	19.0500	21	533.4	30	1.18110
49/64	.765625	19.4469	22	558.8	31	1.22047
25/32	.78125	19.8437	23	584.2	32	1.25984
51/64	.796875	20.2406	24	609.6	33	1.29921
13/16	.8125	20.6375	25	635.0	34	1.33858
53/64	.828125	21.0344	26	660.4	35	1.37795
27/32	.84375	21.4312	27	685.8	36	1.41732
55/64	.859375	21.8281	28	711.2	37	1.4567
7/8	.875	22.2250	29	736.6	38	1.4961
57/64	.890625	22.6219	30	762.0	39	1.5354
29/32	.90625	23.0187	31	787.4	40	1.5748
59/64	.921875	23.4156	32	812.8	41	1.6142
15/16	.9375	23.8125	33	838.2	42	1.6535
61/64	.953125	24.2094	34	863.6	43	1.6929
31/32	.96875	24.6062	35	889.0	44	1.7323
63/64	.984375	25.0031	36	914.4	45	1.7717

UNITS	Pints to Litres	Gallons to Litres	Litres to Pints	Litres to Gallons	Miles to Kilometres	Kilometres to Miles	Lbs. per sq. In. to Kg. per sq. Cm.	Kg. per sq. Cm. to Lbs. per sq. In.
1	.57	4.55	1.76	.22	1.61	.62	.07	14.22
2	1.14	9.09	3.52	.44	3.22	1.24	.14	28.50
3	1.70	13.64	5.28	.66	4.83	1.86	.21	42.67
4	2.27	18.18	7.04	.88	6.44	2.49	.28	56.89
5	2.84	22.73	8.80	1.10	8.05	3.11	.35	71.12
6	3.41	27.28	10.56	1.32	9.66	3.73	.42	85.34
7	3.98	31.82	12.32	1.54	11.27	4.35	.49	99.56
8	4.55	36.37	14.08	1.76	12.88	4.97	.56	113.79
9		40.91	15.84	1.98	14.48	5.59	.63	128.00
10		45.46	17.60	2.20	16.09	6.21	.70	142.23
20				4.40	32.19	12.43	1.41	284.47
30				6.60	48.28	18.64	2.11	426.70
40				8.80	64.37	24.85		
50					80.47	31.07		
60					96.56	37.28		
70					112.65	43.50		
80					128.75	49.71		
90					144.84	55.92		
100					160.93	62.14		

UNITS	Lb ft to kgm	Kgm to lb ft	UNITS	Lb ft to kgm	Kgm to lb ft
1	.138	7.233	7	.967	50.631
2	.276	14.466	8	1.106	57.864
3	.414	21.699	9	1.244	65.097
4	.553	28.932	10	1.382	72.330
5	.691	36.165	20	2.765	144.660
6	.829	43.398	30	4.147	216.990

TECHNICAL DATA

Unless otherwise stated the dimensions are given in inches and the dimensions in brackets in millimetres.

Throughout the appendix 1.1 will refer to the 1098 cc engine, 1.3 will refer to the 1274.86 cc engine, or model fitted with that engine; 1.8 to the 1798 cc engine or model fitted with that engine and TC for models with twin carburetters.

ENGINE (Private Cars, 7 cwt and 10 cwt Vans)

| Type | ... ... | 4 cylinder, in-line, water cooled. OHV using side-mounted camshaft and rocker gear with short pushrods |

Capacities:

1.3	... ...	1274.86 cc (77.8 cu in)
1.8	... ...	1798 cc (109.7 cu in)

Compression ratio:

Standard

1.3	... ...	8.8:1
1.8	... ...	9.0:1
Low-compression	... ...	8.0:1

| **Firing order** | ... ... | 1–3–4–2 |

Bore:

| 1.3 | ... ... | 2.78 (70.61) |
| 1.8 | ... ... | 3.160 (80.26) |

Stroke:

| 1.3 | ... ... | 3.2 (81.38) |
| 1.8 | ... ... | 3.5 (88.9) |

Compression test pressure:

| Standard ... | ... ... | 190 lb/sq in (13.4 kg/sq cm) |
| Low-compression | ... ... | 170 lb/sq in (12 kg/sq cm) |

Crankshaft:

		1.3	*1.8*
Main bearings	... ...	3	5
Bearing shells	... ...	VP3 lead/indium or NFM/3b	Copper/lead or reticular tin
Main bearing clearance	... ...	.002 to .003 (.0251 to .076)	.001 to .0027 (.025 to .068)
Main journal diameter	... ...	2.0012 to 2.0017 (50.83 to 50.843)	2.1265 to 2.127 (54.01 to 54.02)
Minimum journal regrind ...	... ...	1.9612 to 1.9617 (49.815 to 49.827)	2.0865 (52.997)
Big-end bearing shells	... ...	Steel-backed copper/lead, indium-plated	Steel-backed copper/lead or VP3
Big-end clearance	... ...	.0017 to .0032 (.04 to .08)	.0015 to .0032 (.038 to .081)
Crankpin diameter	... ...	1.7497 to 1.7504 (44.442 to 44.46)	1.8759 to 1.8764 (47.648 to 47.661)
Minimum crankpin regrind	... ...	1.7097 to 1.7102 (43.426 to 43.439)	1.836 (46.632)
Undersize bearings available	... ...	−.010, −.020, −.030, −.040 (−.254, −.508, −.762, −1.016)	
Crankshaft end float	... ...	Taken by washers on either side centre main bearing .002 to .003 (.051 to .076)	

Connecting rods:

Type ... ... Horizontal split big-end, interference fit gudgeon pin (some models have fully floating gudgeon pins)

Length between centres ... ... 5.748 to 5.752   6.5
(145.1 to 146)   (165.1)

Pistons:

Type ... ... Aluminium, solid skirt

Clearance of skirt in bore   *1.3*   *1.8*

Top ... ... .0029 to .0037   .0021 to .0037
(.07 to .09)   (.0535 to .0936)

Bottom ... ... .0012 to .0022   .0018 to .0024
(.03 to .06)   (.045 to .061)

Width of piston ring grooves

Compression rings ... ... .064 to .065   .064 to .065
(1.625 to 1.651)   (1.625 to 1.651)

Oil control ... ... .1578 to .1588   .1578 to .1588
(4.01 to 4.033)   (4.01 to 4.033)

Oversizes... ... ... +.010 and +.020   +.010, +.020,
+.030, +.040

Piston rings:

Width

Compression rings ... ... .0615 to .0625 (1.562 to 1.587)

Oil control ... ... .1552 to .1562 (3.94 to 3.96)

Ring to groove ... ... .0016 to .0036 (.04 to .09)

Fitted gap   *1.3*   *1.8*

Compression ... ... .011 to .016   .012 to .017
(.28 to .41) top ring (.304 to .431) All
.008 to .013
(.20 to .33) lower
rings

Oil control ... ... .010 to .040   .015 to .045
(.254 to 1.02) rails   (.381 to 1.147)

Camshaft:

Bearings ... ... 3, steel-backed whitemetal lined renewable reamed to size after fitting

Bearing diametrical clearance ... ... .001 to .002 (.02 to .05)

Journal diameter   *1.3*   *1.8*

Front ... ... 1.6655 to 1.666   1.78875 to 1.78925
(42.304 to 42.316)   (45.424 to 45.437)

Centre ... ... 1.62275 to 1.62325   1.72875 to 1.72925
(41.218 to 41.231)   (43.910 to 43.923)

Rear ... ... 1.37275 to 1.37350   1.62275 to 1.62325
(34.866 to 34.889)   (41.218 to 41.230)

End float ... ... .003 to .007 (.076 to .178)
Controlled by locating plate

Cam followers:

        1.3   *1.8*

Outside diameter... ... ... .81125 to .81175   .812
(20.60 to 20.62)   (20.64)

Length ... ... 1.495 to 1.505   1.495 to 1.505
(37.977 to 38.227)   (37.977 to 38.227)

Rockers:

Shaft length ... ... —   14.032 (355.6)

Shaft diameter ... ... .5615 to .5625   .624 to .625
(14.26 to 14.29)   (15.85 to 15.87)

Bush reamed diameter ... ... .5630 to .5635   .6255 to .626
(14.3 to 14.31)   (15.8 to 15.9)

Valve clearance							*All valves*	
Cold	...	...	...	...	...		.012 (.305)	.013 (.33)
Setting timing	...	...	...	...			.021 (.533)	.020 (.51)

Valves:

Seat angle	...	...	...	...		45 deg.	$45\frac{1}{2}$ deg.
Head diameter							
Inlet (early engines)	...	...	...		1.307 to 1.312 (33.2 to 33.21)	1.625 to 1.630 (41.27 to 41.40)	
Inlet (later engines)	...	...	...		1.562 to 1.567 (39.67 to 39.80)		
Exhaust	...	...	...		1.1515 to 1.1565 (29.24 to 29.37)	1.343 to 1.348 (34.11 to 34.23)	
Stem diameter							
Inlet	...	...	...	...	.2793 to .2798 (7.09 to 7.11)	.3422 to .3427 (8.692 to 8.704)	
Exhaust	...	...	...		.2788 to .2793 (7.08 to 7.09)	.3417 to .3422 (8.66 to 8.692)	
Stem to guide clearance							
Inlet	...	...	...	...	.0015 to .0025 (.0381 to .063)	.0015 to .0025 (.0381 to .063)	
Exhaust	...	...	...		.0015 to .0025 (.0381 to .063)	.002 to .003 (.052 to .076)	
Valve lift	...	...	...	...	.318 (8.07)	.360 (9.14)	

Valve guides:

Length							
Inlet	...	...	...	...	1.6875 (42.87)	1.875 (47.63)	
Exhaust	...	...	...		1.8437 (46.83)	2.203 (55.95)	
Internal diameter	...	...	...		.2813 to .2818 (7.145 to 7.1577)	.3442 to .3447 (8.743 to 8.755)	
External diameter	...	...	...		.4695 to .470 (11.925 to 11.938)	.5635 to .5640 (14.30 to 14.32)	
Fitted height above head							
Inlet	...	...	...	...	.54 (13.72)	.75 (19.05)	
Exhaust	...	...	...		.54 (13.72)	.625 (15.87)	

Valve springs:

Free length	...	...	...	...	1.95 (49.13)	1.92 (48.77)	
Number of working coils	...	...	...		$4\frac{1}{2}$	$4\frac{1}{2}$	
Fitted length	...	...	...	...	1.383 (35.13)	1.44 (36.58)	
Fitted load	...	...	...	...	79.5 lb (36.03 kg)	82 lb (37 kg)	

Valve timing:

						Given in degrees	
Inlet opens	...	...	...	...	5 BTDC	5 BTDC	
Inlet closes	...	...	...	...	45 ABDC	45 ABDC	
Exhaust opens	...	...	...		51 BBDC	40 BBDC	
Exhaust closes	...	...	...		21 ATDC	10 ATDC	

Lubrication:

Pressure							
Running	...	...	...	...	50 to 70 lb/sq in (3.5 to 4.9 kg/sq cm)		
Idling	...	...	...	...	15 to 25 lb/sq in (1.0 to 1.8 kg/sq cm)		
						1.3	*1.8*
Oil pump	...	...	...	...	Internal gear	Hobourn-Eaton	
Oil filter bypass valve opens	...	...		8 to 12 lb/sq in (.56 to .84 kg/sq cm)		
Relief valve opens	...	...	...		70 lb/sq in (4.9 kg/sq cm)		
Relief valve spring						*1.3*	*1.8*
Free length	...	...	...	...	2.86 (72.64)	3 (76)	
Fitted length	...	...	...		2.156 (54.77)	2.156 (54.77)	
Fitted load	...	...	...	...	13 to 14 lb (5.9 to 6.36 kg)	15.5 to 16.5 lb (7.0 to 7.4 kg)	

ENGINE (7 cwt Van)

Capacity	1098 cc (67 cu in)
Bore	2.543 in (64.58 mm)
Stroke	3.296 in (83.72 mm)
Compression ratio	7.5:1

Crankshaft:

Main journal diameter	1.7505 to 1.7510 (44.462 to 44.475)
Minimum regrind...	1.7104 to 1.7110 (43.444 to 43.459)
Crankpin diameter	1.6254 to 1.6259 (41.285 to 41.297)
Minimum regrind...	1.5854 to 1.5859 (40.269 to 40.281)
End float	.002 to .003 (.051 to .076)
Main bearing clearance	.001 to .0027 (.025 to .068)
Big-end clearance	.001 to .0025 (.025 to .063)

Pistons:

Number of rings	4 (3 compression, 1 oil control)

Width of ring grooves:

Compression	.0645 to .0655 (1.638 to 1.663)
Oil control	.1265 to .1275 (3.213 to 3.238)
Fitted gap (compression)	.007 to .012 (.177 to .304)
Ring to groove clearance... ...	.0015 to .0035 (.04 to .09)

Fitted gap (oil control):

Rails	.012 to .028 (.304 to .711)
Side spring	.010 to .015 (.254 to .381)

Valves:

Head diameter, inlet	1.151 to 1.156 (29.23 to 29.36)
exhaust	1.0'to 1.005 (25.4 to 25.53)
Rocker clearance, cold	.012 (.305)
Spring free length	1.750 (44.45)

FUEL SYSTEM

Fuel pump...	SU mechanical

Carburetter:

1.1	SU HS2 or HS4 (after 1974)
1.3	SU HS4
1.8	SU HS6
1.8 TC	Twin SU HS4

Idling speed:

1.1	650 rev/min
1.3	650 rev/min (later HC engines 750)
1.8	800 rev/min
1.8 TC	800 rev/min
Fast idle	1000 to 1100 rev/min for all models

Needle size:

1.1 engines	Up to 1974	AN	After 1974	ABN
1.3 engines	Up to 1972	AAQ	1972-75	AAZ
1.8 engines	Up to 1972	BAQ	1972-74	BAS
	1975	BCW	1975(GT)	ACE
1.8 TC engines ...	Up to 1972	AAS	1972-74	ABA
	After 1974	ABA (manual)		AAS (automatic)

IGNITION SYSTEM

Sparking plugs:

Type	Champion N-9Y
Gap, standard	.024 to .026 (.625 to .660)
1.8 TC and GT	.034 to .036 (.875 to .925)

Distributor:

Type	Lucas 25D4 or 45D4	
Rotation	Anticlockwise, viewed from above	
Dwell angle:		
Up to 1974	60° ± 3°	
1974	51° ± 5°	
Contact gap	.014 to .016 (.35 to .40)	

Ignition settings:

	Static	*Stroboscopic at 1000 rev/min*
1.1	8 deg.	13 deg. BTDC
1.3 HC	9 deg.	14 deg. BTDC
1.3 LC	7 deg.	12 deg. BTDC
1.8 HC	10 deg.	15 deg. BTDC
1.8 LC	9 deg.	12 deg. BTDC
1.8 twin carburetter	7 deg.	15 deg. BTDC
1.8 HC (1975 on)	3 deg.	8 deg. BTDC
1.8 LC (1975 on)	3 deg.	6 deg. BTDC
1.8 GT (1975 on)	7 deg.	10 deg. BTDC

Firing order   1–3–4–2

Ignition coil:

	1.3	*1.8*	*1.8 TC*
Type	Lucas LA12	Lucas 11C12	Lucas 16C6
Primary resistance at			
20°C	3.2 to 3.4 ohms	1.43 to 1.58 ohms	1.43 to 1.58 ohms
Consumption ...	1 amp	1 amp	1 amp
Ballast resistor ...	None	1.3 to 1.4 ohms	1.3 to 1.4 ohms

COOLING SYSTEM

Type	Pressurized with expansion tank
Pressure	15 lb/sq in (1.05 kg/sq cm)
Thermostat:	
Standard	82°C (180°F)
Hot climates	74°C (165°F)
Cold climates	88°C (190°F)
Antifreeze:	
For safety limits see Chapter 4 Section 4:7	
Type	BS 3151 or BS 3152

CLUTCH

Make and type	Borg and Beck, or Laycock diaphragm spring
Driven plate diameter:	
1.3	6.5 (165)
1.8 and Van	8 (203)
Driven plate damper springs:	
1.3	4
1.8 and Van	6
Master cylinder bore	$\frac{1}{2}$ (12.7)
Slave cylinder bore:	
1.3	1 (25.4)
1.8 and Van	$\frac{7}{8}$ (22.2)
Hydraulic fluid	Same as brakes

TRANSMISSION

Gearbox:

Synchromesh ... ... All forward gears

Ratios:

	1.3 and Van	*1.8 and Estate*
Top	1.000:1	1.000:1
Third	1.433:1	1.307:1
Second	2.112:1	1.916:1
First	3.412:1	3.111:1
Reverse	3.753:1	3.422:1
Road speed per 1000 rev/min in top gear ...	15.9 mph (25.6 km/hr)	18.1 mph (29.1 km/hr)

Rear axle:

Type ... ... Hypoid, semi-floating

Ratios

1.3 and 7 cwt Van 4.111:1 (9/37)

1.8 ... ... 3.636:1 (11/40)

10 cwt and later 7 cwt Van 4.556:1 (9/41)

Propeller shafts:

Type ... ... Front and rear tubular with centre bearing

Diameter

Front 3 (76.2)

Rear 2 (50.8)

Universal joints ... ... Hardy Spicer with roller bearings

SUSPENSION

Front:

Type ... ... Independent, torsion bar with lever-type shock absorbers

Kingpin inclination ... ... $7\frac{1}{2}$ deg. positive

Camber angle, twin carburetter models ... 0 deg. 33' positive

others ... ... 0 deg. 46' positive

Caster angle, early cars ... ... 5 deg. positive

cars listed below: ... ... 2 deg. positive

1.3 and 1.8 with servo... ... ... 37879 to 39000 and 40793 onwards

1.3 non-servo ... ... 38248 to 39000 and 41297 onwards

1.8 non-servo ... ... 38168 to 39000 and 40298 onwards

TC and 1.8 automatic ... ... 38168 to 39000 and 41069 onwards

K Series cars from number 101

Hub-bearing end-float ... ... .001 to .005 (.025 to .0127)

Rear:

Type ... ... Semi-elliptic leaf spring with telescopic shock absorbers

Number of spring leaves ... ... 2 (4 on Estate and Van)

Width of leaves 2 (50.8)

Gauge of leaves (Saloon) ... ... .3 to .164 (7.62 to 4.08)

Working load (Saloon) ... ... 270 lb (122.7 kg)

(Van) ... ... 318 lb (144 kg)

STEERING

Type ... ... Rack and pinion

Steering wheel turns—lock to lock ... 4, early cars   3.7, Series 2

Front wheel alignment ... ... $\frac{1}{16}$ (1.6) toe-in

Pinion bearing pre-load ... ... .001 to .003 (.025 to .076)

Oil capacity of rack and pinion ... ... $\frac{1}{3}$ pint (190cc)

BRAKES

Brake fluid:

Disc brake cars	...	...	...	Unipart 550 or SAE.J1703c
Drum brake cars	...	...	...	Unipart 410 or SAE.J1703c

Front:

Drum type

Drum diameter...	...	...	...	8 (203.2)
Lining dimensions	...	...	...	8 x $1\frac{3}{4}$ x $\frac{3}{16}$ (203.2 x 44.45 x 4.76)
Swept area (total)	...	...	...	88 cu in (567.74 cc)
Lining material: Non servo	...	...	...	DON 202
Wheel cylinder diameter	...	...	...	0.750 (17.78)

Disc type

Disc diameter ...	...	...	...	9.785 (248.5)
Pad area (total)	...	...	...	17.4 cu in (286.77 cc)
Swept area (total)	...	...	...	182.8 cu in (2671 cc)
Pad lining material				
Non servo ...	...	...	...	DON 227
With servo ...	...	...	...	F2430

Rear:

Drum diameter ...	...	...	...	8 (203.2)
Lining dimensions	...	...	...	8 x $1\frac{1}{2}$ x $\frac{3}{16}$ (203.2 x 38.1 x 4.76)
Swept area (total)	...	...	...	76 cu in (490.2 cc)
Lining material ...	...	...	...	DON 202
Wheel cylinder diameter				
1.3 ...	...	...	...	.70 (17.78)
1.8 ...	...	...	...	.625 (15.87) with automatic adjuster

Master cylinder:

Diameter

Non servo: 1.3 and 1.8	...	...		0.70 (17.78)
With servo ...	...	...		0.75 (19.05)

ELECTRICAL

System	...	...	...	...	12 volt, negative earth

Battery type:

Lucas	...	...	...	...	A9; A11; A13
Exide	...	...	...	...	6VTP 7–BR; 6VTP 9–BR; 6VTPZ 11BR

Dynamo:

Type	...	...	...	...	Lucas C40/1
Maximum output	...	...	...	22$\pm$1 amps
Cut-in speed	...	...	...	1.585 rev/min at 13.5 volts
Field resistance	...	...	...	6.0 ohms at 20°C (68°F)
Brush spring tension	...	...	...	20 to 34 ozf (567 to 964 gmf)
Brush—minimum length...	...	...	...	.25 (6.5)
Pulley ratio	...	...	...	1.7:1

Control unit:

Type

				RB106	RB340
Lefthand drive ...	...	...	...	Lucas RB 340	
Righthand drive	...	...	...	Lucas RB 106	
Setting at 20°C (68°F)				*RB 106*	*RB 340*
3000 rev/min dynamo...	...	...	16.0 to 16.6 volts	14.5 to 15.5 volts
Cut-in voltage ...	...	...	12.7 to 13.3 volts	12.7 to 13.3 volts
Drop-off voltage ...	...	...	8.5 to 11.0 volts	9.5 to 11.5 volts

Alternator:

Types	Lucas 16, 17 or 18 ACR
Output at 14 volts/6000 rev/min... ...	34, 36 or 45 amps
Brush length (new)	.5 (12.6)
Brush length (minimum)	.3 (7.9)
Brush spring tension	7 to 10 ozf (198 to 283 gmf) with brush face flush with box

Starter motor:

Type	
1.3 Standard	Lucas M418G
1.3 Cold climates	Lucas M35J pre-engaged
1.8 Standard	Lucas 2M100
1.8 Cold climates	Lucas 2M100

	M35J	2M100	M418G
Brush spring tension ...	28 oz (.8 kg)	36 oz (1.02 kg)	30 to 40 oz (.85 to 1.1 kg)
Minimum brush length...	$\frac{3}{8}$ (9.5)	$\frac{3}{8}$ (9.5)	$\frac{5}{16}$ (7.9)
Lock torque	7 lb ft (.97 kg m) with 350 to 375 amp	14.4 lb ft (2.02 kg m) with 463 amp	17 lb ft (2.3 kg m) with 440 to 450 amp
Torque at 1000 rev/min	4.4 lb ft (.61 kg m) with 260 to 275 amp	7.3 lb ft (1.02 kg m) with 300 amp	—
Light running current ...	65 amp at 8000 to 10,000 rev/min	40 amp at 6000 rev/min approx.	45 amp at 6500 to 8500 rev/min
Solenoid pre-engaged types			
Closing coil resistance	.21 to .25 ohm	.25 to .27 ohm	—
Holding coil resistance	.9 to 1.1 ohm	.76 to .80 ohm	—

Wiper motor:

Type	Lucas 14W (two-speed)
Armature end-float	.004 to .008 (.1 to .21)
Light running current	
Normal speed	1 to 5 amp
High speed	2.0 amp
Light running speed	
Normal speed	46 to 52 rev/min
High speed	60 to 70 rev/min

WHEELS AND TYRES

	Maximum load per wheel 715 lb MAX (325 kg) (4 persons and luggage		Maximum load per wheel 740 lb MAX (335 kg) (5 persons and luggage)	
	Front	*Rear*	*Front*	*Rear*
Marina 1.3:				
†5.20—13 cross-ply	26 lb/sq in (1.8 kg/sq cm)	28 lb/sq in (2.0 kg/sq cm)	28 lb/sq in (2.0 kg/sq cm)	30 lb/sq in (2.1 kg/sq cm)
‡145—13 radial ply	24 lb/sq in (1.6 kg/sq cm)	26 lb/sq in (1.8 kg/sq cm)	26 lb/sq in (1.8 kg/sq cm)	28 lb/sq in (2.0 kg/sq cm)
÷165/70—13 radial ply low profile ...			26 lb/sq in min (1.8 kg/sq cm)	28 lb/sq in min (2.0 kg/sq cm)
Marina 1.8:				
†145—13 radial-ply 155—13 radial-ply (later)			26 lb/sq in (1.8 kg/sq cm)	28 lb/sq in (2.0 kg/sq cm)
‡165/70—13 radial-ply low profile ...			26 lb/sq in (1.8 kg/sq cm)	28 lb/sq in (2.0 kg/sq cm)

Marina 1.8 TC:

†165/70—13 radial-ply low profile ...	26 lb/sq in (1.8 kg/sq cm)	28 lb/sq in (2.0 kg/sq cm)

†Standard fit   ‡Optional   ÷Special option

Estate:

155-13 Dunlop SP68 radial, or optional 165-13 ... ...   As Marina 1.8 for normal loads 26 lb/sq in, 32 lb/sq in full loads (2.2 kg/sq cm)

Van:

7 cwt 155SR-13 ... ...   24 lb/sq in (1.68 kg/sq cm)   32 lb/sq in (2.25 kg/sq cm)

10 cwt 155SR-13 reinforced ... ...   24 lb/sq in (1.68 kg/sq cm)   40 lb/sq in (2.81 kg/sq cm)

CAPACITIES

Fuel tank	$11\frac{1}{2}$ gallons ($13\frac{3}{4}$ US gallons, 52 litres)
Engine refill with filter changes:	
1.1 and 1.3	$6\frac{1}{2}$ pints (8 US pints, 3.7 litres)
1.8	$6\frac{3}{8}$ pints (8 US pints, 3.8 litres)
Manual gearbox	$1\frac{1}{2}$ pints ($1\frac{3}{4}$ US pints, .85 litre)
Automatic transmission:	
Borg-Warner Model 35	$9\frac{1}{2}$ pints ($11\frac{1}{2}$ US pints, 5.4 litres)*
With oil cooler when fitted	11 pints (13 US pints, 6.24 litres)*
Borg-Warner Model 65	$11\frac{1}{2}$ pints (13.8 US pints, 6.54 litres)
Rear axle	$1\frac{1}{4}$ pints ($1\frac{1}{2}$ US pints, .71 litre)
Cooling system (including heater):	
1.1 and 1.3	$7\frac{1}{2}$ pints (9 US pints, 4.26 litres)
1.8	9 pints ($10\frac{3}{4}$ US pints, 5.1 litres)
Windscreen washer bottle	3 pints ($3\frac{1}{2}$ US pints, 1.7 litres)

* Includes 5 pints (6 US pints, 3 litres) in torque converter

TORQUE WRENCH SETTINGS

Unless otherwise stated the figures are given in lb ft and the figures in brackets in kg m

Engines, 1.3 and 1.1:

Big-end cap nuts or bolts	35 (4.84)
Main bearing cap bolts	60 (8.3)
Cylinder head nuts	40 (5.5) on 1.1 50 (6.9) on 1.3
Rocker shaft bracket nuts	25 (3.4)
Gearbox adaptor plate bolts	25 (3.4)
Flywheel securing bolts	40 (5.5)
Sump securing bolts	6 (.8)
Oil pump securing bolts	9 (1.2)

Engine 1.8:

Main bearing cap nuts	70 (9.7)
Big-end bearing cap nuts	33 (4.6)
Gearbox adaptor plate bolts	30 (4.15)
Crankshaft rear oil seal retainer bolts	25 (3.5)
Flywheel securing bolts	40 (5.5)
Oil pump cover bolts	10 (1.38)
Oil pump securing bolts	14 (1.9)
Sump securing bolts	6 (.8)
Cylinder head nuts	45 to 50 (6.2 to 6.9)
Rocker shaft bracket nuts	25 (3.4)
Cylinder side cover	3 to 4 (.41 to .55)

Timing cover
$\frac{1}{4}$ inch bolts ... ... 6 (.83)
$\frac{5}{16}$ inch bolts 14 (1.94)
Water pump retaining bolts 17 (2.35)
Water outlet elbow 8 (1.11)
Manifold to cylinder head 15 (2.07)
Rocker cover fixing bolts... ... ... 4 (.55)
Crankshaft pulley nut ... ... 70 to 80 (9.68 to 11.06)
Camshaft nut ... ... 60 to 70 (8.30 to 9.68)
Distributor clamp bolt ... ... 2.5 (.35)
Heater outlet adaptor ... ... 6 to 8 (.83 to 1.11)
Oil release valve dome nut ... ... 40 to 45 (5.53 to 6.22)
Water pump pulley setscrews 18 (2.49)
Thermal transmitter 16 (2.21)

Gearbox (synchromesh):
Flywheel housing retaining bolts ... ... 28 to 30 (3.9 to 4.1)
Rear extension to gearbox bolts ... ... 18 to 20 (2.4 to 2.7)
Drive flange nut ... ... 90 to 100 (12.4 to 13.8)

Automatic transmission:
Drive flange nut ... ... 55 to 60 (7.6 to 8.3)
Drive plate to crankshaft 50 (6.9)
Converter to drive plate bolts ... ... 25 to 30 (3.4 to 4.1)
Transmission case to converter housing bolts ... ... 8 to 13 (1.1 to 1.8)
Rear extension to transmission case bolts ... ... 30 to 55 (4.1 to 7.6)
Filler tube adaptor to case ... ... 20 to 30 (2.8 to 4.1)
Oil pan to gearbox bolts ... ... 9 to 12 (1.2 to 1.6)
Front servo bolts ... ... 8 to 13 (1.1 to 1.8)
Rear servo bolts ... ... 13 to 27 (1.8 to 3.7)
Pump adaptor to housing screw ... ... 2 to 3 (.3 to .4)
Pump adaptor to housing bolts ... ... 17 to 32 (2.3 to 4.4)
Pump adaptor to transmission case bolts ... ... 8 to 18 (1.1 to 2.5)
Manual shaft locknut ... ... 7 to 9 (1.0 to 1.2)
Pressure adaptor plug ... ... 4 to 5 (.5 to .7)
Drain plug ... ... 8 to 10 (1.1 to 1.4)
Upper valve body to lower valve body screws ... ... 20 to 30 lb in (.23 to .34)
Lower valve body to upper valve body screws ... ... 20 to 30 lb in (.23 to .34)
Oil tube and end plate to valve body screws ... ... 20 to 30 lb in (.23 to .34)
Valve bodies to transmission case bolts ... ... 4.5 to 9 (.61 to 1.24)
Cam bracket screws ... ... 20 to 40 lb in (.23 to .46)
Governor to counterweight screws ... ... 4 to 5 (.5 to .7)
Governor coverplate screws ... ... 20 to 48 lb in (.23 to .55)
Front servo adjusting screw locknut ... ... 15 to 20 (2.07 to 2.77)
Rear servo adjusting screw locknut ... ... 30 to 40 (4.1 to 5.5)
Centre support bolts ... ... 10 to 18 (1.4 to 2.5)
Starter inhibitor switch locknut ... ... 4 to 6 (.5 to .8)
Downshift cable adaptor bolts ... ... 8 to 9 (1.1 to 1.2)
Filler tube adaptor to transmission case ... ... 20 to 30 (2.8 to 4.15)
Filler tube units to adaptor 18 (2.5)
Stone-guard screws ... ... 17 to 19 lb in (.19 to .22)

Propeller and drive shafts:
Centre bearing mounting screws... ... ... 22 (3.0)
Flange retaining bolt nuts 28 (3.8)

Rear axle and final drive:
Backplate securing nuts 18 (2.5)
Axle shaft nut 85 (11.7)
Differential case to axle retaining nuts 20 (2.7)

Pinion bearing pre-load ...	...	...	...	...	15 to 18 (.17 to .21)
Drive flange nut	...	...	...	...	90 (12.4)
Axle to spring U-bolt nuts	...	...	...	...	18 (2.4)

Steering:

Rack clamp bracket nuts ...	...	...	...	...	20 to 22 (2.77 to 3.04)
Tie rod ball pin nuts ...	...	...	...	...	20 to 24 (2.7 to 3.3)
Flexible joint pinch-bolt nut	...	...	...	...	6 to 8 (.4 to .5)
Pinion end cover retaining bolts	...	...	...	...	12 to 15 (1.6 to 2.0)
Pinion pre-load	...	...	...	...	15 lb in (.17)
Rack yoke cover bolts ...	...	...	...	...	12 to 15 (1.6 to 2.0)
Tie rod housing locknut ...	...	...	...	...	33 to 37 (4.6 to 5.6)
Tie rod ball spheres pre-load	...	...	...	...	32 to 52 lb in (.37 to .6)
Steering column mounting bolts ...	...	...	...	...	14 to 18 (1.94 to 2.49)
Flexible joint coupling bolts	...	...	...	...	20 to 22 (2.77 to 3.04)
Steering column lock shear screw	...	...	...	...	14 (1.94)
Steering wheel nut	...	...	...	...	43 to 50 (4.5 to 5.0)
Tie rod locknuts	...	...	...	...	35 to 40

Front suspension:

Ball pin retainer locknut ...	...	...	...	...	70 to 80 (9.6 to 11.0)
Eyebolt nut	...	...	...	...	50 to 54 (6.9 to 7.4)
Torsion bar reaction lever lockbolt	...	...	...	...	22 (3.0)
Reaction pad nut...	...	...	...	...	35 to 40 (4.8 to 5.5)
Damper retaining nuts ...	...	...	...	...	26 to 28 (3.5 to 3.8)
Tie rod fork nut	...	...	...	...	48 to 55 (6.6 to 7.6)
Tie rod to fork	...	...	...	...	22 (3.0)
Caliper bracket or mud flap bolts...	...	...	...	...	35 to 42 (4.8 to 5.8)
Brake drum retaining screws ...	...	...	...	...	26 to 28 (3.5 to 3.8)

Rear suspension:

Upper shackle pin nuts ...	...	...	...	...	28 (3.9)
Spring eye bolt nuts ...	...	...	...	...	40 (5.5)
Spring U-bolt nuts ...	...	...	...	...	14 (1.9)
Damper to spring bracket	...	...	...	...	28 (3.9)
Damper to body bracket ...	...	...	...	...	28 (3.9)

Brakes:

Bleed screw	...	...	...	...	4 to 6 (.5 to .8)
Master cylinder retaining nuts	...	...	...	...	15 to 19 (1.7 to 2.1)
Caliper retaining bolts ...	...	...	...	...	50 (6.9)
Wheel cylinder retaining bolts	...	...	...	...	4 to 5 (.55 to .7)

Electrical:

Distributor flange retaining screws	...	...	...	...	8 to 10 (1.1 to 1.4)
Alternator pulley retaining nut	...	...	...	...	20 to 30 (2.77 to 4.16)
Dynamo pulley nut	...	...	...	...	25 to 28 (3.46 to 3.87)

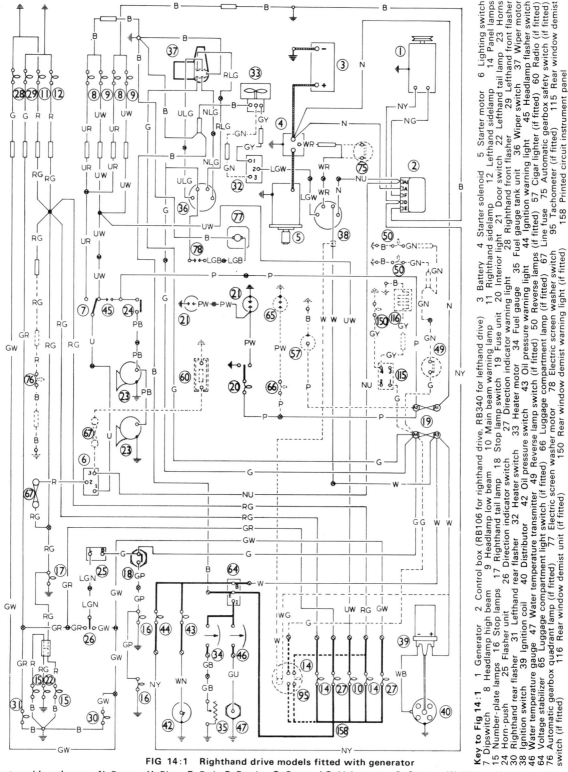

FIG 14:1 Righthand drive models fitted with generator

Key to Fig 14:1 1 Generator 2 Control box (RB106 for righthand drive, RB340 for lefthand drive) 3 Battery 4 Starter solenoid 5 Starter motor 6 Lighting switch 7 Dipswitch 8 Headlamp high beam 9 Headlamp low beam 10 Main beam warning lamp 11 Righthand sidelamp 12 Lefthand sidelamp 14 Panel lamps 15 Number-plate lamps 16 Stop lamps 17 Righthand tail lamp 18 Stop lamp switch 19 Fuse unit 20 Interior light 21 Door switch 22 Lefthand tail lamp 23 Horns 24 Horn-push 25 Flasher unit 26 Direction indicator switch 27 Direction indicator warning light 28 Righthand front flasher 29 Lefthand front flasher 30 Righthand rear flasher 31 Lefthand rear flasher 32 Heater switch 33 Heater motor 34 Fuel gauge 35 Fuel gauge tank unit 36 Wiper switch 37 Wiper motor 38 Ignition switch 39 Ignition coil 40 Distributor 42 Oil pressure switch 43 Oil pressure warning light 44 Ignition warning light 45 Headlamp flasher switch 46 Water temperature gauge 47 Water temperature transmitter 49 Reverse lamp switch 50 Reverse lamps (if fitted) 57 Cigar lighter (if fitted) 60 Radio (if fitted) 64 Voltage stabilizer 65 Luggage compartment light switch (if fitted) 66 Luggage compartment lamp (if fitted) 67 Line fuse 75 Automatic gearbox safety switch (if fitted) 76 Automatic gearbox quadrant lamp (if fitted) 77 Electric screen washer switch 78 Electric screen washer motor 95 Tachometer (if fitted) 115 Rear window demist switch (if fitted) 116 Rear window demist warning light (if fitted) 150 Rear window demist unit (if fitted) 158 Printed circuit instrument panel

Key to cable colours: **N** Brown **U** Blue **R** Red **P** Purple **G** Green **LG** Light green **O** Orange **W** White **Y** Yellow **B** Black
When a cable has two colour code letters the first denotes the main colour and the second denotes the tracer colour.

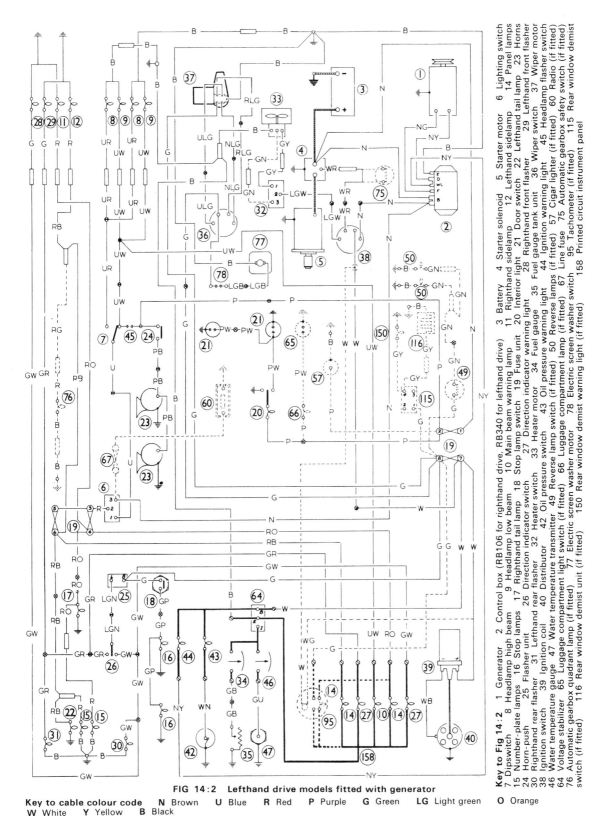

FIG 14:2 **Lefthand drive models fitted with generator**

Key to Fig 14:2 1 Generator 2 Control box (RB106 for righthand drive, RB340 for lefthand drive) 3 Battery 4 Starter solenoid 5 Starter motor 6 Lighting switch 7 Dipswitch 8 Headlamp high beam 9 Headlamp low beam 10 Main beam warning lamp 11 Righthand sidelamp 12 Panel lamps 14 Lefthand sidelamp 15 Number-plate lamps 16 Stop lamps 17 Righthand tail lamp 18 Stop lamp switch 19 Fuse unit 20 Interior light 21 Door switch 22 Lefthand tail lamp 23 Horns 24 Horn-push 25 Flasher unit 26 Direction indicator switch 27 Direction indicator warning light 28 Righthand front flasher 29 Lefthand front flasher 30 Righthand rear flasher 31 Lefthand rear flasher 32 Heater switch 33 Heater motor 34 Fuel gauge 35 Fuel gauge tank unit 36 Wiper motor 37 Wiper switch 38 Ignition switch 39 Ignition coil 40 Distributor 42 Oil pressure switch 43 Oil pressure warning light 44 Ignition warning light 45 Headlamp flasher switch 46 Water temperature gauge 47 Water temperature transmitter 49 Reverse lamps switch (if fitted) 50 Reverse lamps (if fitted) 57 Cigar lighter (if fitted) 60 Radio (if fitted) 64 Automatic gearbox quadrant lamp (if fitted) 65 Luggage compartment light switch (if fitted) 66 Luggage compartment lamp (if fitted) 67 Line fuse 75 Automatic gearbox safety switch (if fitted) 76 Automatic gearbox safety switch (if fitted) 77 Electric screen washer switch 78 Electric screen washer motor 95 Tachometer (if fitted) 115 Rear window demist switch (if fitted) 116 Rear window demist unit (if fitted) 150 Rear window demist warning light (if fitted) 158 Printed circuit instrument panel

Key to cable colour code N Brown U Blue R Red P Purple G Green LG Light green O Orange
W White Y Yellow B Black
    When a cable has two colour code letters the first denotes the main colour and the second denotes the tracer colour.

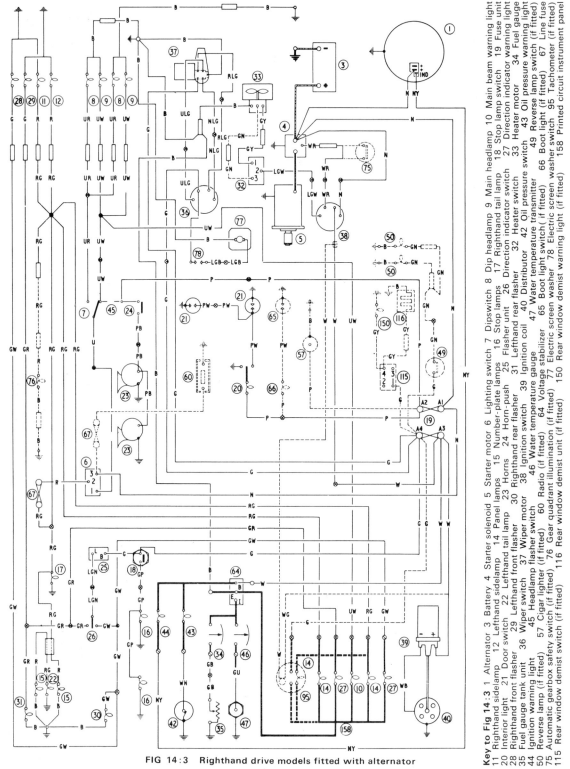

Key to Fig 14:3 1 Alternator 3 Battery 4 Starter solenoid 5 Starter motor 6 Lighting switch 7 Dipswitch 8 Dip headlamp 9 Main headlamp 10 Main beam warning light 11 Righthand sidelamp 12 Lefthand sidelamp 14 Panel lamps 15 Number-plate lamps 16 Stop lamps 17 Righthand tail lamp 18 Stop lamp switch 19 Fuse unit 20 Interior light 21 Door switch 22 Lefthand tail lamp 23 Horns 24 Horn-push 25 Flasher unit 26 Direction indicator switch 27 Direction indicator warning light 28 Righthand front flasher 29 Lefthand front flasher 30 Righthand rear flasher 31 Lefthand rear flasher 32 Heater switch 33 Heater motor 34 Fuel gauge 35 Fuel gauge tank unit 36 Wiper switch 37 Wiper motor 38 Ignition switch 39 Ignition coil 40 Distributor 42 Oil pressure switch 43 Oil pressure warning light 44 Ignition warning light 45 Headlamp flasher switch 46 Water temperature gauge 47 Water temperature transmitter 49 Reverse lamp switch (if fitted) 50 Reverse lamp (if fitted) 57 Cigar lighter (if fitted) 60 Radio (if fitted) 64 Voltage stabilizer 65 Boot light switch (if fitted) 66 Boot light (if fitted) 67 Line fuse 75 Automatic gearbox safety switch (if fitted) 76 Gear quadrant illumination (if fitted) 77 Electric screen washer 78 Electric screen washer switch 95 Tachometer (if fitted) 115 Rear window demist switch (if fitted) 116 Rear window demist unit (if fitted) 150 Rear window demist warning light (if fitted) 158 Printed circuit instrument panel

FIG 14:3   Righthand drive models fitted with alternator

Key to cable colours: **N** Brown **U** Blue **R** Red **P** Purple **G** Green **LG** Light green **O** Orange **W** White **Y** Yellow **B** Black
When a cable has two colour code letters the first denotes the main colour and the second denotes the tracer colour.

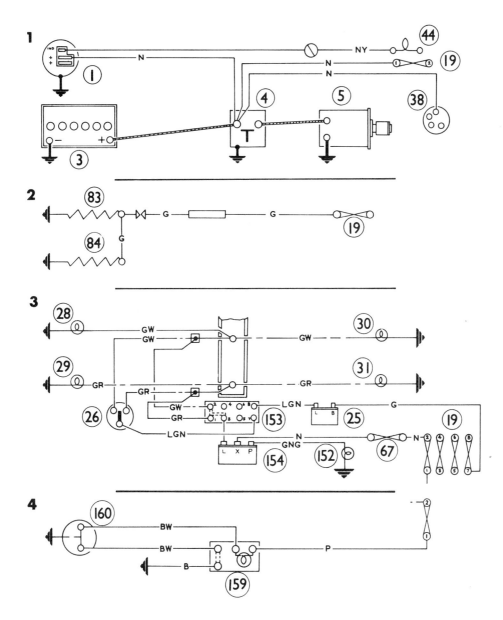

FIG 14:4   Miscellaneous circuits

Key to Fig 14:4
Circuit 1 Alternator circuit   1 Alternator   3 Battery   4 Starter solenoid   5 Starter motor   19 Fuse unit   38 Ignition switch   44 Ignition warning lamp
Circuit 2 Carburetter heater and thermostat circuit   19 Fuse unit   83 Induction heater and thermostat   84 Suction chamber heater
Circuit 3 Hazard warning circuit   19 Fuse unit   25 Flasher unit   26 Direction indicator switch   28 Righthand front direction indicator   29 Lefthand front direction indicator   30 Righthand rear direction indicator   31 Lefthand rear direction indicator   67 Line fuse   152 Hazard warning lamp   153 Hazard warning switch   154 Hazard warning flasher unit
Circuit 4 Split braking circuit   159 Split braking test switch   160 Split braking shuttle valve

NOTES

HINTS ON MAINTENANCE AND OVERHAUL

There are few things more rewarding than the restoration of a vehicle's original peak of efficiency and smooth performance.

The following notes are intended to help the owner to reach that state of perfection. Providing that he possesses the basic manual skills he should have no difficulty in performing most of the operations detailed in this manual. It must be stressed, however, that where recommended in the manual, highly-skilled operations ought to be entrusted to experts, who have the necessary equipment, to carry out the work satisfactorily.

Quality of workmanship:

The hazardous driving conditions on the roads to-day demand that vehicles should be as nearly perfect, mechanically, as possible. It is therefore most important that amateur work be carried out with care, bearing in mind the often inadequate working conditions, and also the inferior tools which may have to be used. It is easy to counsel perfection in all things, and we recognize that it may be setting an impossibly high standard. We do, however, suggest that every care should be taken to ensure that a vehicle is as safe to take on the road as it is humanly possible to make it.

Safe working conditions:

Even though a vehicle may be stationary, it is still potentially dangerous if certain sensible precautions are not taken when working on it while it is supported on jacks or blocks. It is indeed preferable not to use jacks alone, but to supplement them with carefully placed blocks, so that there will be plenty of support if the car rolls off the jacks during a strenuous manoeuvre. Axle stands are an excellent way of providing a rigid base which is not readily disturbed. Piles of bricks are a dangerous substitute. Be careful not to get under heavy loads on lifting tackle, the load could fall. It is preferable not to work alone when lifting an engine, or when working underneath a vehicle which is supported well off the ground. To be trapped, particularly under the vehicle, may have unpleasant results if help is not quickly forthcoming. Make some provision, however humble, to deal with fires. Always disconnect a battery if there is a likelihood of electrical shorts. These may start a fire if there is leaking fuel about. This applies particularly to leads which can carry a heavy current, like those in the starter circuit. While on the subject of electricity, we must also stress the danger of using equipment which is run off the mains and which has no earth or has faulty wiring or connections. So many workshops have damp floors, and electrical shocks are of such a nature that it is sometimes impossible to let go of a live lead or piece of equipment due to the muscular spasms which take place.

Work demanding special care:

This involves the servicing of braking, steering and suspension systems. On the road, failure of the braking system may be disastrous. Make quite sure that there can be no possibility of failure through the bursting of rusty brake pipes or rotten hoses, nor to a sudden loss of pressure due to defective seals or valves.

Problems:

The chief problems which may face an operator are:
1 External dirt.
2 Difficulty in undoing tight fixings
3 Dismantling unfamiliar mechanisms.
4 Deciding in what respect parts are defective.
5 Confusion about the correct order for reassembly.
6 Adjusting running clearances.
7 Road testing.
8 Final tuning.

Practical suggestion to solve the problems:

1 Preliminary cleaning of large parts—engines, transmissions, steering, suspensions, etc.,—should be carried out before removal from the car. Where road dirt and mud alone are present, wash clean with a high-pressure water jet, brushing to remove stubborn adhesions, and allow to drain and dry. Where oil or grease is also present, wash down with a proprietary compound (Gunk, Teepol etc.,) applying with a stiff brush—an old paint brush is suitable—into all crevices. Cover the distributor and ignition coils with a polythene bag and then apply a strong water jet to clear the loosened deposits. Allow to drain and dry. The assemblies will then be sufficiently clean to remove and transfer to the bench for the next stage.

On the bench, further cleaning can be carried out, first wiping the parts as free as possible from grease with old newspaper. Avoid using rag or cotton waste which can leave clogging fibres behind. Any remaining grease can be removed with a brush dipped in paraffin. If necessary, traces of paraffin can be removed by carbon tetrachloride. Avoid using paraffin or petrol in large quantities for cleaning in enclosed areas, such as garages, on account of the high fire risk.

When all exteriors have been cleaned, and not before, dismantling can be commenced. This ensures that dirt will not enter into interiors and orifices revealed by dismantling. In the next phases, where components have to be cleaned, use carbon tetrachloride in preference to petrol and keep the containers covered except when in use. After the components have been cleaned, plug small holes with tapered hard wood plugs cut to size and blank off larger orifices with grease-proof paper and masking tape. Do not use soft wood plugs or matchsticks as they may break.

2 It is not advisable to hammer on the end of a screw thread, but if it must be done, first screw on a nut to protect the thread, and use a lead hammer. This applies particularly to the removal of tapered cotters. Nuts and bolts seem to 'grow' together, especially in exhaust systems. If penetrating oil does not work, try the judicious application of heat, but be careful of starting a fire. Asbestos sheet or cloth is useful to isolate heat.

Tight bushes or pieces of tail-pipe rusted into a silencer can be removed by splitting them with an open-ended hacksaw. Tight screws can sometimes be started by a tap from a hammer on the end of a suitable screwdriver. Many tight fittings will yield to the judicious use of a hammer, but it must be a soft-faced hammer if damage is to be avoided, use a heavy block on the opposite side to absorb shock. Any parts of the steering system which have been damaged should be renewed, as attempts to repair them may lead to cracking and subsequent failure, and steering ball joints should be disconnected using a recommended tool to prevent damage.

3 It often happens that an owner is baffled when trying to dismantle an unfamiliar piece of equipment. So many modern devices are pressed together or assembled by spinning-over flanges, that they must be sawn apart. The intention is that the whole assembly must be renewed. However, parts which appear to be in one piece to the naked eye, may reveal close-fitting joint lines when inspected with a magnifying glass, and, this may provide the necessary clue to dismantling. Left-handed screw threads are used where rotational forces would tend to unscrew a righthanded screw thread.

Be very careful when dismantling mechanisms which may come apart suddenly. Work in an enclosed space where the parts will be contained, and drape a piece of cloth over the device if springs are likely to fly in all directions. Mark everything which might be reassembled in the wrong position, scratched symbols may be used on unstressed parts, or a sequence of tiny dots from a centre punch can be useful. Stressed parts should never be scratched or centre-popped as this may lead to cracking under working conditions. Store parts which look alike in the correct order for reassembly. Never rely upon memory to assist in the assembly of complicated mechanisms, especially when they will be dismantled for a long time, but make notes, and drawings to supplement the diagrams in the manual, and put labels on detached wires. Rust stains may indicate unlubricated wear. This can sometimes be seen round the outside edge of a bearing cup in a universal joint. Look for bright rubbing marks on parts which normally should not make heavy contact. These might prove that something is bent or running out of truth. For example, there might be bright marks on one side of a piston, at the top near the ring grooves, and others at the bottom of the skirt on the other side. This could well be the clue to a bent connecting rod. Suspected cracks can be proved by heating the component in a light oil to approximately 100°C, removing, drying off, and dusting with french chalk, if a crack is present the oil retained in the crack will stain the french chalk.

4 In determining wear, and the degree, against the permissible limits set in the manual, accurate measurement can only be achieved by the use of a micrometer. In many cases, the wear is given to the fourth place of decimals; that is in ten-thousandths of an inch. This can be read by the vernier scale on the barrel of a good micrometer. Bore diameters are more difficult to determine. If, however, the matching shaft is accurately measured, the degree of play in the bore can be felt as a guide to its suitability. In other cases, the shank of a twist drill of known diameter is a handy check.

Many methods have been devised for determining the clearance between bearing surfaces. To-day the best and simplest is by the use of Plastigage, obtainable from most garages. A thin plastic thread is laid between the two surfaces and the bearing is tightened, flattening the thread. On removal, the width of the thread is compared with a scale supplied with the thread and the clearance is read off directly. Sometimes joint faces leak persistently, even after gasket renewal. The fault will then be traceable to distortion, dirt or burrs. Studs which are screwed into soft metal frequently raise burrs at the point of entry. A quick cure for this is to chamfer the edge of the hole in the part which fits over the stud.

5 **Always check a replacement part with the original one before it is fitted.**

If parts are not marked, and the order for reassembly is not known, a little detective work will help. Look for marks which are due to wear to see if they can be mated. Joint faces may not be identical due to manufacturing errors, and parts which overlap may be stained, giving a clue to the correct position. Most fixings leave identifying marks especially if they were painted over on assembly. It is then easier to decide whether a nut, for instance, has a plain, a spring, or a shakeproof washer under it. All running surfaces become 'bedded' together after long spells of work and tiny imperfections on one part will be found to have left corresponding marks on the other. This is particularly true of shafts and bearings and even a score on a cylinder wall will show on the piston.

6 Checking end float or rocker clearances by feeler gauge may not always give accurate results because of wear. For instance, the rocker tip which bears on a valve stem may be deeply pitted, in which case the feeler will simply be bridging a depression. Thrust washers may also wear depressions in opposing faces to make accurate measurement difficult. End float is then easier to check by using a dial gauge. It is common practice to adjust end play in bearing assemblies, like front hubs with taper rollers, by doing up the axle nut until the hub becomes stiff to turn and then backing it off a little. Do not use this method with ballbearing hubs as the assembly is often preloaded by tightening the axle nut to its fullest extent. If the splitpin hole will not line up, file the base of the nut a little.

Steering assemblies often wear in the straight-ahead position. If any part is adjusted, make sure that it remains free when moved from lock to lock. Do not be surprised if an assembly like a steering gearbox, which is known to be carefully adjusted outside the car, becomes stiff when it is bolted in place. This will be due to distortion of the case by the pull of the mounting bolts, particularly if the mounting points are not all touching together. This problem may be met in other equipment and is cured by careful attention to the alignment of mounting points.

When a spanner is stamped with a size and A/F it means that the dimension is the width between the jaws and has no connection with ANF, which is the designation for the American National Fine thread. Coarse threads like Whitworth are rarely used on cars to-day except for studs which screw into soft aluminium or cast iron. For this reason it might be found that the top end of a cylinder head stud has a fine thread and the lower end a coarse thread to screw into the cylinder block. If the car has mainly UNF threads then it is likely that any coarse threads will be UNC, which are not the same as Whitworth. Small sizes have the same number of threads in Whitworth and UNC, but in the $\frac{1}{2}$ inch size for example, there are twelve threads to the inch in the former and thirteen in the latter.

7 After a major overhaul, particularly if a great deal of work has been done on the braking, steering and suspension systems, it is advisable to approach the problem of testing with care. If the braking system has been overhauled, apply heavy pressure to the brake pedal and get a second operator to check every possible source of leakage. The brakes may work extremely well, but a leak could cause complete failure after a few miles.

Do not fit the hub caps until every wheel nut has been checked for tightness, and make sure the tyre pressures are correct. Check the levels of coolant, lubricants and hydraulic fluids. Being satisfied that all is well, take the car on the road and test the brakes at once. Check the steering and the action of the handbrake. Do all this at moderate speeds on quiet roads, and make sure there is no other vehicle behind you when you try a rapid stop.

Finally, remember that many parts settle down after a time, so check for tightness of all fixings after the car has been on the road for a hundred miles or so.

8 It is useless to tune an engine which has not reached its normal running temperature. In the same way, the tune of an engine which is stiff after a rebore will be different when the engine is again running free. Remember too, that rocker clearances on pushrod operated valve gear will change when the cylinder head nuts are tightened after an initial period of running with a new head gasket.

Trouble may not always be due to what seems the obvious cause. Ignition, carburation and mechanical condition are interdependent and spitting back through the carburetter, which might be attributed to a weak mixture, can be caused by a sticking inlet valve.

For one final hint on tuning, never adjust more than one thing at a time or it will be impossible to tell which adjustment produced the desired result.

NOTES

GLOSSARY OF TERMS

Allen key   Cranked wrench of hexagonal section for use with socket head screws.

Alternator   Electrical generator producing alternating current. Rectified to direct current for battery charging.

Ambient temperature   Surrounding atmospheric temperature.

Annulus   Used in engineering to indicate the outer ring gear of an epicyclic gear train.

Armature   The shaft carrying the windings, which rotates in the magnetic field of a generator or starter motor. That part of a solenoid or relay which is activated by the magnetic field.

Axial   In line with, or pertaining to, an axis.

Backlash   Play in meshing gears.

Balance lever   A bar where force applied at the centre is equally divided between connections at the ends.

Banjo axle   Axle casing with large diameter housing for the crownwheel and differential.

Bendix pinion   A self-engaging and self-disengaging drive on a starter motor shaft.

Bevel pinion   A conical shaped gearwheel, designed to mesh with a similar gear with an axis usually at 90 deg. to its own.

bhp   Brake horse power, measured on a dynamometer.

bmep   Brake mean effective pressure. Average pressure on a piston during the working stroke.

Brake cylinder   Cylinder with hydraulically operated piston(s) acting on brake shoes or pad(s).

Brake regulator   Control valve fitted in hydraulic braking system which limits brake pressure to rear brakes during heavy braking to prevent rear wheel locking.

Camber   Angle at which a wheel is tilted from the vertical.

Capacitor   Modern term for an electrical condenser. Part of distributor assembly, connected across contact breaker points, acts as an interference suppressor.

Castellated   Top face of a nut, slotted across the flats, to take a locking splitpin.

Castor   Angle at which the kingpin or swivel pin is tilted when viewed from the side.

cc   Cubic centimetres. Engine capacity is arrived at by multiplying the area of the bore in sq cm by the stroke in cm by the number of cylinders.

Clevis   U-shaped forked connector used with a clevis pin, usually at handbrake connections.

Collet   A type of collar, usually split and located in a groove in a shaft, and held in place by a retainer. The arrangement used to retain the spring(s) on a valve stem in most cases.

Commutator   Rotating segmented current distributor between armature windings and brushes in generator or motor.

Compression ratio   The ratio, or quantitative relation, of the total volume (piston at bottom of stroke) to the unswept volume (piston at top of stroke) in an engine cylinder.

Condenser   See capacitor.

Core plug   Plug for blanking off a manufacturing hole in a casting.

Crownwheel   Large bevel gear in rear axle, driven by a bevel pinion attached to the propeller shaft. Sometimes called a 'ring gear'.

'C'-spanner   Like a 'C' with a handle. For use on screwed collars without flats, but with slots or holes.

Damper   Modern term for shock-absorber, used in vehicle suspension systems to damp out spring oscillations.

Depression   The lowering of atmospheric pressure as in the inlet manifold and carburetter.

Dowel   Close tolerance pin, peg, tube, or bolt, which accurately locates mating parts.

Drag link   Rod connecting steering box drop arm (pitman arm) to nearest front wheel steering arm in certain types of steering systems.

Dry liner   Thinwall tube pressed into cylinder bore

Dry sump   Lubrication system where all oil is scavenged from the sump, and returned to a separate tank.

Dynamo   See Generator.

Electrode   Terminal, part of an electrical component, such as the points or 'Electrodes' of a sparking plug.

Electrolyte   In lead-acid car batteries a solution of sulphuric acid and distilled water.

End float   The axial movement between associated parts, end play.

EP   Extreme pressure. In lubricants, special grades for heavily loaded bearing surfaces, such as gear teeth in a gearbox, or crownwheel and pinion in a rear axle.

Fade	Of brakes. Reduced efficiency due to overheating.	**Journals**	Those parts of a shaft that are in contact with the bearings.
Field coils	Windings on the polepieces of motors and generators.	**Kingpin**	The main vertical pin which carries the front wheel spindle, and permits steering movement. May be called 'steering pin' or 'swivel pin'.
Fillets	Narrow finishing strips usually applied to interior bodywork.	**Layshaft**	The shaft which carries the laygear in the gearbox. The laygear is driven by the first motion shaft and drives the third motion shaft according to the gear selected. Sometimes called the 'countershaft' or 'second motion shaft.'
First motion shaft	Input shaft from clutch to gearbox.		
Fullflow filter	Filters in which all the oil is pumped to the engine. If the element becomes clogged, a bypass valve operates to pass unfiltered oil to the engine.		
FWD	Front wheel drive.	**lb ft**	A measure of twist or torque. A pull of 10 lb at a radius of 1 ft is a torque of 10 lb ft.
Gear pump	Two meshing gears in a close fitting casing. Oil is carried from the inlet round the outside of both gears in the spaces between the gear teeth and casing to the outlet, the meshing gear teeth prevent oil passing back to the inlet, and the oil is forced through the outlet port.	**lb/sq in**	Pounds per square inch.
		Little-end	The small, or piston end of a connecting rod. Sometimes called the 'small-end'.
		LT	Low Tension. The current output from the battery.
Generator	Modern term for 'Dynamo'. When rotated produces electrical current.	**Mandrel**	Accurately manufactured bar or rod used for test or centring purposes.
Grommet	A ring of protective or sealing material. Can be used to protect pipes or leads passing through bulkheads.	**Manifold**	A pipe, duct, or chamber, with several branches.
		Needle rollers	Bearing rollers with a length many times their diameter.
Grubscrew	Fully threaded headless screw with screwdriver slot. Used for locking, or alignment purposes.	**Oil bath**	Reservoir which lubricates parts by immersion. In air filters, a separate oil supply for wetting a wire mesh element to hold the dust.
Gudgeon pin	Shaft which connects a piston to its connecting rod. Sometimes called 'wrist pin', or 'piston pin'.		
Halfshaft	One of a pair transmitting drive from the differential.	**Oil wetted**	In air filters, a wire mesh element lightly oiled to trap and hold airborne dust.
Helical	In spiral form. The teeth of helical gears are cut at a spiral angle to the side faces of the gearwheel.	**Overlap**	Period during which inlet and exhaust valves are open together.
Hot spot	Hot area that assists vapourisation of fuel on its way to cylinders. Often provided by close contact between inlet and exhaust manifolds.	**Panhard rod**	Bar connected between fixed point on chassis and another on axle to control sideways movement.
		Pawl	Pivoted catch which engages in the teeth of a ratchet to permit movement in one direction only.
HT	High Tension. Applied to electrical current produced by the ignition coil for the sparking plugs.	**Peg spanner**	Tool with pegs, or pins, to engage in holes or slots in the part to be turned.
Hydrometer	A device for checking specific gravity of liquids. Used to check specific gravity of electrolyte.	**Pendant pedals**	Pedals with levers that are pivoted at the top end.
Hypoid bevel gears	A form of bevel gear used in the rear axle drive gears. The bevel pinion meshes below the centre line of the crownwheel, giving a lower propeller shaft line.	**Phillips screwdriver**	A cross-point screwdriver for use with the cross-slotted heads of Phillips screws.
		Pinion	A small gear, usually in relation to another gear.
Idler	A device for passing on movement. A free running gear between driving and driven gears. A lever transmitting track rod movement to a side rod in steering gear.	**Piston-type damper**	Shock absorber in which damping is controlled by a piston working in a closed oil-filled cylinder.
		Preloading	Preset static pressure on ball or roller bearings not due to working loads.
Impeller	A centrifugal pumping element. Used in water pumps to stimulate flow.	**Radial**	Radiating from a centre, like the spokes of a wheel.

Radius rod	Pivoted arm confining movement of a part to an arc of fixed radius.
Ratchet	Toothed wheel or rack which can move in one direction only, movement in the other being prevented by a pawl.
Ring gear	A gear tooth ring attached to outer periphery of flywheel. Starter pinion engages with it during starting.
Runout	Amount by which rotating part is out of true.
Semi-floating axle	Outer end of rear axle halfshaft is carried on bearing inside axle casing. Wheel hub is secured to end of shaft.
Servo	A hydraulic or pneumatic system for assisting, or, augmenting a physical effort. See 'Vacuum Servo'.
Setscrew	One which is threaded for the full length of the shank.
Shackle	A coupling link, used in the form of two parallel pins connected by side plates to secure the end of the master suspension spring and absorb the effects of deflection.
Shell bearing	Thinwalled steel shell lined with antifriction metal. Usually semi-circular and used in pairs for main and big-end bearings.
Shock absorber	See 'Damper'.
Silentbloc	Rubber bush bonded to inner and outer metal sleeves.
Socket-head screw	Screw with hexagonal socket for an Allen key.
Solenoid	A coil of wire creating a magnetic field when electric current passes through it. Used with a soft iron core to operate contacts or a mechanical device.
Spur gear	A gear with teeth cut axially across the periphery.
Stub axle	Short axle fixed at one end only.
Tachometer	An instrument for accurate measurement of rotating speed. Usually indicates in revolutions per minute.

TDC	Top Dead Centre. The highest point reached by a piston in a cylinder, with the crank and connecting rod in line.
Thermostat	Automatic device for regulating temperature. Used in vehicle coolant systems to open a valve which restricts circulation at low temperature.
Third motion shaft	Output shaft of gearbox.
Threequarter floating axle	Outer end of rear axle halfshaft flanged and bolted to wheel hub, which runs on bearing mounted on outside of axle casing. Vehicle weight is not carried by the axle shaft.
Thrust bearing or washer	Used to reduce friction in rotating parts subject to axial loads.
Torque	Turning or twisting effort. See 'lb ft'.
Track rod	The bar(s) across the vehicle which connect the steering arms and maintain the front wheels in their correct alignment.
UJ	Universal joint. A coupling between shafts which permits angular movement.
UNF	Unified National Fine screw thread.
Vacuum servo	Device used in brake system, using difference between atmospheric pressure and inlet manifold depression to operate a piston which acts to augment brake pressure as required. See 'Servo'.
Venturi	A restriction or 'choke' in a tube, as in a carburetter, used to increase velocity to obtain a reduction in pressure.
Vernier	A sliding scale for obtaining fractional readings of the graduations of an adjacent scale.
Welch plug	A domed thin metal disc which is partially flattened to lock in a recess. Used to plug core holes in castings.
Wet liner	Removable cylinder barrel, sealed against coolant leakage, where the coolant is in direct contact with the outer surface.
Wet sump	A reservoir attached to the crankcase to hold the lubricating oil.

NOTES

INDEX

Alfa Romeo Giulia 1600,
1750, 2000 1962 on
Aston Martin 1921-58
Auto Union Audi 70, 80,
Super 90, 1966-72
Audi 100 1969 on
Austin, Morris etc.
1100 Mk. 1 1962-67
Austin, Morris etc. 1100
Mk. 2, 3, 1300 Mk. 1, 2, 3
America 1968 on
Austin A30, A35, A40
Farina 1951-67
Austin A55 Mk. 2, A60
1958-69
Austin A99, A110 1959-68
Austin J4 1960 on
Austin Allegro 1973 on
Austin Maxi 1969 on
Austin, Morris 1800
1964 on
Austin, Morris 2200 1972 on
Austin Kimberley, Tasman
1970 on
Austin, Morris 1300, 1500
Nomad 1969 on
BMC 3 (Austin A50, A55
Mk. 1, Morris Oxford
2, 3 1954-59)
Austin Healey 100/6,
3000 1956-68
Austin Healey, MG
Sprite, Midget 1958 on
Bedford CA Mk. 2 1964-69
Bedford CF Vans 1969 on
Bedford Beagle HA Vans
1964 on
BMW 1600 1966 on
BMW 1800 1964-71
BMW 2000, 2002 1966 on
Chevrolet Corvair 1960-69
Chevrolet Corvette V8
1957-65
Chevrolet Corvette V8
1965 on
Chevrolet Vega 2300
1970 on
Chrysler Valiant V8
1965 on
Chrysler Valiant Straight
Six 1963 on
Citroen DS 19, ID 19
1955-66
Citroen ID 19, DS 19, 20,
21 1966 on
Citroen Dyane Ami 1964 on
Daf 31, 32, 33, 44, 55
1961 on
Datsun Bluebird 610 series
1972 on
Datsun Cherry 100A, 120A
1971 on
Datsun 1000, 1200 1968 on
Datsun 1300, 1400, 1600
1968 on
Datsun 240C 1971 on

Datsun 240Z Sport 1970 on
Fiat 124 1966 on
Fiat 124 Sport 1966 on
Fiat 125 1967-72
Fiat 127 1971 on
Fiat 128 1969 on
Fiat 500 1957 on
Fiat 600, 600D 1955-69
Fiat 850 1964 on
Fiat 1100 1957-69
Fiat 1300, 1500 1961-67
Ford Anglia Prefect 100E
1953-62
Ford Anglia 105E, Prefect
107E 1959-67
Ford Capri 1300, 1600 OHV
1968 on
Ford Capri 1300, 1600,
2000 OHC 1972 on
Ford Capri 2000 V4, 3000 V6
1969 on
Ford Classic, Capri
1961-64
Ford Consul, Zephyr,
Zodiac, 1, 2 1950-62
Ford Corsair Straight
Four 1963-65
Ford Corsair V4 1965-68
Ford Corsair V4 2000
1969-70
Ford Cortina 1962-66
Ford Cortina 1967-68
Ford Cortina 1969-70
Ford Cortina Mk. 3
1970 on
Ford Escort 1967 on
Ford Falcon 6 1964-70
Ford Falcon XK, XL
1960-63
Ford Falcon 6 XR/XA
1966 on
Ford Falcon V8 (U.S.A.)
1965-71
Ford Falcon V8 (Aust.)
1966 on
Ford Pinto 1970 on
Ford Maverick 6 1969 on
Ford Maverick V8 1970 on
Ford Mustang 6 1965 on
Ford Mustang V8 1965 on
Ford Thames 10, 12,
15 cwt 1957-65
Ford Transit V4 1965 on
Ford Zephyr Zodiac Mk. 3
1962-66
Ford Zephyr Zodiac V4,
V6, Mk. 4 1966-72
Ford Consul, Granada
1972 on
Hillman Avenger 1970 on
Hillman Hunter 1966 on
Hillman Imp 1963-68
Hillman Imp 1969 on
Hillman Minx 1 to 5
1956-65
Hillman Minx 1965-67

Hillman Minx 1966-70
Hillman Super Minx
1961-65
Jaguar XK120, 140, 150,
Mk. 7, 8, 9 1948-61
Jaguar 2.4, 3.4, 3.8 Mk.
1, 2 1955-69
Jaguar 'E' Type 1961-72
Jaguar 'S' Type 420
1963-68
Jaguar XJ6 1968 on
Jowett Javelin Jupiter
1947-53
Landrover 1, 2 1948-61
Landrover 2, 2a, 3 1959 on
Mazda 616 1970 on
Mazda 808, 818 1972 on
Mazda 1200, 1300 1969 on
Mazda 1500, 1800 1967 on
Mazda RX-2 1971 on
Mazda R100, RX-3 1970 on
Mercedes-Benz 190b,
190c, 200 1959-68
Mercedes-Benz 220
1959-65
Mercedes-Benz 220/8
1968 on
Mercedes-Benz 230
1963-68
Mercedes-Benz 250
1965-67
Mercedes-Benz 250
1968 on
Mercedes-Benz 280
1968 on
MG TA to TF 1936-55
MGA MGB 1955-68
MGB 1969 on
Mini 1959 on
Mini Cooper 1961-72
Morgan Four 1936-72
Morris Marina 1971 on
Morris (Aust) Marina
1972 on
Morris Minor 2, 1000
1952-71
Morris Oxford 5, 6 1959-71
NSU 1000 1963-72
NSU Prinz 1 to 4 1957-72
Opel Ascona, Manta
1970 on
Opel GT 1900 1968 on
Opel Kadett, Olympia 993 cc
1078 cc 1962 on
Opel Kadett, Olympia 1492,
1698, 1897 cc 1967 on
Opel Rekord C 1966-72
Peugeot 204 1965 on
Peugeot 304 1970 on
Peugeot 404 1960 on
Peugeot 504 1968 on
Porsche 356A, B, C 1957-65
Porsche 911 1964 on
Porsche 912 1965-69
Porsche 914 S 1969 on
Reliant Regal 1952-73

Renault R4, R4L, 4 1961 on
Renault 5 1972 on
Renault 6 1968 on
Renault 8, 10, 1100 1962-71
Renault 12, 1969 on
Renault 15, 17 1971 on
Renault R16 1965 on
Renault Dauphine
Floride 1957-67
Renault Caravelle 1962-68
Rover 60 to 110 1953-64
Rover 2000 1963-73
Rover 3 Litre 1958-67
Rover 3500, 3500S 1968 on
Saab 95, 96, Sport
1960-68
Saab 99 1969 on
Saab V4 1966 on
Simca 1000 1961 on
Simca 1100 1967 on
Simca 1300, 1301, 1500,
1501 1963 on
Skoda One (440, 445, 450)
1955-70
Sunbeam Rapier Alpine
1955-65
Toyota Carina, Celica
1971 on
Toyota Corolla 1100,
1200 1967 on
Toyota Corona 1500 Mk. 1
1965-70
Toyota Corona Mk. 2
1969 on
Triumph TR2, TR3, TR3A
1952-62
Triumph TR4, TR4A
1961-67
Triumph TR5, TR250,
TR6 1967 on
Triumph 1300, 1500
1965-73
Triumph 2000 Mk. 1, 2.5 PI
Mk. 1 1963-69
Triumph 2000 Mk. 2, 2.5 PI
Mk. 2 1969 on
Triumph Dolomite 1972 on
Triumph Herald 1959-68
Triumph Herald 1969-71
Triumph Spitfire, Vitesse
1962-68
Triumph Spitfire Mk. 3, 4
1969 on
Triumph GT6, Vitesse
2 Litre 1969 on
Triumph Stag 1970 on
Triumph Toledo 1970 on
Vauxhall Velox, Cresta
1957-72
Vauxhall Victor 1, 2, FB
1957-64
Vauxhall Victor 101
1964-67
Vauxhall Victor FD 1600,
2000 1967-72

Continued on following page

Vauxhall Victor 3300,
Ventora 1968-72
Vauxhall Victor FE
Ventora 1972 on
Vauxhall Viva HA 1963-66
Vauxhall Viva HB 1966-70

Vauxhall Viva, HC Firenza
1971 on
Volkswagen Beetle 1954-67
Volkswagen Beetle 1968 on
Volkswagen 1500 1961-66

Volkswagen 1600 Fastback
1965-73
Volkswagen Transporter
1954-67
Volkswagen Transporter
1968 on

Volkswagen 411 1968-72
Volvo 120 series 1961-70
Volvo 140 series 1966 on
Volvo 160 series 1968 on
Volvo 1800 1960-73